Evaluating community care

Evaluating community care

*Services for people
with learning difficulties*

Ken Wright
Alan Haycox
Ian Leedham

Open University Press
Buckingham · Philadelphia

Open University Press
Celtic Court
22 Ballmoor
Buckingham
MK18 1XW

ILTG

and
1900 Frost Road, Suite 101
Bristol, PA 19007, USA

W

First Published 1994

copy 2

A catalogue record of this book is available from the British Library

ISBN 0 335 09496 1 (pbk)   0 335 09497 X (hbk)

Library of Congress Cataloging-in-Publication Data
Haycox, Alan, 1957–
    Evaluating community care : services for people with learning
difficulties / Alan Haycox, Ian Leedham, Ken Wright.
       p. cm.
    Includes bibliographical references and index.
    ISBN 0–335–09497–X (hb). –ISBN 0–335–09496–1 (pb)
    1. Mentally handicapped–Services for–Great Britain–Evaluation.
    2. Learning disabled–Services for–Great Britain–Evaluation.
    3. Mental health services–Great Britain–Evaluation.   I. Leedham,
    Ian, 1964–   . II. Wright, Ken, 1937–   . III. Title.
    HV3008.G7H39   1994
    362.3'8'0941–dc20   94–5535
                                                                        CIP

Typeset by Graphicraft Typesetters Ltd., Hong Kong
Printed in Great Britain by Biddles Ltd, Guildford and King's Lynn

94   02731

To people with learning difficulties and their supporters who are continually working to turn the vision of community living into a practical reality.

Contents

Acknowledgements

The original ideas for this book arose from discussions with Professor Martin Knapp (Personal Social Services Research Unit at the University of Kent). Martin's encouragement, advice and practical involvement in the early stages is gratefully acknowledged. A similar debt of gratitude is owed to Alan Shiell of CHERE (Centre for Health Economics Research and Evaluation, Westmead Hospital, Australia) whose work on the costs of residential care is reflected in Chapters 7 and 8.

Sue Hennessy undertook an invaluable editorial role on our behalf. In addition, Paula Press and Kerry Atkinson typed the manuscript with their usual speed and efficiency. Any remaining deficiencies remain the responsibility of the authors.

1 Introduction

This book has been written for those people who are interested in appraising the development and management of services for people with learning difficulties. The material presented in the following chapters draws heavily on the microeconomic principles of policy evaluation but does not demand any prior knowledge of economics. However, economics is not the only science exploited; sociology, for example, is the foundation for a considerable amount of the material in the chapters on outcome measurement. The literature on the evaluation of services for people with learning difficulties has also been built up through a multi-disciplinary approach.

The concepts of efficiency and effectiveness dominate the following chapters. Again these concepts are of concern to many intellectual disciplines as well as many service purchasers or providers. Generally we take the concept of effectiveness to mean the achievement of predetermined objectives. We also take the position that improving the welfare of people with learning difficulties and their carers is a major policy objective. Efficiency means achieving the predetermined objectives at the lowest possible cost. Since it is possible to be efficient but not effective (by pursuing unwanted objectives at least cost), the need to specify and agree the objectives by which effectiveness is to be assessed is taken to be of paramount importance.

The contents of the book have been planned to follow a logical sequence which is derived from the methodology of evaluation. Chapter 2 is designed to explore the evaluation framework and is concerned with the importance of specifying objectives and the general concept of the production of welfare in terms of combining inputs or resources into services that produce benefits or the improved well-being or welfare of users. Chapter 3 contains a discussion of the recent policy background against which more detailed evaluations are undertaken. The technical aspects of evaluation, such as the measurement of outcomes and costs, are set out and discussed in Chapters 4 to 8. The final chapter is used to pull together the evidence that has been described in the evaluation literature and relates this to the current and future policy agenda.

An immediate terminological challenge faces all those who wish to discuss services for people with learning difficulties. As has become obvious, we have used the term 'learning difficulties' to describe the people who are the subject of this book. Over the years terms such as 'mental handicap', 'mental retardation' or, more recently in the UK, 'learning disabilities' have been used. Our initial temptation was to follow the official line of the Department of Health and use the term 'learning disabilities'. However, our personal contacts and enquiries revealed that the term 'learning difficulties' was generally preferred by people with learning difficulties and by the organizations to which they and their carers belong.

We were further challenged by the question of whether or not to talk about different categories of people, for example people with mild, moderate or severe difficulties, people with behaviour disorders, people of different age groups and people with concomitant impairments, such as blindness, deafness or speech difficulties. Any categorization immediately raises the problems of definition. It can also lead to charges of discrimination and stigmatization. However, while these definitional problems are widely discussed and their dangers recognized, in the end some categorization is deemed necessary more often than not. Anyone who is familiar with the epidemiology of learning difficulties or who is concerned with the planning, development, delivery and administration of the relevant services will be familiar with the most common ones. Thus intelligence quotients are used as one method of distinguishing between profound, severe, moderate and minor learning difficulties. The generally accepted measures are that people with an IQ of under fifty are considered to have 'severe' learning difficulties and those with an IQ of between fifty and seventy to have 'moderate' difficulties (Fraser and Green 1991).

Using these approaches it is generally accepted that the prevalence of severe learning difficulties is around three people per 1,000 population, which suggests that there are around 160,000 people with severe learning difficulties in the United Kingdom. However, there could well be around another 2 per cent of the population who have an IQ between fifty and seventy and could therefore be labelled as having a 'moderate' learning difficulty.

In total, therefore, there are just over a million people in the UK who may have a moderate or severe learning difficulty. Around 60,000 people with severe learning difficulties will be under six years of age (Taylor and Taylor 1986). In the main, the services for people with learning difficulties, especially for people beyond compulsory school age, will be targeted at those with severe difficulties, but there are a number of initiatives in day services and in employment schemes that will be of particular benefit to people with moderate difficulties.

The demand for and use of services is determined by not only the severity of intellectual or physical impairments, but also environmental factors such as housing problems, low income, family circumstances and knowledge of the existence of and access to the providing agencies. Thus, the proportion of people with learning difficulties in any area who are known to use services will vary for social and environmental reasons, but generally it is to be expected that the greatest proportion in receipt of services will live in areas with the highest levels of social deprivation.

This book has been written at a time of great change in health and social care policies for people with learning difficulties. The key to these changes is the concept of the purchaser–provider split, which is, at the time of writing, more visible in health than in social care. The provisions of the National Health Service and Community Care Act 1990 were applied immediately to the organization of health care. The implementation of the new arrangements for community care was delayed until 1 April 1993. In addition, there is a clear organizational split between purchasers and providers of health care, whereas social services departments are expected to differentiate these functions internally with no clearly prescribed management system for the effective achievement of the different objectives. One clear guiding principle applies to purchasers irrespective of their organizational location. Services must be purchased according to the needs of the population served. This is a major challenge facing purchasing organizations and is discussed in more detail in Chapter 3. However, at this point it can be seen that needs-led purchasing will be very reliant on local and wider evaluations that indicate the efficiency and effectiveness of services in meeting needs or at the very least identify the criteria by which efficiency, quality and effectiveness need to be assessed.

The problem with having needs-led services is that it is always difficult to define 'needs'. A search of the academic literature reveals different meanings. Perhaps one of the best known is Bradshaw's taxonomy (Bradshaw 1972), which distinguishes between:

- 'normative need', which is need defined by a relevant professional or expert;
- 'felt need', which is what the relevant population believe they want;
- 'expressed need', which is felt need expressed or made explicit;
- 'comparative need', which is evident when people are not receiving help that is made available to other people who are in identical circumstances.

'Need' was not defined in the government papers that presaged the recent changes in health and social care. Our interpretation is that the principal concept at work is one of normative or professionally defined need, with a pinch of felt need added. Thus, purchasers of health care will rely heavily on professional (mostly medical) assessments of the health needs of their local populations, while purchasers of social care will rely on professional assessment of people with a community care need. For example, guidance to NHS authorities in the assessment of health need (Department of Health 1990: 13) accepted that there was very little evidence available on how to assess the health needs of a given population, but 'information about incidence and prevalence (e.g. by sex, age and condition), linked with that about the evaluation of different treatments' provides one basis. In the White Paper on the new community care arrangements (Secretaries of State for Health, Social Security, Wales and Scotland 1989) one of the key responsibilities to be laid on social services departments was the 'appropriate assessment of an individual's need for social care' (p. 17). In guidance offered on the new community care arrangements, need was defined as the 'ability of an individual or collection of individuals to benefit from care' (Department of Health 1993: 6). This definition does not really take the debate any further since there will be considerable debate about how 'benefit' is measured, by whom and for what cost. How is a clash of opinion between professionals and potential users on the 'ability to benefit' to be resolved? Generally, NHS purchasers are charged to assess population needs, but the term will be open to varied interpretation between agencies, professionals, localities and users. It would be possible to spend a considerable amount of space discussing the meaning of need, but this has been done at length elsewhere (Doyal and Gough 1991) and we have chosen to concentrate on the theory and practice of measuring costs and outcomes, which are essential items of information for determining, setting and agreeing priorities for service development and delivery.

These organizational changes have been implemented while the policy for the transition to community care for people with learning difficulties has been making steady if slow progress. In fact, the origin of the reform of the management of community care was a response to the criticisms of the Audit Commission that the pace of change in terms of both closure of long-stay hospitals and the build-up of community-based facilities had been too slow (Audit Commission 1986). The flavour of this book is very much in terms of providing community-based care that gives people with learning difficulties the opportunities to experience as full a life as possible within the community in which they live. No attempt is made to defend or discuss the retention of the large long-stay hospitals. The recommendations of the White Paper which recognized the value of the transition to community care in the early 1970s (Department of Health and Social Security 1971) have been treated as the starting point. It must be remembered that these recommendations stated that people with learning difficulties should maintain as normal a life as possible, should develop life skills to a personal maximum capacity and should be integrated into, not segregated from, the general life of the community. The modern interpretation of these values into present service provision is a recurring theme through this book, especially in Chapters 2 to 6.

The economic language of the market place, of purchasing and providing, of buying and selling, of consumer sovereignty and satisfaction, of costs and revenue, of inputs and outputs and of production and exchange is used throughout nearly all of the ensuing chapters. Such blatant commercialism is anathema to those people who regard public services, especially health, education and social care services, as being above the competitive world of marketeering. However, we make no apologies for being concerned with the efficient allocation of resources, with promoting consumers' rights and with insisting that managers are accountable for what their services achieve as well as what they spend. The great financial reforms of the nineteenth century in the British civil service and local government emphasized the need for financial stewardship of public monies to prevent misappropriation of funds. Public officials could not spend public money in an unsanctioned way and were accountable for every pound and penny so disbursed. Although this is still a proper concern of public accountability, recent progress has increasingly focused not only on whether monies were spent in accordance with correct financial procedures, but also on whether they were spent efficiently and effectively; that is, did they achieve some pre-declared purpose or objective, did they result in a better life for the people who used the services, could they have achieved these ends with less expenditure or could the same expenditure have produced even better results?

Use of this language is not a surrender to some harsh uncaring set of people who consider that public services are unproductive or to those who believe that people with learning difficulties should be neither seen nor heard but locked away in some secure, remote environment with only the bare essentials of life to ensure their survival. It is a recognition that caring for people demands the efficient allocation of resources. Meeting objectives at the lowest possible cost is ethical because of the inescapable fact that resources are scarce and if they are used to care for person X they cannot be used to care for person Y. All of us are constantly having to make choices about how we use our limited resources, in common everyday decisions knowing that if we buy one set of goods or services we cannot afford to buy another set, that if we use some space in our house for one purpose we have to forgo it for some other purposes. Even our time is a scarce resource. If we choose to use our limited time in one way (for example, go to work) we cannot use it in another (for example, recreation).

Such choices and dilemmas occur repeatedly in the public sector. How much should total public expenditure be this year? How much of this total should be devoted to defence, education, law and order, health and social care, housing, roads, social security payments and so on. Within each major government department choices have to be made about the expenditure to be devoted to different areas and services. Health and social services are no exception. How much is to be spent on primary health care services, on preventive or curative or long-term care, on children, adults, elderly people, people with disabilities or children in need of protection? Eventually we arrive at making choices between different services and, at service level, between meeting the needs of one person and not another. All these choices are the result of the scarcity of resources. Hence good choices will be made and resource use will be improved if decision-makers at all levels in the hierarchy are well informed about not only the expenditure or costs of services to be provided but also the outcomes or benefits that are to be achieved.

The state of our knowledge about outcomes in public services is very lacking in terms of deciding the optimum allocation of resources between the major government departments as well as between different groups of users in the social services departments. The allocation of resources between caring for children, elderly people, people with physical disabilities, people with mental health problems and people with learning difficulties has to be made by the subjective judgement of the responsible officers and politicians. Yet this is no reason for despair. Rather it is a good reason for showing that the services provided are meeting their objectives to improve the well-being of people with learning difficulties and their carers. This in itself (as explained in Chapters 4, 5 and 6) is not easy, but if we make some progress with this task, not only are we ensuring that we serve as many people as our limited resources allow in the best possible way, we shall also be making a strong case for the continuing development of the services provided, by informing the subjective judgements at a higher level of the good that comes from expenditure on our services.

There is also a general good to be served. Some people regard the public sector as the 'non-productive' part of the economy. It is easy to see why people have this opinion. Public expenditure is mostly met from taxation of one kind or another at either central or local government level. Unchecked increases in public expenditure have the potential danger of causing taxation to rise to levels many people would regard as intolerable. Obviously, the proportion of public expenditure in the economy has to be limited and closely monitored. However, public services are productive. They ensure peace, law and order, they promote social and personal development through education, they maintain and restore good health, they protect the disadvantaged, they protect the environment and they aid the transport of people and goods throughout the country.

Most services provide indispensable outputs vital to the welfare of the whole population. The logic of the 'non-productive public sector' school of opinion is that the manufacture of cigarettes is 'productive', but the treatment of all the ill-health that arises from cigarette smoking is 'non-productive'. However, if all those people who are concerned that the public sector continues to produce desirable products (such as increases in the well-being of people with learning difficulties) are to make their case, they have to ensure not only that the services are provided effi ciently and effectively but also that they are seen to be so provided. It is a formidable challenge, but the welfare of people with learning difficulties demands that it is met.

Similarly, although the reorganization of health and community care have commercial overtones, it is possible to view the changes in a public service perspective. One of the major benefits of the purchaser–provider split is to give greater weight and voice to users' preferences. Under the previous arrangements NHS budgets were held by managers at unit (e.g. hospital) or at departmental (e.g. nursing, pharmacy, pathology) level. In local authority social services departments, budgets were delegated to service managers (e.g. home care, day care, residential care) and to individual 'cost centres' (an area manager, a day centre, a residential home). The implication of this budget allocation system was that each budget holder 'rationed' service delivery, each manager determined how many and which people could receive the service. Different sources of referral could be used, but generally the referrers depended on the service managers to make decisions on whether referrals could be accepted and what level of service should be provided. Service managers would sometimes be in the position that although they were responsible for the disbursement of a budget, outside demands gave them little discretion in how it was allocated. Thus, in some areas service managers were able to use their discretion about the quantity and quality of service to be provided for people who were referred to them, and in other cases service managers had very little discretion and found their budgets exhausted by people who did not have any responsibility for it. The former model was common in community care and social workers had no guarantee that their requests for home care, day care, short-term care or whatever would be met. The latter model was common in hospitals, where consultant physicians ordered tests, prescribed drugs or requested therapies that individual service managers in pathology, pharmacy or physiotherapy, for example, had difficulty in refusing. A major objective of the new arrangements in health and social care is to give purchasing power to people who are responsible for the users' health or welfare. Service managers will obtain their budgets in the form of sales revenue and will only be able to maintain or expand provision if the services provided meet the purchasers' requirements on cost, quantity, quality and outcome.

Purchasing in community care will differ from purchasing in health care. Health care purchasers are operating in the main at the rather macro level of identifying the configuration of services that meet the needs of their local population. These services will normally be provided in the internal NHS market, with some relatively minor use of the outside private health care market. Purchasers of community care will operate at both macro and micro levels. At macro or community-wide level they need to make strategic decisions about the service needs of the population, the resources to be allocated between different groups of users and to different forms of care. But they will also need to operate at the individual or micro level because, as is explained in Chapter 3, managers need to organize (or purchase) the set of services that meets the assessed needs of the people in their care. At both macro and micro levels, local authority social services will be expected to make thorough use of private and voluntary provision and thereby to operate in a local mixed economy. In some areas that will not be too difficult in the provision of residential or nursing home care. The mix of private, voluntary and public provision is well developed in residential care in some localities; nursing home provision is generally dominated by private care (Darton and Wright 1993). Day and domiciliary care is dominated in almost all areas by public provision. In some areas, especially in Inner London and Northern England, there is relatively sparse provision by the independent sector even in residential care (Hamnett and Mullings 1992). Thus, we can expect a slow development of a mixed economy of private, voluntary and public services.

There is a further consideration that ought to be taken into account. Since people with a community care need will frequently require both health and social care, purchasers of both health and social care services need to take a strategic view of provision. It is clearly acknowledged that many of the boundaries between health and social care are extremely fuzzy. This is particularly true for people with learning difficulties, for whom residential, day and respite care may be regarded as health and social care needs. Most health services are available free of charge, but the charging for social care provided by local authorities adds to the confusion and tends to blur this issue even more. Consequently, the Audit Commission (1992) advocated close cooperation in the strategic planning process between NHS and local authority purchasers in order to pool their knowledge and coordinate their purchasing policies and agreed priorities. If these recommendations are put into effect, the new purchasing role will not differ markedly from the strategic planning arrangements that existed before 1993.

There is no need to fear these new approaches of internal markets and care management together with all their accompanying jargon. They can in fact be used to general advantage. By responding to the 'non-productive public sector' opinion, by showing the value of health, social care and other services for people with learning difficulties and their carers, and by ensuring that resources are used efficiently and effectively the doubts of the sceptics can be erased for all our benefits. It is in this spirit that we examine the way in which evaluation of services and policies can show the worth of services, and how this evaluation is itself dependent on clearly defined objectives, comprehensive measurement of resource use and costs, and the clear specification and measurement of outcomes.

2 The evaluation framework

Introduction

Evaluation is about establishing the worth of a policy, service, activity or whatever is under consideration. It is about effectiveness and efficiency as defined in the previous chapter. It is, therefore, an examination of the objectives of service provision, how well these objectives are achieved and at what cost. Evaluation involves the following procedures (Evans *et al*. 1991):

1 The systematic collection of information; that is, collecting information in an explicit way that allows those who have to use the results of the evaluation to assess whether it has been collected in ways that avoid any bias against or in favour of the activities in question.
2 Description of activities, characteristics and outcomes of the service or policies in question.
3 Description of the programmes, personnel, products or other elements of inputs into the services or policies in question.
4 Involvement of all interested persons, who include service providers, service users, the evaluation team itself and decision-makers who will use the results of the evaluation.
5 The making of judgements on the results of the evaluation.
6 Distinguishing between the structure of service provision (inputs), the way in which it works (process) and the achievement of objectives (outcome).

These six procedures lead to the classic framework of economic evaluation, which poses six main questions (Drummond 1981):

1 What is the question/topic to be answered or evaluated?
2 What alternative services, procedures and activities are to be evaluated in answer to this question?

3 What are the costs of these alternatives and how are they to be measured?
4 What are the benefits (effectiveness) of these alternatives and how are they to be measured?
5 What conclusions can be drawn from these analyses of costs and benefits?
6 What allowances have to be made for the doubts, assumptions and uncertainties that were encountered in these analyses?

The final step reminds us that all evaluations concern judgement of some kind, that those judgements are based on prevailing conditions which change over time and that service innovations increase the range of alternative ways of achieving an objective. Thus, the results and consequences of evaluations need to be reviewed from time to time to check whether changes in conditions, new services or perhaps the failure to meet objectives as originally estimated alter the original decisions made on the basis of previous work.

Evaluation is the key to appraising the efficiency and effectiveness of service provision. It is therefore the keystone to ensuring the efficient allocation of resources. In economic theory there are two major considerations in achieving an efficient allocation of resources: consumer satisfaction and productive efficiency. Thus an efficient allocation of resources is achieved where the set of goods, commodities or services that maximizes consumer satisfaction is produced at minimum cost per unit of output. Economic theory shows how this allocative efficiency can be achieved through 'the unseen hand' of the pricing system using a particular set of market considerations under which the owners of the means of production (the entrepreneurs) or firms have a major overriding objective to maximize their profit, or the difference between the monies they spend in inputs (costs) and the revenue they receive from selling their goods and services. We do not need to go into detail here, but the usefulness of this paradigm lies in the way it concentrates attention on the main actors in the system – consumers, suppliers of inputs (labour, land, capital, enterprise) and sellers – as well as on the underlying objectives (maximization of consumer satisfaction, minimizing costs, maximizing profit), the production process and the working of markets.

The emphasis throughout this chapter is on the efficient allocation of resources. The fairness or equity of resource allocation is not discussed. This is for reasons of clarity, to concentrate on one major issue and does not reflect any opinion that equity is less important than efficiency in resource allocation. The efficiency calculus of maximizing net income or profit in the private sector or maximizing effectiveness less costs in the public sector is not purely technical. As discussed later in this chapter, judgement is always needed in valuing the goods and services produced and in assessing the final results of an evaluation. However, the idea of 'fairness' is essentially judgemental. It rests on what people believe to be a fair distribution of costs and benefits falling on different groups in society and this topic is taken to be beyond the scope of this book.

A major starting point in the factors which govern efficiency is the role of consumers in deciding the quantity and variety of the goods and services they wish to buy. Theoretically, it is possible to start from the point of view that it is consumers who demand the range and mix of goods and services which determine what firms will produce at various prices. Of course, in the real world we know that there is a whole industry devoted to persuading consumers that they really need what firms produce, but that debate does not concern us here. Even without advertisements, consumers' subjective opinions and tastes would be important components of market demand.

Theoretically, consumers' demands and the prices they are willing to pay to obtain them are signals to the entrepreneurs in the economy that they will collect the forecasted income if they can produce the goods and services demanded by consumers. They can enjoy part of this income for themselves provided that they organize the purchase and use of the required resources at a cost that is below the total income or revenue they expect to receive. This profit is an incentive for them to enter into and maintain the production of the good or service they have selected. It is also an incentive to economize on resource use.

Although the profit motive is a potent force in ensuring the efficient use of resources within firms, we also need to assess the forces that ensure the efficient allocation of resources between firms producing different goods or services. How do we know the correct quantity to be produced? Much depends on what is meant by 'correct'. Firms are producing too much total output if it cannot all be sold at its current price and this requires them either to reduce the price of the commodity and sell the surplus off or to reduce production and maintain price. Similarly, if firms are unable to produce a sufficient quantity of a commodity to meet existing consumer demand at current prices, the obvious answers are either to let the price rise and reduce total demand or to increase production at the current price.

Prices, therefore, play an important role in determining the quantity and range of goods and services to be provided by signalling to producers whether they are producing too much or too little. However, in terms of efficiency they do not in themselves bring about an optimum allocation of resources. Nor are they operating in a vacuum. The extra force working to ensure efficiency is competition in the markets for goods and services. The market is an important but simple concept in economics. Put simply, it is 'a place' in which buyers and sellers meet to trade, but 'a place' may be several different types of location. It might include, for example, the traditional market in the sense of a market in the square of a country town. The stock market provides another example. It is also possible to talk about the motor car market or the gold market, which are much more nebulous concepts. Markets can be very local, nationwide or international; they exist wherever buying and selling occurs. Competition between buyers and sellers occurs in a market. As we shall see later, the idea of the competitive market underlies the major changes that have occurred recently in the reorganization of the health and community care services in Britain.

Competition limits the power of producers or sellers to exploit consumers, provided that there are no barriers to new firms entering the market. For example, if demand for a commodity increases and the resulting shortage causes its price to increase, the profits of the producers will also rise. These higher profits will be an incentive for new firms to start producing and the consequent increase in the quantity of the good being put on to the market will help to reduce price and profits to a level where no more new firms are encouraged to enter the industry. Conversely, if demand and prices fall, causing profits to reduce, some firms will start to make losses and leave the industry. This will reduce output until the remaining firms enjoy enough profit to make it worth their while to continue production. Competition encourages the more efficient firms to continue in production and forces inefficient firms to quit.

As most economic theory textbooks explain (e.g. Culyer 1986), the price system and competition in markets ensure the efficient allocation of resources between and within the production of goods and services in the economy. At its most efficient the competitive economy is working in a way in which it is not possible to move any resource from one use to another without decreasing output. Provided that there is freedom of movement for all goods, services and the resources needed to produce them, no entrepreneur will earn 'excess' profit. And the beauty of this theoretical world is that it is necessary only to say to each entrepreneur 'maximize your profits!' for such an efficient allocation to be achieved.

Of course, this is theory and the real world is different, but the theory provides three important lessons for practice: first, the importance of consumer sovereignty and demand; second, the efficient production of goods and services; third, the maximization of profit. For this chapter, there is another lesson to examine: the application of these very commercial concerns of consumerism, profit maximization and efficient use of resources to social and health care. Each idea will be considered separately, starting with consumer sovereignty, moving on to notions of the efficient production of social welfare and finally the achievement of efficiency by the maximization of net social benefit from health and social care services. At the end of the chapter we also raise some questions about the way in which markets work or fail to work, and discuss the need for regulation.

Consumer sovereignty

It is a basic tenet of classical economics that consumer choice determines the quantity and variety of goods and services to be produced. Theoretically, each consumer is armed with knowledge of the prevailing prices of all goods and services and has complete access to them, provided that he or she has sufficient income. The consumers are the sole judge of the choices that maximize their total satisfaction. We know that this theoretical world is far removed from the real one where consumers do not have perfect information on the prices of goods available, where access costs vary greatly between localities and where firms produce goods and then subsequently use advertising to create the demand for them.

There are even more complicating factors where public services are concerned. They are free or zero-priced at point of delivery to many consumers. They are financed wholly or in part from general taxation rather than from sales. Some services, like defence and policing, are not susceptible to pricing because the nation consumes them collectively rather than individually. Some services, such as education, produce benefits not just for those directly receiving them but also for the rest of the nation in terms of economic growth, cultural enhancement and social cohesion. However, this does not imply that users or consumers of public services should not have a voice in the way in which they are produced. Recently we have seen the development of pressure or other special groups who have taken a keen interest in the organization and delivery of public services. This movement has led to the development of methods of improving user participation in services for people with learning difficulties, and of giving a voice to service users.

The starting point: the rationale and objectives of service interventions

Quite clearly, people with learning difficulties have the same dignity, the same value, the same rights, the same aspirations and the same basic needs and wants as every other member of the human family. We all want and need to be acknowledged and treated as individual, complete human beings and as full and valued citizens in our own neighbourhood. We all place tremendous importance on being able to participate in the community in ways that are respected and valued. Such participation revolves around having a range of two-way relationships with ordinary people (family, friends) and ordinary places (home, work, shops and so on).

More specifically, we need and want various positive life experiences. The following list is based on the 'accomplishments' framework, set out by O'Brien (1987) and developed by Leedham (1991):

- Community presence – the sharing of the ordinary places that define community life.
- Choice – autonomy in small and big matters, freedom to define who we are and what we value.
- Awareness of opportunities and constraints – information, informed choice etc.
- Competence – the opportunity to perform functional and meaningful activities, with whatever help needed.
- Self-determination – associated with ownership of one's own life and positive self-identity.
- Respect – having valued roles in community life.
- Community participation – being part of a network of two-way relationships with other people (this defines 'community') reflects our deep needs to love and to be loved, to give, to receive, to share.
- Personal continuity – ongoing relationships with people, places and possessions.

These eight accomplishments are positive life experiences that we all seek to increase. Consequently, they are the *raison d'être* of service interventions and a measuring rod for assessing the effectiveness or quality of services. It follows from this that the key questions to ask throughout our work are: what do/would I need and want for myself or my family, and what do/would valued citizens in Britain today want for themselves or their families?

The process of achieving what we need and want

At all the different stages in our lives, we all need and want various relationships and various goods, services, help, and support in order to participate in local community life in valued ways. Most of us achieve this by participating in three main markets.

1 The 'commercial market'. We buy the goods and services that we need and want, for example shopping at the supermarket or at the travel agent. We decide what we need and want, collect information on what is or might be available, and then go and buy the goods or services. The state of our bank balance is obviously a constraint, and this forces us to think about priorities. Consequently, it is important to be well informed about alternative ways of using our money.
2 The 'informal market'. We arrange the multitude of everyday helps and supports (where payment is often not appropriate) that we need and want, for example using the 'services' of family, friends and neighbours. The proper role for services here is to enable informal support to operate more effectively and, as part of this, to promote the development of a supportive and caring community.

2. it's a social network not a market.

3 The 'social market'. We use/receive professional, specialist, and technical services that are funded largely by taxation and provided by the state-regulated 'social market'. Obvious examples are the NHS or the education service. The social market is somewhat different from the free and informal markets in that decisions on what is needed and wanted are typically not made directly by the consumer. The main rationale for this concerns the need for professional, specialist or technical knowledge (e.g. with regard to the diagnosis and treatment of medical conditions). Instead, decisions are made indirectly by professionals, managers or politicians, and the consumer's influence is mediated through these people.

It is important to note that there is a fundamental separation of prescription and provision in the commercial and informal markets. Simplistically, the consumer decides, the provider provides. There would, of course, be a major conflict of interest if, say, the supermarket or the travel agent decided what you needed and wanted and then provided you with it. The result would be a lot of frustration and wasted money. Hence comes the trend towards greater separation of prescription and provision – and prescription and funding – in the social market (where the same agency has traditionally performed both functions).

The issues related to user choice and the provision of social care are discussed further in Chapter 3 and is a recurring theme in Chapters 4 to 6, which contain major discussions of the outcomes of health and social services.

The production of welfare

In the first part of this chapter we set out the role of profit maximization and competition in determining the efficient allocation of resources. The question now is: can these roles be mimicked by public service provision? In the private sector world, the clarion cry to producers was to maximize profit. The equivalent in the public sector is to maximize the net benefit (benefits less costs) of services. However, although costs can be expressed in monetary units, the measurement of 'benefit' makes this a particularly difficult goal for public sector managers to pursue. The benefits of public services are related to improving the well-being of people who receive them (and wider society at times) and are usually assessed in terms of goal achievement. The crucial questions surrounding public services are:

• What objectives are the services attempting to achieve?
• How well are these objectives achieved?

The combination of resources (inputs) to achieve the desired benefits (outputs) in social care has been conceptualized in the framework of 'the production of welfare'.

Services for people with learning difficulties pursue a variety of objectives, such as the improvement of client skills, the minimization of the burden falling on parents or the integration of people with learning difficulties into 'ordinary' community living. By reference to the objectives we have a measure of the need for intervention, and by examining movements towards these objectives we gain an indication of achievement, effectiveness, outcome or benefit. In order to meet needs and to achieve outcomes we usually require some organized intervention by way of service provision. Services are provided by combining the appropriate resources, particularly buildings and the skills of paid or unpaid staff, and these resources are usually obtained at a price. There is nothing particularly new about such a set of dimensions, nor is there anything particularly controversial. However, in this paragraph we have captured the essentials of the economist's approach to the evaluation of services for people with long-term needs, whether they are related to learning difficulty or other conditions. This is the 'production of welfare' approach, which provides us with a framework to link these various concepts, running from objectives to needs and from costs to outcomes, and thereby offering a conceptual base for the examination and pursuit of policy and practice criteria such as equity and efficiency.

There are considerable problems in measuring the output of services for people with learning difficulties. A full discussion of the issues is set out in Chapters 4 to 6. Many of these measurement problems result from attempts to define the 'well-being' of people with learning difficulties and their families and other carers. Consequently, the evaluation of services has sought other ways of assessing achievements. These range from simple measures of the quality of the resources used (e.g. proportion of qualified staff, suitability of buildings) to more complex measures of the quality of service delivery (e.g. staff attitudes to users) and the attitudes of users (user/carer satisfaction with respite care facilities). These attempts at assessing quality of input or process have been termed intermediate outcomes, and the term final outcome is retained for measurement of changes in user/carer well-being. These relationships are illustrated in Figure 2.1.

We can therefore define a service, intervention or activity to be effective if it results in an identifiable increase in outcomes, that is if it moves towards achieving service or policy objectives. Objectives are rarely discussed without reference to the various factors known or believed to have an impact on their achievement. The range of characteristics that may exert an influence is wide: the personal characteristics, experiences and circumstances of clients will be of particular importance not only in

Figure 2.1   Inputs, processes, outcomes

The production of welfare involves:

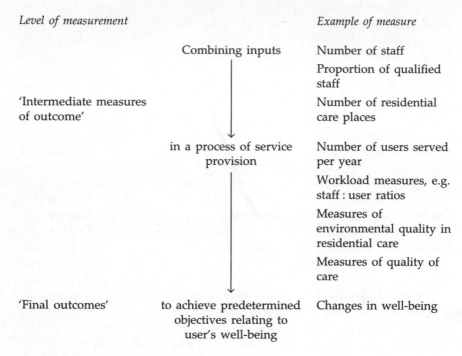

Level of measurement		*Example of measure*
	Combining inputs	Number of staff
		Proportion of qualified staff
'Intermediate measures of outcome'		Number of residential care places
	in a process of service provision	Number of users served per year
		Workload measures, e.g. staff : user ratios
		Measures of environmental quality in residential care
		Measures of quality of care
'Final outcomes'	to achieve predetermined objectives relating to user's well-being	Changes in well-being

assessing the success of care, but also in the definition of objectives at the outset; psychologists stress the importance of a 'good' social environment and supportive and stimulating staff attitudes and roles in moving towards the improvement of behavioural problems; and the characteristics of the physical environment, for example choice over single and shared bedrooms in residential homes, can also be influential factors.

So far we have simply drawn out some of the underlying theoretical perspectives and empirical conclusions of a large body of research on long-term care. However, set out in this way the argument stresses a similarity between the social welfare literature and the basic premises of what the economist calls the theory of production. The economist's basic assumption is that inputs – some of them resources, with a clear imputed price, others with no market value simply because markets do not exist – combine together to produce outcomes (goods and services). This is not implying that long-term care is perceived as a simple process that feeds resources in at one end and mechanically churns out client well-being at the other. Rather, the production analogy helps us to be clear and precise about issues which, when they reach the decision-making stage, require clear and precise policies. Nor do we mean to suggest that we take the power of decision away from the individual professional or worker. The aim of the economist's perspective is not to replace the need for decision-taking, but rather clarity of thought, clarity of assumption and hence clarity of policy. If you are not clear where you are going, how can you be sure you have got there? Anything less is a recipe for confusion. The production analogy underlies the arguments of this book. It should lay to rest the misconceptions that 'economists know the price of everything and the value of nothing' and that they are concerned solely with money, profit and markets.

The production of welfare model, therefore, has five major components. On the achievement side are the final and intermediate outcomes. On the other side of the production relationship are the inputs. Resource inputs are the conventional factors of production. In our case these include staff, physical capital (including buildings and vehicles), provisions and other consumable items. Associated with them are costs. In contrast, the non-resource inputs are determinants of final and intermediate outcome that are neither physical nor tangible: they are embodied in the personalities, activities, attitudes and experiences of the principal actors in a support or care process, particularly the users, their relatives and care staff.

The distinction between resource and non-resource inputs is important. The characteristics of the physical environment, which are included in the resource inputs, are often stressed in policy and planning documents. But it is a common assumption among professional and practitioner groups, and among some associated policy-makers, that non-resource factors such as sympathetic or stimulating staff attitudes are more important. Certainly, much of the social work and health care literature on people with learning difficulties has focused upon these non-resource influences. However, to neglect the influences of the resource inputs will limit the practicable usefulness of any evaluation concerning the association between non-resource factors and outputs. Differences in resource inputs will be partly responsible for observed differences in the extent to which care objectives are achieved, because of both their direct influence upon a client's welfare and their indirect influences on the quality of the service delivered. Similarly, many of the influences of the resource inputs upon final outputs are brought about by the non-resource inputs. It is the resource inputs that enter the financial accounts of health and social care agencies and that, in the economist's terminology, have identifiable costs. Cost, in fact, is a summary measure of the resource inputs. The theoretical and practical issues of measuring costs are discussed in Chapters 7 and 8.

The production of welfare approach is thus a simple summary of the complex linkages between service and client achievements and the resource and non-resource factors that make them possible. The various influences on outcome – the inputs – are highly intercorrelated but this should not be a cause for conceptual concern or empirical difficulty. The production of welfare approach is quite capable of disentangling these intercorrelations and using them to good effect in the development of policy recommendations.

This approach can therefore contribute to the understanding of care practice and the development of policy in a number of ways. It offers a theoretical framework within which to locate many of the current views on the organization and delivery of services for people with learning difficulties. Because it offers clear, hypothetical links between different resource availabilities, personnel activities, client preferences and iden-tifiable changes in circumstances and characteristics, the framework is empirically testable. If it is sensitively structured and responsively re-structured, the framework can embody the results of empirical research. The material in Chapters 3 to 5 illustrates a number of relationships between aspects of care, carers and clients.

In examining the achievements of services for people with learning difficulties we must not confine our evaluative attentions solely to the impacts on the welfare of service users; we should not ignore the effects on society at large. The vast majority of outcome evaluations of services or interventions for people with learning difficulties have focused on the impacts of services on individual users, and rightly so. Yet it was not many decades ago that British society was investing heavily in the high-walled, remote asylums that gave every impression of pursuing objectives which benefited only the relatives of people described as 'lunatics' or 'mental defectives', or which benefited sensitive members of society who would otherwise have had the 'misfortune' of meeting them on the street or in the ale house. Relatives' and society's outcomes assumed precedence over outcomes for people with learning difficulties. In today's more enlightened times we pursue a more equitable balance between the sometimes competing outcomes for users and others, though perhaps few would take the view that public policy or practice has yet got the balance right.

In economics the term 'externality' is used to summarize the many side-effects of consumption or production that are not traded on the market or taken into account in the setting of prices. Some externalities are desirable, such as the pleasure I derive from my neighbour's beauti-ful garden. These are external benefits or positive externalities. Others, termed social costs or negative externalities, are less desirable and in-clude environmental pollution, traffic jams and loud, unwanted noises. Externalities, therefore, are either benefits that one can enjoy for free or at a low price, or costs that one suffers without adequate compensa-tion. Just as the users of services can enjoy both intermediate and final outcomes – such as the receipt of high quality services and the achievement of improvements in skills or higher levels of morale – so the external effects of a policy can be couched in intermediate and final terms. For example, it might be argued that grouping large numbers of people with learning difficulties in remote, bleak asylums generated external benefits to Victorian society, as well as some direct disbenefits to those so accommodated. However, Victorian policy registered some concern lest these asylums damage the well-being of inmates. Thus Victorian society derived 'intermediate external benefits' from the remoteness of the accommodation, and what one might call 'final external benefits' from knowledge that residents were receiving an acceptable quality of care, notwithstanding their separation from society. Bringing the discussion up to date, we can observe numerous effects at play in policy and practice decisions. Most people are reasonably tolerant of oddly dressed or oddly mannered citizens, and the sartorial impact of years of institutionalization may be less a cause for ridicule and victimization than once it was. Nevertheless, it is claimed by some people that discharging hospital patients puts the community at risk. Thus potential external effects might include the assumed rising crime rate as a result of the discharge of people with inadequate resources into inadequately funded community settings, an increase in victimization attacks on people with learning difficulties, longer queues for public sector housing and increased burdens on general practitioner and other local services funded from general sources. A recent government-sponsored survey (Leighton 1988) reported that half the general population were either 'strongly opposed' to integrating people with learning difficulties into the community or 'opposed' to integration that would affect their families or neighbourhoods.

These external effects are examples of market failure. Many beneficial effects, such as the pleasure one derives from another's garden display, cannot be charged for. My neighbours do not have a property right over my enjoyment of their gardens. Similarly, detrimental effects often remain uncompensated for: my neighbours find it difficult to charge me for the weed seeds that blow out of my garden into theirs. Health and social care markets may well experience uncompensated external effects. The common example is where one agency fails to provide a service and pushes costs on to other agencies or individuals. The failure to provide good respite care pushes the costs of care on to family carers.

Markets may also fail to provide services where users need them. Residential homes provide a good example because they may not be in the places where potential residents wish to live but are provided where suitable property is available. Residents may wish to live in ordinary housing accommodation on suburban estates, but other residents may object and prevent the use of the preferred location (Knapp *et al.* 1992). It may well then be necessary for purchasing authorities to use their purchasing or persuasive powers to 'fix' the market to meet users' needs. Some providers may find it difficult to meet the needs of some users who present special care problems. Again, purchasers may wish to intervene by subsidizing some providers to encourage them to accommodate people with special needs. They may also subsidize providers who are needed in certain areas, for example subsidizing residential homes that are needed in areas where property prices are high.

Market regulation may include interference in quality as well as in prices of services. Although user involvement is to be encouraged, assessment of the quality of service provision and delivery may require professional knowledge. It would be very difficult, for example, for users to assess the quality of health rehabilitative services. People who are using some services or living in some residential homes may feel too vulnerable to complain about quality and fear exclusion or eviction.

Thus, although the competitive market provides a useful analogy for the provision of efficient health and social services, it has to be remembered that markets fail and there is a need for general regulation to ensure that overall efficiency is achieved. Without regulations, the enterprise that is the great strength of the competitive spirit and drive towards personal efficiency targets may, through self-interest, fail users or the public at large. This is why economic evaluations attempt to cost all resources used in the policies pursued or the services provided, irrespective of who or which agency owns them, as discussed in Chapter 7. The market analogy provides a framework, but its limitations are clearly recognized.

An introduction to techniques of economic analysis

Economic analysis and decision-making

Evaluation of service provision normally relates to the potential expansion or contraction of an existing service or the appropriate level of service provision for a proposed service. Under such circumstances, knowledge of the way in which costs alter in response to changes in the level of service provision (the cost function) is required to address these issues. Knowledge of the total cost function allows gradual increases in costs (marginal costs, see Chapter 7) to be calculated. The vast majority of evaluations undertaken within the public services require careful calculations of these changes in costs in order to achieve accurate assessment of the resource commitment or resource savings that would result from alterations in the scale or nature of the service provided. Costs that are not sensitive to these changes may invalidate the analysis undertaken.

The economic approach to 'cost' is also distinct from that of other disciplines. The comprehensive approach of the economist encompasses all the resources consumed by society in undertaking any policy or programme. This approach emphasizes that resource costs are equally valid irrespective of whether the resource is actually traded through the market. Thus the effort and commitment of the six million 'informal carers' is no less valid in economic terms than the millions of pounds spent upon carers within the statutory services. The actual conceptualization of 'cost' is equally distinct from the perspective of the economist. These issues are discussed in greater detail in Chapter 7.

Efficiency in service provision

The efficiency of service provision in the public sector depends on the maximization of benefit less income. Therefore, evaluation techniques have sought to estimate the costs and benefits of various alternative ways of providing services. The measurement problems involved are formidable and consequently Chapters 4 to 6 have been devoted to the measurement of benefit or outcome and Chapters 7 and 8 to the measurement of costs. In this section three broad approaches to economic appraisal are discussed.

Cost–benefit analysis (CBA)

Cost–benefit analysis attempts to translate all the costs and benefits from any resource into monetary values. Such an approach is necessary when comparing options that would provide significantly different outcomes. The impact of the outcome variations needs to be reduced to the common scale of money for comparison purposes. The practical difficulties involved in evaluating all costs and benefits in money terms are enormous but the presentation of the cost and benefit issues in this form of a checklist facilitates more rational decision-making by emphasizing the need to analyse symmetrically both the costs and benefits arising from each policy option. In this manner the method of thinking introduced by the use of CBA is more crucial than the practical calculations underlying the analysis. There is no full-blown CBA in health and social care services because of the difficulty of expressing benefits in monetary forms.

Cost–utility analysis (CUA)

Since CBA is so very difficult to complete, analysts have tried to develop other ways of helping decision-makers to choose between alternative methods of delivering services. The problem in the main is the measurement of benefits, although costings are never very straightforward. If benefits are not expressed in money terms, the compromise is to find other suitable units so that services can be assessed in terms of cost per unit of outcome. These outcomes are still difficult to achieve since, as we saw in the previous section, final outcome is about improving the well-being of service users, and defining and measuring 'well-being' in an acceptable way is fraught with difficulty.

The best examples of CUA in health services have come from attempts to measure health-related quality of life in acute medical treatments (Williams 1985). In these studies, various treatments are assessed for improving length of life and improving quality of life. If quality of life is not included some appraisals might stop at just the number of extra years of survival brought about by the different treatments and therefore each treatment would be assessed solely in terms of cost per extra year of life produced. The obvious difficulty with this approach is that unless people are returned to their original state of health the quality of each extra year produced will not be equal. Thus, there have been several attempts to adjust each added year of life by a quality of life index based on pain or distress-free social functioning. In these circumstances, the cost–utility appraisal assesses treatments in terms of the cost per quality adjusted year of life. The use of this technique is still very much at the developmental stage as controversy rages over how to develop an index of quality of life. Thus, cost–utility analyses are still the subject of immense debate. There are no applications in services for the care of people with learning difficulties.

Cost–effectiveness analysis (CEA)

Cost–effectiveness analysis avoids the problems inherent in converting all outcomes to a common unit by focusing on a more restricted set of problems. CEA assesses alternative methods of achieving the same objective and attempts to isolate either the most effective or the lowest cost option. This restriction obviously reduces the applicability of the approach, as only rarely do two options lead to precisely the same outcome. In cases where programme outcomes are 'similar', CEA can be utilized by scaling the results to take account of perceived variations in the effectiveness of options being analysed. The results of a CEA can be divided into four broad categories:

1 The policy is found to be both more effective and cheaper or the same cost.
2 The policy is found to be both less effective and more expensive or the same cost.
3 The policy is found to be more effective but also more expensive.
4 The policy is found to be less effective but also cheaper.

In the first case the policy is unambiguously supported as it both improves outcome and saves resources. In the second case the policy is unambiguously rejected as it reduces outcome and requires additional resources. In the third case the outcome is ambiguous and requires the use of judgement relating to the extent of change in effectiveness and cost. In essence we are addressing the issue of whether the greater effectiveness resulting from this policy is 'worth' the investment of the additional resources. The outcome is also ambiguous in the fourth case, in which a less effective policy saves resources. Again the issue revolves around the extent to which resources are saved and the extent of the reduction in effectiveness. The aim of CEA, especially in the latter two cases, is to supplement, not supplant, the thought processes underlying decision-making.

Conclusion

The evaluative framework shows why concepts of user involvement, efficiency and effectiveness of service provision, the purchaser–provider split, the creation of the internal market and the development of the mixed competitive economy of welfare have formed the basis for the recent reorganization of health and community care in Britain. The analogy of the competitive market is particularly apt because service providers who are unable to meet consumer demand (as expressed by purchasers) at a price that reflects the best use of the resources employed will be driven out of business by more efficient providers. The competitive edge will remain as long as new producers are free to enter the market and can cover their costs. The framework also presents evaluators with some formidable problems of measuring costs and outcomes, which include consumer satisfaction with the services provided and the effectiveness of services in meeting needs and policy objectives. We now proceed to examine these problems in greater detail.

3 The policy background

Introduction

The purpose of this chapter is to set out the policy issues that have influenced the development of services for people with learning difficulties over the past 20 years. In particular, the main concerns are the prevention of conditions that promote learning difficulties, the health care of people with learning difficulties, the changing pattern of care, in particular the transition to community care, and the acceptance of 'ordinary life' objectives. The funding of community care is discussed in the final section.

Prevention policies

This section is concerned with reduction of the incidence of conditions that cause learning difficulties, such as brain defects or abnormalities which occur during pregnancy or birth as well as traumatic incidents or illnesses which cause brain damage in infancy, childhood or other stages of the life cycle. The medical causes of impairments that result in learning difficulties are not addressed here, but it is recognized that the reduction of the relevant impairments is a major objective of good antenatal, obstetric and paediatric services. Thus, preventive policies can be discussed in terms of preconceptual measures, antenatal, neonatal, perinatal and post-natal care. As far as economics is concerned, the major focus has settled on the provision of methods of antenatal screening and, therefore, most of the discussion is concentrated on this issue.

Preconception measures

One of the most important prevention measures that has developed over the past 20 years is the provision of programmes for the immunization of adolescent girls against rubella. Currently the take-up rate for females under the age of 14 in England is over 80 per cent (Department of Health 1992). It has been argued that this important step is still insufficient and that girls should be given the first immunizing dose at 18 months of age, along with immunization against mumps and measles (Taylor and Taylor 1986).

Where impairments are likely to arise from hereditary factors, genetic counselling has a key role to play. In addition, health education is necessary to warn couples of the risks of hereditary conditions and to encourage those likely to be affected to seek advice and help. In cases where impairments arise from poor environmental conditions, poor nutrition or known pollutants, general public health measures such as housing improvements, dietary advice and reduction in pollution will play an important part. Although there may be little evidence of the relationship between learning difficulties and unwanted pregnancies, general contraceptive advice and family planning services play an important role in ensuring desired and planned pregnancies, which will tend to produce healthy and well-nurtured infants (Taylor and Taylor 1986).

Antenatal care

In general, good antenatal care that ensures the birth of a healthy baby is as important in prevention policies as good preconceptual care and services. This applies across all pregnancies irrespective of the risk of impairments that cause learning difficulties. However, some of the most problematic issues have arisen with the development of methods of antenatal screening that accurately detect affected fetuses and the provision of the subsequent option to terminate the pregnancy. The religious and ethical considerations are highly relevant and important here, but given the orientation of the book towards evaluation, attention is focused on the appraisals of the costs and benefits of these techniques.

A number of prenatal fetal screening techniques have been pioneered over the past 20 years and progress is being made continuously in developing new techniques or improving existing ones. One of the major economic concerns has been about the costs and benefits of providing the service to all or a limited number of expectant mothers. In a nutshell, the problem is that the risks of certain defects vary within the population and the costs of total coverage are likely to be very high. Thus, where risks are very low, it may be more worthwhile to invest resources in other programmes, within either antenatal care or some other programme, than in a large-scale specialized screening programme.

The development of screening techniques that detect an affected fetus provides a good example of the appraisals undertaken and the discussions they have provoked. Approximately 15 per cent of fetuses are lost by spontaneous miscarriage in early pregnancy and over one-half of such fetal loss is caused by an unbalanced chromosome abnormality. In many cases, miscarriage can be perceived as being nature's response to severe fetal abnormality and the role of prenatal screening is to complement this natural process by identifying the remaining affected pregnancies. In the past, women were identified as being at high risk entirely on the basis of maternal age. The rationale for such selection was the strong relation-ship between the risk of a pregnancy affected by Down's syndrome and maternal age. The overall risk for women of all ages is 1 in 650. However, a mother who conceives at age 25 has only a 1 in 1,500 risk of giving birth to a Down's syndrome baby. This rises to a 1 in 350 risk at age 35, and a 1 in 30 risk at age 45 (Ferguson-Smith 1988). Unfortunately, selec-tion on the basis of age alone excludes the vast majority of pregnancies given the significantly higher birth rate among younger women. In ad-dition, selection on the basis of age alone exposes women to a hazardous procedure that could have been avoided if it were possible more accur-ately to select the women at highest risk.

Methods have been developed to improve detection above levels exhi-bited by systems based only on an age factor. Wald *et al.* (1988) reported that with age as a basis for screening only 30 per cent of all pregnancies affected by Down's syndrome could be detected by amniocentesis, and the actual detection rate was much lower because fewer than 50 per cent of older women had chosen to accept an amniocentesis. A new selection criteria using age and the results of simple blood tests could identify about 60 per cent of all affected pregnancies in the high risk group (Wald *et al.* 1988). The extra costs of the improved selection criteria appear to be small. One test (for alphafetoprotein, AFP) is already employed as a screening process for spina bifida (looking for high maternal serum AFP), and the analysis for low AFP (indicative of Down's syndrome) should not require any additional resources. The other test, on human chorionic gonadotrophin (HCG), is a highly mechanized process and the major cost involved would be that of reagent kits. The benefits of spreading screening protection to all women and improving the selection process would appear to outweigh by far the small additional costs involved.

Current government policy indicates the provision of amniocentesis to all women over the age of 35. A study in North Western Regional Health Authority showed that approximately 100 children per year are born with Down's syndrome out of a total of approximately 60,000 pregnancies (Haycox and Walsworth-Bell 1988). A survey of women who had amniocentesis suggested a strong propensity to terminate abnormal pregnancies: of the 24 women detected by NWRHA current screening service in 1988, only one decided not to have an abortion when informed that she was carrying a child with Down's syndrome. On this basis it was assumed that 95 per cent of women who are informed that they are carrying an affected child will choose to have a termination. Assuming

Table 3.1 Impact of composite risk screening

Current system	Composite system
Stage 1: selection of women for amniocentesis	
Age alone – no extra cost, only older women covered.	Composite risk calculated from age. AFP and HCG. Increased cost of HCG reagents but all women covered.
Stage 2: provision of amniocentesis	
30–40% of older women take up the service – approximately 4% of all pregnancies.	Higher take-up rate as more accurate test – approximately 5–6% of all pregnancies. Marginally increased workload of obstetrics and gynaecology service to cope with additional spontaneous abortions. Increased workload of cytogenetic laboratory in analysing samples of amniotic fluid.
Stage 3: implications of improved information	
Approximately 20% detection implications of termination or better preparation of family for baby with Down's syndrome. Approximately 80% liveborn to families unaware of risk.	Approximately 60% detection – three times as many terminations and well prepared families. Approximately 40% liveborn to families unaware of risk.

that 120 fetuses would be born in the absence of any screening service, and that there would be a 60 per cent detection rate using the composite risk factor, then an enhanced service could detect 72 affected fetuses, of which an estimated 68 would be terminated. In comparison to the current service the birth of an additional 45 fetuses would be prevented within NWRHA.

The resources required to implement the system of composite screening in 1988 into the North Western Regional Health Authority were estimated at £250,000 per annum (Haycox and Walsworth-Bell 1988). The increased accuracy of the screening system, however, would be expected to detect an additional 48 fetuses with Down's syndrome, of which 45 would be expected to be terminated. The anticipated costs and benefits that would be expected to be derived from this improvement in screening for Down's syndrome within the North Western Region (population four million) are provided in Table 3.1.

Economists have had great difficulties in getting to grips with the

appraisal of prenatal screening techniques. The only aspect of the economic appraisal that gathers any general consensus is the financial cost
of the screening programme and of subsequent terminations of pregnancy. After this, the methodological problems become increasingly tricky.
As a point of departure, it is possible to look at the earliest appraisals of
prenatal screening and see how they identified the benefits that might
accrue from the introduction of the programme. These benefits take the
form of 'cost savings' from the extra costs that a disabled person places
on his or her family and the rest of society (Hagard and Carter 1976). The
implication of this argument is that disabled people impose extra costs
(but no benefits) on society over the length of their lives. This cannot be
right. A complicating factor is that women who agree to the termination
of an affected pregnancy may subsequently conceive and bear a healthy
child. Thus, studies then became even more complex by talking about
only the costs of rearing a disabled child that exceed those of a 'normal'
child.

Methodologically, it is always tricky to use cost savings as a measure
of benefits. Assuming for a while that disabled people did impose
uncompensated costs on society, it is possible to calculate the financial
costs of a screening programme and subsequent termination and deduct
the estimated life-long cost savings from this total, for both 'replacement'
and 'non-replacement' scenarios. If this approach were acceptable, it is
possible that the financial costs of screening would be completely offset
by the savings, at least for women over 35 years of age.

There are, of course, non-financial benefits to these screening programmes. Information provided by the results of the screening process
has a number of benefits. The reassurance of a negative result is an
obvious one. Even people who choose not to terminate an affected pregnancy will have time to prepare for any special care needs their baby
may require. It has also been suggested (Modell 1986) that the availability
of the screen encourages people who feared the risk of producing a disabled infant to start a family, knowing that it would be possible to terminate an affected pregnancy. Against this are the disbenefits of the risks
of false positives or harm done by the screen. Thus, a considerable argument for introducing, widening and continuing screening would be that
it gives potential parents the chance of being reassured about the health
of the fetus or having a choice of termination or going to full-term pregnancy if the test detected an abnormality.

It is, therefore, possible to avoid becoming embroiled in the discussion
about whether or not disabled people 'cost' more than 'normal' people.
It is easy to see, especially in a world of continuing financial crises and
severely restrained public expenditure, why analysts were attracted to
offset the costs of screening with hypothesized cost savings. The general
discomfort of the logic of treating disabled people in this way and of the

resulting undervaluation has made economists much more careful in their approach (Callan 1988). The general mood of the discussion is settling towards the cost of screening, the development of safer methods and the lowering of the age limit of women to be included in the programme. It has to be remembered, though, that decisions have to be made as to whether the benefits are worth the cost, both on an individual basis, in balancing the risks involved, and at a societal level, in terms of the general demand on resources for health care and their allocation between this programme and other forms of screening or treatment.

General health care

People with learning difficulties will use post-natal, paediatric and general health services along with the general population. Two special aspects of health care, though, should be mentioned. First, people with learning difficulties may need special help to access and use general services. This has been recognized at ministerial level (Department of Health 1989) and specific recommendations have been made to health services to introduce the necessary arrangements. In particular, it was recommended that a designated person in a hospital should be responsible for ensuring that people with learning difficulties who are referred for treatment there receive the individual care that they need, for example in finding their way around the different departments, communicating with staff and developing nursing care plans.

The second aspect is more difficult. It relates to the special conditions or extra medical attention that may need to be given, but are frequently missed in the primary health care services. For example, learning difficulties may be accompanied by physical disability, sensory impairment or susceptibility to fits. A recent survey from the Royal College of General Practitioners (1990) found a number of impairments or disabilities among people with learning difficulties, including fits or epilepsy, difficulty with walking or inability to walk at all, and hearing and sight problems.

In other instances, medical problems may go undetected or undertreated, either because people with learning difficulties are at special risk or because their general disability masks other treatable conditions. One small study of 151 people attending a training centre found that there was a considerable unmanaged set of problems affecting circulatory, respiratory, nervous and metabolic systems as well as poor management of hearing and sight problems (Howells 1986).

There are no special screening methods or requirements for the detection of these unmanaged conditions, either in the primary health sector or in hospitals. The need for careful, routine checking of health problems of people with learning difficulties and discussions with carers should be stressed in the training of doctors, nurses, paramedical and social care workers. It takes time to change attitudes and to complete necessary training, but at least in the short term in each health authority it would be possible to give the responsibility of managing the medical and nursing care of people with learning difficulties in general hospitals to one or two designated staff, and to use a nurse, possibly a health visitor, in primary care to assist with the identification and management of concurrent health problems in this population alongside general practitioners and their practice nursing staff. It is also possible that health care needs will be recognized as part of the assessment and service delivery components of care management, which are discussed below. If this is so, there will be considerable pressure on general practitioners and the NHS providers to deliver the appropriate treatments.

The transition to community care

Background

Throughout the 1960s there was a long-running debate about the relative merits of community and hospital care. By the beginning of the 1970s, the balance of advantage was tipping towards the community, with growing discontent with hospital care, as revealed in specific studies of the care provided in institutions (Goffman 1961) and by a number of scandals arising from the poor standards of care offered. Some motivation for community care may also have come from a belief that its costs were below those of hospital care.

The publication of the White Paper, *Better Services for the Mentally Handicapped* (Department of Health and Social Security 1971), was a watershed in this debate. One of its main recommendations was a replacement of about half the 60,000 hospital places in England and Wales by residential home care. This substitution would take place gradually over 20 years. These days, with hindsight, it is possible to say that too many hospital places and too few residential places were recommended. The transition to community care was given a further impetus by the publication of the Jay Committee's recommendations on the principles of community-based care (Committee of Enquiry into Mental Handicap Nursing and Care 1979). These principles emphasized the rights and individuality of people with learning difficulties and the reduction of their isolation and segregation in society. The principles were put into practice as health and local authorities began to accept policies that developed services in line with the objectives of 'ordinary living', which are discussed later.

Throughout the 1970s, hospital closures occurred at a very slow pace and in 1981 a decision was made to accelerate community-based care (Department of Health and Social Security 1981). A major cause of slow progress had been the difficulty of financing the replacement residential

Table 3.2 Places available in hospitals and residential care in England 1980–1990

	1980	1990	% change
Beds available in NHS hospitals	51,500	32,700	−37
Places in local authority residential homes	12,062	16,886	+40
Places in voluntary homes	2,129	7,894	+271
Places in private homes	1,298	8,383	+546
Total	66,989	65,862	−2

Sources: Department of Health and Social Security 1984; Department of Health 1991.

care, since the cash savings from the closures accrued at least in the first instance to health authorities, but the responsibility for providing residential care generally lay with local authorities. New financing arrangements were recommended to ensure that the inter-agency cash transfers were more rapidly and effectively transacted.

Since 1981 there has been steady progress towards the replacement of hospital by residential care. Priority was given to the discharge of children and to the prevention of their admission. This policy has been almost completely and successfully achieved. However, few hospitals have been completely closed and there has been some concern that the pace of change has failed those people with learning difficulties who still remain in what is considered to be unsatisfactory accommodation. As discussed later, a major reason for this alleged failure has been the difficulties in financing care in the community, which on the whole is proving to be more expensive than hospital care, as discussed in Chapter 8.

Despite the criticisms that have been levelled at the pace of change in the transition to community care, the 1980s have seen some matching of hospital closures by the provision of residential homes in a most fascinating, but possibly accidental, development of a mixed economy of welfare. Between 1980 and 1990 the balance of residential care across public and independent providers in England changed as shown in Table 3.2. In 1980, 75 per cent of people with severe learning difficulties in long-term care were accommodated in hospitals and only 5 per cent were in independent residential homes. By 1990, about half were in hospitals while 25 per cent were in independent homes.

Finance again played an important role in these changes. The expansion of private and voluntary residential care has been financed by social security payments, which cover all or the major part of the changes made for accommodation for a large proportion of residents with learning difficulties. This expenditure has supplemented the budgets of the other public agencies and many health and local authorities might well have had to pace their closure programme even more slowly if they had had to rely solely on their own resources. In addition, unlike the programme for the resettlement of people from psychiatric hospitals, which has generated many criticisms over the failure to provide suitable alternative accommodation, the transition to community care for people with learning difficulties has been accomplished without a stream of stories and scandals about homelessness or unsatisfactory standards of care.

The 'ordinary life' objectives

Throughout the 1980s there has been widespread, though not universal, support for the application of the objectives of 'ordinary living' to people with learning difficulties. A fuller discussion of the principles of an 'ordinary life' and of normalization is set out in Chapter 4. The point of raising the issue at this stage is that the transition to community care and the provision of services for people cared for at home have been affected by the debate on these philosophies and the resource implications of their acceptance and implementation. In residential care, for example, there has been a long-running controversy over the type of accommodation that should be used for people leaving hospital, with the strongest advocates of the 'ordinary life' principles recommending that people with learning difficulties should live in 'ordinary' domestic-scale housing accommodation within their local communities. As discussed in Chapter 8, this has raised a number of issues on the costs of residential homes and the number of people accommodated. The move has also affected thinking about the appropriate nature and size of day services, about employment opportunities and about helping families to care for a relative with learning difficulties.

The general principles behind the 'ordinary life' objectives are well set out in a policy statement issued by the North Western Regional Health Authority (1990). The statement explains how 'ordinary life' principles are to be applied in the strategy for caring for people with learning difficulties by posing and outlining answers to five key questions:

1 *Who am I?* Answering this question involves valuing people in terms of giving them positive identity, treating them as individuals, accepting them for who they are and giving them opportunities to make worthwhile contributions to the community.
2 *Whom do I know?* Knowing people means having the opportunity to develop a number of social contacts, having a wide circle of friends, having help to communicate, if necessary, and keeping in touch with family, friends and relatives.
3 *How do I live?* Having a valued lifestyle means sharing ordinary places, sharing ordinary activities, meeting ordinary people and sharing in ordinary facilities.

4 *What can I do?* Having a valued lifestyle means doing things that are important to oneself, being encouraged and helped to develop skills and interests, keeping fit and having opportunities to try out new activities.
5 *How can I influence and control my life?* Having control of one's own life means having the opportunities to choose and to be able to influence events, having choices respected and having someone to help with decision-making if necessary.

The acceptance of this philosophy of care implies the full integration of people with learning difficulties into their own communities, and an end to segregation in specialized large units, such as hospitals, large residential homes, large specialized day centres and special employment or occupation centres. As stated above, these principles are now widely accepted, but there is some opposition from people who believe that specialized facilities can care best for people with learning difficulties, and although these views are recognized in official government policy, they still have only limited support. The dilemma posed by the different opinions is well illustrated in a recent circular (Department of Health 1991) on residential care, which advocated the provision of domestic-scale living accommodation but recognized that there were still arguments being put forward for specialized residential care facilities (including village communities).

Day services

The 'ordinary life' principles have led to doubts about the effectiveness of many traditional day services, in particular the use of large day centres, which were originally named occupation centres, then adult training centres and then social education centres (with or without special needs or special care units). The aforementioned circular (Department of Health 1991) said that 'local authorities should plan to shift away from services based on the traditional adult training centre' (para. 15). New services should be based on assessment of individual needs, which would then be met by personalized, planned programmes of day-time activities using ordinary community facilities. The buildings that housed the social education centres need not be abandoned, but could be converted to 'resource centres' providing assessment facilities, some services and a staff base. However, the main thrust of policy should be towards encouraging people to use schools, colleges, recreation facilities, social clubs, shops, cinemas and open spaces enjoyed by the general population.

The implementation of these policy guidelines is bound to occur gradually because of the resource implications involved, as discussed in Chapter 8. Day services are moving towards a more intensively staffed form of provision than existed in social education centres. Although the guidance suggested the use of volunteers to accompany people who need help to access general community facilities, it is doubtful that this change could take place without the increasing involvement of trained staff.

Employment services

Contract work was part of the service provided in social education centres. There were advantages to such work because it provided an approximation to a normal family routine of going to work, it provided revenue for the centre and it could give opportunities to 'the workers' of earning a 'wage'. However, critics pointed out the repetitive nature of the work, the boredom, the failure to widen and deepen individual skills, the segregation and at times the lack of demand for the products. If 'ordinary life' principles are to apply, would it not be more effective to place people with learning difficulties in general, open employment?

Of course, especially over the past 10 years, finding and keeping a job has been a problem for the entire population. The performance of the British economy has not been conducive to experiments in new methods of employing people with either learning difficulties or physical disabilities. Nevertheless, attempts have been made to get some initiatives under way. The Pathways Employment Service, developed by MENCAP in collaboration with local authorities, has attempted to place people with learning difficulties in paid employment: 'regular jobs earning the going rate for the work they do and as an accepted member of the workforce' (MENCAP undated). The Pathway Officer plays a key role in assessing anyone who is referred to the service for suitable employment and assisting the person to gain employment. This assistance may include improving existing skills, approaching prospective employers, attendance at interviews and follow-up visits after the start of work.

Supported employment is still in its infancy for people with learning difficulties, and their earnings potential was severely limited until recently by social security regulations and the effects of regular wages on benefit paid (Disability Alliance 1992). Some schemes that specially cater for providing employment for people with learning difficulties have been developed in the United States and have potential for application in the UK (Campaign for People with Mental Handicaps 1985). However, progress has been very slow; this applies to employment opportunities for many people with chronic illnesses and disabilities, not just to people with learning difficulties. In addition, in the past 10 years there have been additional problems of training unemployed school-leavers, unemployed people in declining industries and those whose skills are no longer relevant. The labour market has generally suffered excess supply, and until a lower level of unemployment is achieved it is going to continue to be difficult to place disabled people in work. There is no lack of general ideas, principles and experimental schemes, but there are very few initiatives that lead to the widespread, permanent employment of people with learning difficulties.

Family care

As stated in Chapter 1, about one-half of the total number of people with severe learning difficulties live at home with their families. Most of the people with moderate learning difficulties live at home with their families. There has been concern that the transition to community care has led to a 'two-tier' service, with priority given to people leaving hospital, while those at home have received little help beyond traditional day care (Audit Commission 1989). Generally, a number of services are available to help a family care for a relative with learning difficulties but the coverage of these services is rather inadequate. There is little firm evidence on a UK scale to back up these opinions, but evidence from the All Wales Strategy suggests that, if the picture revealed there is true on a national level, there is a major problem of unmet need in the community. The last report from the All Wales Strategy (Welsh Office 1991a) identified a need for more day services, respite care and domiciliary care. Given that in many parts of the UK there is a total lack of domiciliary care specially designed to meet the needs of people with learning difficulties, the picture for areas outside Wales is likely to be worse rather than better than that revealed in these surveys.

Improvement of family-based care has several elements. Day and employment services have already been mentioned. There are three other important aspects: short-term care, professional support and financial help.

Short-term care

Short-term care can be provided in a number of settings: as part of a residential home, in temporary family-based foster care or in the person's own home. It is possible for such care to be something of a mixed blessing, in that temporary separation can be distressing for carers and for people with learning difficulties but at the same time the rest granted to carers renews their strength to continue with their caring activities. As usual, the needs of individuals will differ for several reasons and they will have different preferences for different types of care. This is shown in some areas where families obtain care from a variety of sources (Robinson and Stalker 1991).

Short-term care, especially in the variety needed to meet individual needs and preferences, is in short supply. This means that families have to manage with less than satisfactory provision or with no provision at all. The strain of caring for a person with severe learning difficulties in a family setting over a long period of time is well known and the absence of suitable care for those who wish to use it means that carers are left to carry all the burden on their own shoulders. As with day care and employment services, there are accepted principles and a good deal of experience of what constitutes a high-quality service. The major cause of the shortage of facilities is likely to be financial and this problem is raised at the end of this chapter.

Professional support

Many areas benefit from the work of teams of professionals from different backgrounds, who can provide families with counselling, support, access to services and advice on welfare benefits and other facilities that help in the caring situation (Brown and Wistow 1990). Psychiatrists, psychologists, community nurses with specialized training in the care of people with learning difficulties, occupational therapists and social workers belong to such teams. How adequate their coverage is and how much unmet need there is for this support is not clear. The new arrangements for community care contained in the National Health Service and Community Care Act 1990 will give new prominence to this work.

One of the major effects of the 1990 Act is the development of case or care management. The aim behind this service is to ensure that people living in the community who need any service receive effective support in obtaining it. There are five key tasks to care management:

- identifying need;
- assessing needs;
- organizing a set of services to meet the assessed needs;
- mobilizing resources to meet needs;
- monitoring the effectiveness of the services provided.

There have been experiments in care management that give a good guide to the way in which an effective service can be provided. Most of the pioneering work in Britain has been carried out in the care of elderly people (Challis and Davies 1986) but people with learning difficulties have been able to benefit in some areas of the country from innovative schemes (National Development Team 1991). If the lessons of the experimental and development work in care management are put into practice, the implementation of the 1990 Act should provide people with learning difficulties with a wonderful new opportunity to benefit from individually tailored packages of services.

The main strength of care management is its emphasis on the identification and assessment of individual needs and the provision of services tailored to meet them. In an ideal situation, each person with learning difficulties will be allocated a care manager who will carry out the tasks listed above. In theory, therefore, people with learning difficulties will find that they are receiving the care that will benefit them most. The care manager may be any of the professionals who provide support at the moment and it is by no means clear that any profession will be specially singled out for the role. Indeed, it would be possible for a team to carry out the core tasks of care management.

In practice, care management will run into the same financial constraints that have operated on all other services for people with learning difficulties. In the first place there is a need to determine the caseload of one or a team of care managers. In the work on the care of elderly people, care managers carried a caseload of around 25 people (Challis *et al.* 1990). In the Andover scheme for people with learning difficulties the caseload of one and a half full-time equivalent managers was 50 people (National Development Team 1991). The resource implications of different caseloads will no doubt be assessed from one locality to another and it will be some time before the full resource consequences are established.

The establishment of care managers is only the first step, though. If care managers effectively achieve their objectives, especially in identifying all the needs of the people in their locality with learning disabilities, and the extent of unmet need in day, respite and domiciliary care is of the scale suspected, they will produce a whole new set of service requirements, each with its own resource consequences. Unless the finance is available to meet the new demands, it is easy to envisage that the actual situation will fall far short of the ideal. In addition, care management will touch closely on the systems that are being designed to bring greater user and carer involvement in service planning and provision.

Financial help

The benefits provided by the social security system help to compensate for some of the extra costs of caring for a person with learning difficulties at home. These benefits are in addition to income support, family credit and housing benefit payments, which are available to supplement low incomes in general. They include:

1 Attendance Allowance, which is paid for children aged six months to five years or people aged 65 or more who need a considerable amount of care by day and/or by night.
2 Disability Living Allowance, which is paid for people aged between five and 65 years who need a considerable amount of care by day and/or by night.

3 Disability Working Allowance, for people aged 16 years or over who are working 16 hours a week or more and who are considered to be at a disadvantage because they are employed (or self-employed).
4 Severe Disablement Allowance, paid to people who have been incapable for work for at least 28 weeks but do not have sufficient national insurance contributions to qualify for sickness pay or invalidity benefit.
5 Community Care Grants, which may be paid to assist a person to be resettled in the community following a stay in hospital or residential care or to remain in the community instead of entering hospital or residential care.

Certain charitable funds can also be drawn on, including:

6 The Independent Living Fund, a charitable organization set up with government funds to help severely disabled people who need domestic support if they are to live in their own homes. The original arrangements for the fund came to an end in March 1993 and two new administrative bodies were created. One body administers the funds for the people who received payments before November 1992 and the second body is concerned with people funded after April 1993.
7 The Family Fund, financed out of government funds but administered by the Joseph Rowntree Foundation. The Fund is used to help families caring for a severely handicapped child under 16 years old by awarding a lump sum granted for a specific item, for example a washing machine, tumble drier, clothing, telephone and holiday.

These sources of support compensate to some extent for the extra costs imposed on households where one family member suffers a major, chronic disability. The other financial effect that influences the household economy is the loss of employment opportunities for the principal carer. Again it is possible that the payment of a social security benefit – Invalid Care Allowance – will provide some compensation for lost earnings. Invalid Care Allowance is paid to people who have not been able to maintain or take up employment because of the time they have to devote to caring for a disabled person.

It is difficult to assess the degree to which these different forms of financial support actually compensate for the higher costs of coping with a disability.

People with behaviour disorders

About 10 to 15 people with learning difficulties per 100,000 general population present special challenges for service providers (Emerson *et al.* 1987b). There have been a number of efforts to define these special challenges, for example in terms of inappropriate behaviour or behaviour that is dangerous to that person or others (Zarkowski and Clements 1988), or in terms of using services: 'behaviour of such intensity, frequency and duration that the physical safety of the person or others is placed in serious jeopardy or behaviour which is likely to seriously limit or delay access to and use of ordinary community facilities' (Emerson *et al.* 1987a). In a study in the area of the North Western Regional Health Authority, Qureshi and Alborz (1992) found that the prevalence of this type of behaviour varied from one locality to another from 9 to 25 persons per 100,000 general population. The higher prevalence occurred in the more socially deprived districts.

There is a major policy question concerned with how appropriate the 'ordinary life' model is for people with challenging behaviour. Those who have developed and advocated the model would suggest that many people with challenging behaviours do not need to be segregated and that 'ordinary life opportunities together with methods which promote and support adaptation to the environment are possible ways of preventing challenging behaviour' (Welsh Health Planning Forum 1992: 41, para. 125). It is, however, acknowledged by this Forum that a small number of individuals with learning difficulties (about 5 per cent) require special facilities because they offend or are deemed to be dangerous. There has been no special service prescription on treating people with challenging behaviour although relevant services have received close study (Department of Health 1989). Instead, NHS authorities and social services departments have been left to develop their own local responses to the problems posed. This has led to a wide variety of approaches, including specialized teams, specialized facilities and integrated services, with or without occasional withdrawal when behaviour becomes too challenging for the service to handle (Harris 1991). Very few of these approaches have been evaluated, so no single model of best practice has emerged. Thus, there is a considerable need to share experience and to disseminate the lessons learned from different approaches as well as to carry out formal evaluations of alternative methods of care for people with challenging behaviour.

Empowerment and brokerage in health and social care

Principles of empowerment and brokerage

If people with learning difficulties have the same basic needs and wants as everyone else, there is no reason why the process of achieving needs and wants should be any different from that applying to the general population. 'That means becoming more compatible with communities, and valuing the ways in which ordinary people and communities operate' (Dowson 1991: 26).

The general idea of empowerment and brokerage is tremendously 'natural' and simple. The purpose is to enable people to exercise the rights and responsibilities of citizenship. Towards this end, the objective is to empower consumers and their support networks by giving them:

- control over resources – individualized funding, which gives consumers the ability to make effective *demands* (and should maximize system flexibility, responsiveness and accountability);
- information on how best to spend their resources;
- technical support with making the necessary arrangements.

The aim is to enable people with disabilities to achieve what they want and need in basically the same way that you or I would. Empowerment and brokerage is therefore a natural extension of ordinary community processes.

It is important to emphasize three points. First, the objective is genuine consumer control, not just participation in decision-making. This is reflected in the titles of the two most comprehensive UK publications to date on empowerment and brokerage: *Free to Choose* (Brandon and Towe 1989) and *Direct Power* (Brandon 1991). Second, consumers are helped by the people closest to them, typically family and friends. This is often referred to as the consumer's personal network, or 'Joshua Group'. Third, service brokers are independent from service providers and funding agencies.

The obvious separation of service provision from the other steps conforms with general expectations of consumers outside health and social services, where we expect people to provide a product or service, not to give us reliable advice about whether we need it or can afford it (Dowson 1990: 17).

Brokers may come from a variety of professions or voluntary societies and provide a technical, mediating, support service, acting on the agenda of the person served. They act like travel agents, mixing and matching services from various sources (existing and new sources in an infinitely mixed economy of provision) and being accountable to the consumer and his or her support network. They also act as catalysts in stimulating the community to respond to consumers' needs and demands. This increases the ability of families and communities to help themselves. It also means that services are interwoven with families and neighbourhoods, which is beneficial in terms of:

- making maximum use of existing and potential resources;
- promoting fuller community participation by people with disabilities;
- gaining support from the community and building as stronger pressure-group power base.

A service brokerage system revolving around consumer power has its own in-built accountability mechanisms and 'quality action process' in that providers would have to deliver the goods in order to survive, yet alone grow and develop. This would help to overcome various problems and constraints that tend to dominate the existing system. More specifically, it would help to:

- spread good practices;
- overcome the major problems of inter-agency and inter-professional fragmentation of funding, responsibility and accountability, and the resulting 'buck-passing approach';
- overcome the low priority given to people with learning difficulties;
- provide promising ways of improving pessimistic, sceptical and demoralized climates.

Service brokerage provides coherent frameworks and powerful mechanisms for improving opportunities and supports. This will facilitate and support the development of a number of core services, which will include:

- flexible and mobile staff teams, to enable and support people to take advantage of community resources and opportunities, from going to the pub with friends to undertaking full-time employment;
- supported ordinary housing (of various types);
- various family support services.

These services will be very different from most existing services. They will be more flexible and, as part of this, more labour-intensive (and much less facility-based). Furthermore, they will build on the activities and motives of ordinary people and communities, and will thus be much more 'ecologically sound'.

The existing service system

The existing system does not wholly reflect a genuine commitment to enabling the positive life experiences considered above.

The arrangements before April 1993 actually undermined ordinary community processes. Most services were organized and provided in a very much top-down and paternalistic way, with a considerable reliance on 'expert' judgements made by professionals and managers. Prescription, funding decisions and provision were performed by the same agency, even the same people. This encourages block-funding, block-provision and 'fitting people in' to the best (least bad) alternative. The result was that people had few rights, few choices and no real power as consumers. They became 'clientized', passive and dependent on the services offered.

While the new arrangements for community care have some laudable objectives for the social care sector, for example enabling people to live in their own homes, caring for the carers, clarifying responsibilities and accountability, and developing care management, they still do not address the real issues of the need for empowerment and brokerage as ways of achieving objectives. As the pressure group Values into Action puts it, the *Caring for People* proposals (Secretaries of State for Health *et al*. 1989) indicate a continuing belief that the service machine can deliver, if only it can be put together in the right way. 'The evidence would suggest that is either a deception or a gross conceit . . . Where in the UK has there been any large scale success in helping people with learning difficulties to achieve a socially valued, integrated lifestyle? As far as we know, nowhere' (Values into Action 1989).

The underlying problem with the new legislation is that it does not attempt a fundamental separation of prescription and provision, or of prescription and funding. Care management combines these conflicting functions, and consequently is likely to lead to 'more of the same'. It could fail to achieve the radical change that is needed.

The need for a new approach: ways forward

Approaches revolving around rights, empowerment and service brokerage represent an essential precursor of good practice: (a) they build on the 'ordinary life' philosophy, which reflects the major objective of service interventions and provides a measuring rod for assessing effectiveness and quality; (b) they are 'ecologically sound' extensions of the ordinary processes by which most people achieve what they want and need. Thus they also provide process-based measures of success. Furthermore, empowerment and brokerage could act as a powerful base mechanism for achieving the main objectives of the community care legislation:

- enabling people to live in their own homes;
- caring for the carers;
- making 'assessment and care management' the cornerstone of high quality provision;
- promoting a flourishing independent sector;
- clarifying responsibilities and accountability;
- improving value for money.

Moreover, the lack of direction and coherence in the legislation leaves ample scope for forward-looking players to make significant advances towards empowerment and brokerage.

Given this scenario, it is surprising to find that there is not a tremendous amount of work being done on the rights, empowerment and brokerage topic in this country, and certainly very little in a systematic way. Consequently, there is a major need for new project work.

The following five tasks need to be undertaken:

1 Review (and develop) the relevant literature on theory and practice, much of which is Canadian.
2 Develop and disseminate thinking in the UK context, in terms of opportunities, challenges and strategies.
3 Promote the development and implementation of the new approaches by means of written materials, promotional events, workshops, direct work with key players and training.
4 Encourage the setting-up and development of one or more small-scale demonstration projects to develop the case for consumer empowerment and offer practical pointers. As Brandon and Towe (1989: 36) say: 'We need to get the whole machinery right from the basis of a very limited experience of real consumer empowerment.'
5 Learn lessons from tasks 1–4 and do everything to ensure that the lessons are disseminated and acted upon.

Some key questions to be addressed are as follows:

1 Organization of brokers. How is it possible to ensure that brokers are organized, managed and trained most effectively, that standards are as high as possible and that they always remain accountable to consumers and personal networks?
2 Information for informed choice. How is it possible to ensure that brokers provide the best possible information – and thus a solid basis for informed choice – to the consumer? Consumers will sometimes make choices that appear to be against their own best interests and there may sometimes be a conflict of interest between the consumer and his or her personal network.
3 Targeting and equity. How are individualized funding allocations to be decided, and by whom? The financing body would have to balance consumer demands with its own resource ceilings and targeting priorities. This is discussed in the next section.
4 Political climate for radical reform. How can commitment to and support of the necessary reforms be mobilized? What is the best way to influence the political climate, given the lack of a clear policy, the powerful political and professional interests that are vested in maintaining the status quo and the fact that the legal basis of service provision remains weak in the UK (e.g. as opposed to some US states and Scandinavia, where clear legal rights have been powerful levers for change).
5 Demonstration projects. How is a demonstration programme to be designed to develop the case further and offer practical pointers? The aim would be to demonstrate that the new system is not just idealistic but also offers benefits in terms of cost-effectiveness, equity and

externalities (e.g. helping other social policies). The demonstrations would also act as powerful levers for change, both directly and through their impact on public attitudes.

Funding community care

The funding of community care has been a major focus of debate since the publication of the Audit Commission's (1986) concerns about the slow progress made in achieving the transition from hospital to community care. The financial system is bewilderingly complex, involving a multiplicity of agencies working to different resource constraints and financial rules. Service availability and standards vary from one part of the country to another and there is probably a major under-provision of many needed services.

The organizational complexity of funding care is illustrated in Figure 3.1 (Felce *et al*. 1993). It shows all the different agencies, both statutory and voluntary, at local and national levels, that are involved in providing the necessary finance. There are three important central government departments involved and each plays a different role. The Department of Social Security, for example, plays a vital role in providing income support for people with learning difficulties and their families, and in providing a range of financial benefits for both the disabled person and for carers. However, income support was also an important element in the provision of residential care because it was used to meet residents' charges. Although the Audit Commission's concern about the growth of expenditure on social security for long-term care was prompted by the growth of residential and nursing home care for elderly people, exactly the same points can be made about caring for people with learning difficulties. The social security budget is one of the few budgets that is not strictly cash limited. Consequently, as previously mentioned, there has been until recently a great incentive for health and local authorities to encourage the use of private and voluntary residential homes, knowing that the costs of care will fall on the social security budget rather than their own.

Local health services are financed by the Department of Health via Regional Health Authorities. Personal social services are financed by local taxation and by the grants in aid made by the Department of the Environment to local authorities. The finance of local government, in terms of both the working of the grant arrangements and the controversy over poll tax and other forms of local taxation, has become extremely complicated. Consequently, services for people with learning difficulties that are administered by both health and local authorities are affected by the operation of financial controls imposed by two separate government departments. Health authorities work generally to cash-limited budgets.

Figure 3.1 The funding of health and social care for people with learning difficulties

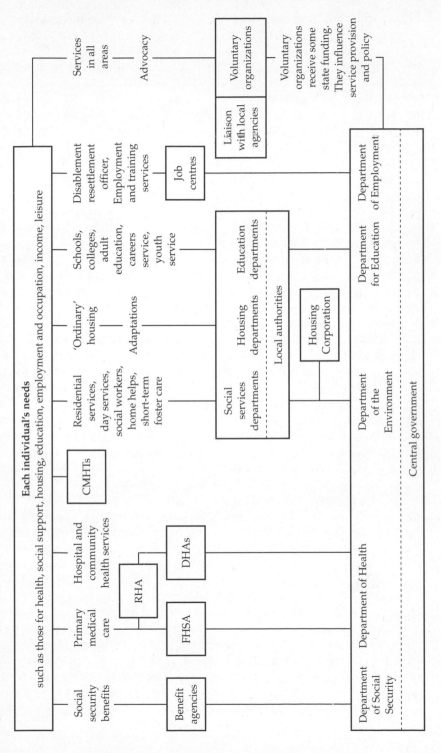

Local authorities have both cash limits and restrictions such as tax-capping to restrain their expenditures.

The problem of local government finance is particularly acute. A large proportion of local authority budgets comes from a grant from central government, administered by the Department of the Environment. Although the details of the grant are based on the expected expenditure on important local government services, such as education and social services, the grant is paid as one general payment to the authorities. No expenditure is specifically earmarked for one service or another. Consequently, it is not possible for central government to insist that specified parts of the grant, which is based on expected expenditure in one local authority on social services, actually be spent on social services. This leads to interminable, indeterminate arguments between central and local politicians as to whether the former has or has not increased the money available for spending on social services and whether it has or has not been spent on other services. Although knowledge of the expected expenditure on social services might help a director of social services to bargain in local budget-making exercises for a particular level of expenditure, there is no obligation on the council to meet these demands.

The development of social services generally, and services for people with learning difficulties in particular, might have been helped if the general grant had been replaced, at least in part, by specific grants in aid. Specific grants have never been popular with local authorities because of the control required to ensure that the money claimed on a specific grant is paid out in conformity with the specialized, identified services. Strict auditing of accounts is needed to ensure that monies spent on non-grant-aided services are not 'slipped into' the specific grant claim. Nevertheless, this policy was used to develop local education and health services in the 1950s and is a major incentive to ensure that service provision is targeted at the services to which policy-makers have allotted greatest priority.

The whole position is exacerbated by the financing of the transition to community care, where the costs of new community-based services have been greater than the costs of hospital care. While this is bound to be true over the short term, as community care services need to be built up at a pace greater than the run down of hospital care, there is growing evidence that long-term costs of community care are also above those of hospital care (see Chapter 8). Given that local authority social services play the leading role in developing community care, they need extra finance to meet both the short-term and long-term financial consequences of these extra responsibilities. In the short term a form of bridging finance would ease the situation, but although this is possible, it has not been used comprehensively throughout the country. The longer-term financial consequences have not been confronted and they quickly enter the debate about general versus specific grants for local authorities. There is also considerable suspicion that all the monies released from hospital closures are not being allocated to the people discharged from them or to those who might have been admitted. Instead, there is considerable fear that NHS authorities have used the money to meet general demands on their budgets (Glover *et al.* 1993). Despite the lack of firm evidence, there was sufficient concern for the Audit Commission to call for the monies to be specially protected or 'ring-fenced' to ensure that they are spent on community services for people who used or would have used hospital services (Audit Commission 1986).

Generally, the financial system is not designed to encourage authorities to provide services, but rather to pass on costs to others and thereby remain within the cash limits set at either central or local level. The example of the social security budget in the 1980s has already been cited. The other worry is that costs get shunted on to the informal care sector, sometimes explicitly in the form of user charges, but usually implicitly by a failure to provide necessary support to caring families. The shortfall in short-term and family care services mentioned above exemplifies this policy.

When the Audit Commission investigated the organization and financing of community care, it made several recommendations for funding community care (Audit Commission 1986). These were:

- a rationalization of funding policies from the centre in order to remove the policy conflicts that blighted the development of community care;
- adequate short-term funding to meet the demands of running two services in parallel during the transition to community care;
- the coordination of social security and community care policies.

Following the criticisms of existing policy and the recommendations made by the Audit Commission for the reorganization of the finance of community care, Sir Roy Griffiths was asked to report on possible future strategies, which were then set out in his *Agenda* (Griffiths 1988). Generally, the *Agenda* supported the recommendation to give local authorities the lead in the organization and funding of community care. The development of care management as set out previously was recommended, but this was to be supported by: transferring resources from the social security budget to local authorities to fund an efficient mix of community-based, residential and nursing home care; supporting social services with general and targeted specific grants. The main differences between the recommendations of the Audit Commission and Sir Roy's *Agenda* arose in the transfer of NHS funds for community care to local authorities. Sir Roy did not accept that local authorities should hold this part of the budget and purchase NHS services for their clients, but recommended that these funds be retained but ring-fenced in order to protect them from predatory raids from other sectors of the NHS.

The Audit Commission's recommendations were further diluted by the National Health Service and Community Care Act 1990. No provision was made for ring-fencing of community care expenditure and specific grants were used only for limited development of services for people with mental health problems. The preceding White Paper (Secretaries of State for Health *et al.* 1989) rejected the idea of ring-fencing on the grounds that it removed the necessary flexibility to alter budgets as community care needs changed. Specific grants were rejected on the grounds of their disadvantages of increasing central control and removing local discretion in determination of the allocation of resources to local services.

The result of these rejections of the Audit Commission's recommendations is that the new arrangements for community care face the same problems that were responsible for the slow improvement of services in the 1980s. There is still a multiplicity of agencies holding different budgets and working to different types of financial control. Collaboration between agencies depends on good will between managers. Community care funds are not protected from the grasping hands of other services. The only major reform has been the transfer to local authorities of part of the income support used for caring for people in residential and nursing homes. However, this is ring-fenced for only a temporary period and could, therefore, become the subject of continual discussion about how much money should go from the general grant to social services departments in general and, more specifically, to people with learning difficulties or other long-term disabilities. When care managers assemble packages of care that include health, housing or services provided by other budget holders, they will not have the purchasing power to command the services they need. They will be dependent on their own powers of persuasion and the good will of other service managers to obtain the prescribed packages. If packages cannot be assembled because of shortages of resources in other agencies, who takes the responsibility for failure? The story of inter-agency collaboration since the NHS and local authority reforms of 1974 is not a happy one (Hunter and Wistow 1986). The separation of organizational from financial responsibility in community care still threatens effective inter-agency collaboration.

There is no doubt that despite the lack of a hospitable financial climate, there is sufficient ingenuity within the staff of health and local authorities and representatives of the private sector to overcome the difficulties and to work together to improve the well-being of all people with a community care need. Several models for integrating care management into the NHS purchasing and the primary care management systems have been set out by the Audit Commission (1992). In addition, they have set out principles of financial management that emphasize the need to ensure command over resources, responsibility for financial control and managerial responsibility. However, probably the most important aspect is the highlighting of the need to ensure quality of care in the new system, assisted by effective financial and outcome information. The Commission has also promised to audit the new arrangements, to identify good practice, to draw attention to gaps and inadequacies as they arise and to address the issues of policy-making, operational arrangements and inter-agency coordination. Our fervent hope must be that the picture that emerges in 1996 will show a considerable improvement on that of 1986 in terms of: the achievement of the objectives of improved domiciliary, day and respite services, a high priority accorded to carers, efficient and effective care management (involving users of advocates or service brokers) and, generally, the ensuring of better value for money by the effective and efficient funding of social care.

4 Outcomes 1: definition and methodology

Introduction and context

As we saw in Chapters 1 and 2, a fundamental aim or objective of most policy and service interventions in the social care field is to meet the needs of the user and thus enable his or her quality of life, welfare or general well-being to be improved. Such objectives are based on fundamental human rights and needs. Deficiencies in respect of the objectives are needs (welfare shortfalls), while outcomes represent progress towards the objectives and thus the reduction of welfare shortfalls. Resources are central to the production of welfare: the process of translating needs into outcomes by means of service interventions.

As set out in Chapter 2, service interventions produce three main types of outcomes, as follows:

1 Final outcomes (user outcomes), which reflect the ultimate goals of welfare provision, and thus reflect user welfare. These are outcomes valued in their own right.
2 Intermediate outcomes (service/organizational outcomes), which are closely related to resources, examples being the actual services received, throughput, and quality and standards of care. These may be of interest in themselves but are mostly important via their associations with final outcomes.
3 External outcomes (externalities), which include external benefits (which one can enjoy free or at a low price) and external costs (which one suffers without adequate compensation).

These are discussed in the remainder of this chapter and in Chapters 5 and 6. There is a special emphasis on final (user) outcomes.

Final (user) outcomes

The need for a frame of reference

We need to be clear about what it is that service interventions in the human services should aim to achieve or produce. In other words, we need a frame of reference for defining and evaluating quality of life (welfare), needs (welfare shortfalls) and outcomes (the reduction of welfare shortfalls by means of policy and service interventions and production processes).

Such a frame of reference – labelled the 'social welfare paradigm' by Davies and Challis (1986), a 'standards matrix' by Evans (1988), a 'mission statement' by Leedham (1991) and a 'charter' by NCVO (1991) – consists of various normative/value propositions that together help to define (a) an ideal pattern of outcomes and, consequently, (b) the *raison d'être* of service interventions. Such a framework is essential if we are even to begin the process of defining and measuring quality in terms of the infinitely complex impact of services on people's lives. The ideal transcends the actual objectives of policy and service interventions (but these, nevertheless, remain very important), which are: 'complex, multiple, conflicting and vary over time and between contexts. They are variously interpreted, notoriously ambiguous, and are sometimes difficult to locate at all' (Smith and Cantley 1985a: 5). The frame of reference also acts as a statement of mission in terms of foundations, principles and minimum standards, and consequently provides a process-based measure of achievement.

The starting point

Quite clearly, people with learning difficulties – or any special needs – are first and foremost people, with the same dignity, the same value, the same rights, the same aspirations and the same basic needs and wants as every other member of society.

Individual people and society as a whole constitute a continuum of abilities and disabilities; we all depend on each other to a greater or lesser degree. We are all handicapped to a certain extent (for example, see Williams 1978), although most of us can conceal our disabilities most of the time. The difficulties and needs of people with learning difficulties are different in degree rather than in kind from those of us all (Novak 1980; Shearer 1981; Atkinson and Williams 1990).

Consequently, 'handicap' is determined both by the individual's disability and by social responses to that disability. Individuals with disabilities are handicapped to the extent that society allows their disabilities to block mainstream social participation (Apolloni 1980; Finkelstein 1981; Heron and Myers 1983). Handicap, in other words, is at least partly socially constructed and is imposed over and above disability to make it more limiting than it must necessarily be (Gunzburg and Gunzburg 1973; Shearer 1981).

We all want and need to be acknowledged and treated as individual, complete human beings and as full and valued citizens in our own neighbourhood. We all place tremendous importance on being able to participate in the community in ways that are respected and valued. Such participation revolves around having a range of two-way relationships with ordinary people (family, friends) and places (home, work, shops and so on).

This is basically what the normalization principle is all about. Normalization originated in Scandinavia in the late 1960s and has since then been most often associated with the American, Wolf Wolfensberger (see, for example, Nirje 1969; Wolfensberger 1972). It is often referred to as ordinary life principles (King's Fund Centre 1980). Normalization, as currently perceived, is fundamentally about human value and rights – it means the acknowledgement and treatment of disadvantaged people as individual, complete human beings and as full and valued citizens in their own community, in order that they may enjoy all that we value for ourselves (e.g. Bronston 1980a; Lakin and Bruininks 1985; Renshaw 1986). A better term for normalization would be valorization.

Normalization principles help to provide an essential framework for evaluating outcomes and processes of achieving outcomes. The key questions to ask are: (a) What do/would I need and want for myself or my family? (b) What do/would valued citizens in Britain today want for themselves or their families? As Tyne (1986: 14) argues, people should

> judge the quality of what happens in the lives of people with handicaps by the same criteria and standards as they would apply in their own lives and those of other valued people. Too often people make hidden and unquestioned assumptions about what is okay for people with handicaps, but which would be intolerable in their own lives.

User-level accomplishments

Normalization principles are most easily understood in terms of the 'five accomplishments' framework developed by John O'Brien (1987) and others. The accomplishments – community presence, choice, competence, respect and community participation – are positive life experiences of which it makes sense for a person to seek more. 'Together they indicate a balance of valued day-to-day experiences that constitute a [good] quality adult life' (O'Brien 1987: 177). The accomplishments have been used to define effectiveness by Bolton CHC (1987), Blunden (1988), Evans (1988), Leedham (1989) and Wilkinson (1989), among others.

The first accomplishment, community presence, is 'the sharing of the ordinary places that define community life' (O'Brien 1987: 177). The most important place is the home,

> the place of our security and the base of our exploration, the place where we can express and develop our own personality, where we can find our privacy and our closest relationships. It is our stake in our own community, the place from which we meet the neighbours and tradespeople around us and to which we return for comfort when the world outside seems confusing and hostile. Or if it isn't, then we wish it was.
>
> (Shearer 1986: 127)

Integration in ordinary residential, educational, work and recreational settings is a right and a need shared by all of us. Such settings spatially represent people's place within society; they are powerful mediums of personal identity and value (Bronston 1980b; Towell 1985; Robinson 1987).

The second accomplishment, choice, is

> the experience of autonomy both in small, everyday matters (e.g. what to eat or what to wear) and in large, life-defining matters (e.g. with whom to live or what sort of work to do).
>
> (O'Brien 1987: 177)

Each choice we make is an expression of our personal autonomy – our freedom to define who we are and what we value. Making choices provides us with the power to determine to a great extent what happens to us on a moment to moment basis as well as over a span of time.

> (North-East CMH and Carle 1986: 1)

A related accomplishment is that of awareness of opportunities and constraints. The provision of good quality information is central here (NCVO 1991).

Choice – and particularly informed choice – is closely related to the third accomplishment, competence. This is 'the opportunity to perform functional and meaningful activities with whatever level or type of assistance . . . required' (O'Brien 1987: 178).

Closely related to the choice and competence accomplishments is the concept of self-determination. In Western culture, the most highly valued aspects of people's lives – such as identity, dignity, respect, participation and moral and life satisfaction – stem from the ability to be largely self-determining in most of the core activities of daily living, particularly those related to personal care and other everyday needs. Self-determination is associated with ownership of one's own life (i.e. an internal locus of control) and, subsequently, with positive self-identity. In contrast, an external locus of control tends to be associated with dependence, powerlessness and a dependent, controlled or stigmatized identity. Seevers (1980: 43) refers to 'indecent dependency with its resulting degradation of the human spirit'.

Another important concept here is that of risk-taking, which is a normal indeed essential, part of the learning process. There are many risks associated with developing greater self-determination and a more valued lifestyle (Cambridge 1987). There is a conflict between the need for risk-taking and the need for protection, and a need for an optimal balance between over-protection and under-protection. People need to develop an understanding of the predictable outcomes of their choices and actions. Successful choice leads to the person being perceived as competent and able to participate in valued ways.

The fourth and fifth accomplishments, respect and community participation, are both central to the ultimate goal of full and valued participation in community life. Respect is 'having a valued place among a network of people and valued roles in community life', while community participation is the experience of being part of a network of personal relationships with other people, like family, friends, neighbours and colleagues (O'Brien 1987: 178). Such ties and connections define 'community' (King's Fund Centre 1988): 'People establish who they are, and where they belong, through their relationships with others' (Atkinson and Williams 1990: 60).

Both the respect and community participation accomplishments reflect the deep needs, shared by us all, to love and to be loved, to give, receive and share. Horizontal relationships of the 'gift relationship' and 'life-sharing' kind are more valuable than traditional, more vertical and directive, helper–user relationships because they are based on mutual consent, reciprocity and fellowship; the horizontal or gift relationship 'means that individuals want to give of themselves rather than simply give as a response to a pay check' (Sumarah 1987: 166). This is perhaps the ultimate reflection of the perceived value and dignity of any person, particularly someone with disabilities. As Taylor *et al.* (1987: 4) note, 'no amount of professional services can replace the need people have for friendship'. Similarly, O'Brien (1987: 176) notes that 'the benefits of friendship with a sibling or a neighbor cannot be purchased at any price'.

An additional accomplishment is personal continuity. Ongoing relationships and ties with other people, places and possessions help us to sustain our sense of identity and belonging. Continuity in these relationships is very important.

It is generally assumed that the above accomplishments and the various research dimensions they span are crucial determinants of – or at least are closely related to – personal (user) experience of life and life quality, which in many ways reflects the ultimate 'final' outcome. Cattermole (1987), among others, argues that quality of life is ultimately a perception by the individual of his or her life. While this is undoubtedly true, we should not proceed to argue that the accomplishments are only valid in cases where they are positively correlated with personal experience of life quality. A person could be very 'satisfied' and yet score very badly on all of the accomplishments (or vice versa), one of the main reasons being that the determinants of personal satisfaction are immensely complex and so the accomplishments can by no means account for all of them. There are some very complex dilemmas and potential trade-offs between morale and the accomplishments. Despite this, personal experience of life and life quality remains of crucial importance.

Moral imperative

The framework of user-level accomplishments discussed above is based on fundamental human rights and needs. Consequently, it is much more than just another theory or philosophy. It reflects our very status as human beings.

Following on from this, a note on the context and role of research in relation to user-level accomplishments is called for. As Pieper and Cappuccilli (1980: 60) point out, 'We need to be honest in admitting that normalization is based upon values and beliefs about people . . . It may be supported by research, but it is not dependent upon research for its validity.'

Thus certain policies and practices can be justified primarily on moral, ethical and humanitarian grounds. Relationships between needs, resources and outcomes remain of crucial importance if services are to be improved and user welfare enhanced.

Intermediate or service-based outcomes

The production of final outcomes

The production of final outcomes involves effort directed towards change at three levels: change in the pattern of community norms and opportunities, in the services and informal resources that support the person and in the person himself or herself (O'Brien 1987). Intermediate objectives and outcomes are concerned with means of achieving final objectives and are usually based on inputs and processes of producing welfare. They focus on the quantity and quality of inputs, the process of service delivery and methods of organizing care. These many different factors represent the plethora of practical means by which policy and service interventions attempt to achieve their final outcomes.

Change at the community and service levels is often referred to as 'environmental normalization': the process of developing culturally valued and appropriate opportunities, living environments and services. This echoes the original Scandinavian conception of normalization (i.e. valorization). Change at the individual level is often referred to as 'user normalization': the acquisition and development of the skills, abilities and behaviour necessary for assuming culturally valued social roles and responsibilities (see Wolfensberger 1972). Environmental and user normalization are 'reciprocally reinforcing' (Wolfensberger 1983a) and are closely linked to the developmental model, which is based on the premise that every person has the capacity to learn and develop, and thus emphasizes the potency of environmental conditions and the malleability of the human organism (Gunzburg and Gunzburg 1973; Roos 1980).

Service or organizational-level accomplishments

People with learning difficulties are – or should be – full citizens, and it is the role of services to enable them to exercise the rights and responsibilities of citizenship. Most of us need little or no organized support in order to work towards achieving this vision for our lives. However, people with learning difficulties generally need help to identify the support they need to achieve as good and satisfying a life as full citizens. History shows that people with (severe) disabilities are likely to miss ordinary positive experiences unless the people they rely on work hard on their behalf.

The help and support required will often be to access mainstream resources like a house, a job, a college or a leisure centre. It will probably involve having people to help with housework and cooking, with travelling around and with going to the shops. Most people will need financial help, while some will need aids and adaptations. In addition, because many people with learning difficulties have had and are still experiencing damaging lifestyles (for example, abnormal environments, absent or poor quality relationships, loss of identity and frequent moves) they may have emotional and behavioural difficulties that need understanding and extra support.

All of this help and support needs to be organized and coordinated at both the individual level and the collective level. Each individual in need of services has unique and complex need-related characteristics and circumstances. These relate particularly to the individual's strengths, wishes and needs, and to his or her existing or potential networks of support. Services should be needs-based and user-led, aiming for user-level accomplishments. They should aim to empower users and empower, support and strengthen networks of support.

Crucially, services must tailor resources to the needs and wishes of individual users and their support networks. Consequently, they need:

• to be highly flexible, so they can respond to changing needs, wishes and opportunities;

- to make maximum use of existing and potential resources, for example by stimulating and supporting local communities to respond in appropriate ways;
- to be much more labour-intensive and much less building-based than many current services.

The use of care management supported by service brokerage, empowerment and user involvement is an important method in meeting these needs.

External outcomes

An analysis of final and intermediate outcomes needs to be supplemented by consideration of external outcomes, in other words the effects – in terms of costs and benefits – of policy and service interventions on carers and society at large. Sometimes, there is competition and conflict between improving the welfare of users and improving that of carers or the general population. Consequently, we need to pursue an equitable balance between final outcomes and external outcomes.

External costs

The physical, emotional and financial costs incurred by carers have been the focus of increased research and media attention in recent years (e.g. Buckle 1983; Flynn and Saleem 1986; Cattermole *et al.* 1987; Yorkshire TV 1987; BBC TV 1989). There are also some less obvious costs incurred by the general population.

Family and other informal carers have traditionally had a straight choice between unsupported informal care or long-term hospitalization of their son or daughter, institutions traditionally being the only services available. Consequently, many carers have to struggle on with little or no appropriate help or support. Many of the people involved are being placed under intolerable stresses and strains. The situation is bad for all concerned.

- For families and people with learning difficulties, who are denied an ordinary family life and often face poverty and social isolation. Furthermore, the care-giving family members often face extreme physical and/or emotional difficulties.
- For service agencies, who have to pick up the pieces in the end. This often takes the form of crisis management, which is notoriously inefficient and unjust as a service intervention.
- For society as a whole, which has to live with all of the social problems that are part and parcel of this scenario. Examples include the breakdown of families, social marginalization, problems of physical and mental health, and reduced economic productivity.

Many carers fear a time when their children or siblings will be neglected, isolated and victimized. They have to struggle on until the intolerable strains and burdens simply become too much for them. Old age and/ or ill-health often precipitate such a crisis, and institutional care often results (sometimes for the carer as well). Hardly surprisingly, this is a much-feared scenario. Other concerns and fears focus on the children or siblings moving from one kind of care to another, typically from family or institutional care to care in the community. A number of carers are very anxious about such moves – particularly about issues of security and the permanence of placements – while some actively oppose them (e.g. Segal 1987; Spreat *et al.* 1987; Tonkin 1987).

The costs incurred by the general population are, of course, less direct. They are mostly emotional costs. First, many people with no direct experience appear to believe popular myths of the stereotyped 'mental person' and 'mental home'. Consequently, they tend to see care in the community as bringing 'unpredictable', 'dangerous' or 'odd' individuals into otherwise 'nice' neighbourhoods, hitting property values, threatening the children and so on (Seltzer and Seltzer 1987; Leighton 1988). A number of people seem to have the view that community integration is acceptable provided their own particular neighbourhoods are not affected (Seltzer 1985). Second, there are costs associated with the knowledge or belief that people are not being cared for properly.

External benefits

The provision of appropriate support for people with learning difficulties and their carers will enable the achievement of user-lever accomplishments. It will also lead to positive physical, emotional and financial benefits for carers, reflected in an ordinary family life and peace of mind.

The benefits for carers will, in turn, lead to benefits for society as a whole, for example through the reduction of social problems, like the breakdown of families, and health problems. In addition, ordinary people will come to realize that people with learning difficulties can live successfully in the community and can make a useful contribution to improving community life. A more general benefit for ordinary people will come from the knowledge that people are being helped and supported in appropriate ways.

Towards specific research dimensions

Previous sections have provided a framework for a set of research dimensions by attempting to specify what it is that policy and service interventions in the learning difficulty field should aim to achieve or produce. The various accomplishments are pitched at a high level of generality. If practical evaluations are to be undertaken, they need to be translated into research dimensions or indicators that are at a lower level of generality and thus more specific. The results of the translation process are detailed in Chapter 5. However, in order to place these dimensions in context it is necessary first to consider some key aspects of research design and methodology in the evaluation of outcomes.

Measurement basics: issues of research design

Measures of outcomes

The accomplishments framework discussed above reflects the objectives of policies and services. Consequently, it enables us to measure outcomes (i.e. the achievement of objectives). There are three main and overlapping types of outcomes, as follows:

- static, point-in-time outcomes – we can compare the existing situation with the accomplishments framework, i.e. compare reality with ideals;
- dynamic, across-time outcomes – we can assess changes over time, for example following an individual through a change in service arrangements;
- relative or comparative outcomes – we can compare outcomes either with what would have happened in some other circumstances or with some norm.

Consider the accomplishment of community participation as an example. The ideal outcome measure would:

1 Adopt a valid, reliable and easy-to-use scale focusing on key dimensions of community participation (various aspects of relationships with ordinary people and places etc.).
2 Use this scale to measure community participation now and/or at regular intervals before, during and after the service intervention (remembering that the impact of some interventions may take some time to work through).
3 Compare the results of (1) and (2) with various alternatives, including no intervention and the situation of people *without* disabilities.
4 Make comparisons between people with learning difficulties and, if necessary, use some aggregate measures of outcomes. (Note that the myriad outcomes dimensions are far too complex – for example, in terms of causality and interconnections – for them to be combined into a single measure of outcome.)

Data quality and level of measurement

Good quality data have three main desirable properties:

1 Validity. Data should measure what they are intended to measure and indicate what kinds of conclusions can be drawn from the results. A related property is that of generalizability.
2 Reliability. Data should be dependable, consistent and stable.
3 Sensitivity. Data should be sufficiently sensitive to reflect any (often small) changes over time that may occur.

Statistical analyses, both descriptive and inferential, rely on good quality data for their usefulness.

Level of measurement is crucial with regard to the analysis of quantitative data, especially when inferential statistical techniques are involved. Ratio and interval data – collectively known as cardinal data – are superior to ordinal and nominal data. Ratio data are ordered numbers with intervals of regular size and with an absolute zero (e.g. temperature, weight, length). Interval data are the same as ratio data with one exception – there is no absolute zero. Ordinal data represent a rating or grading scale (e.g. ranks from 1 to 5, from very dissatisfied to very satisfied). Nominal data are simply labels used to classify things (e.g. male/female; type of accommodation).

Some important recent developments in health economics have attempted to produce cardinal scales for assessing health status (Gudex *et al.* 1993). The basic approach is to examine the trade-offs people are prepared to make between two or more different states of health. For example, the magnitude estimation approach of Fanshel and Bush (1970) assigns a value of 1,000 to perfect health and 0 to death. Fifty other health states are described in detail and interviewees are invited to place values (0–1,000) on them. A scale consists of the average ratings from a sample of interviewees.

This approach underpins the QALY (Quality Adjusted Life Year) developed by Rosser and Kind (1978) and quite widely used in the UK today. Despite this, it is not widely accepted that the combination of scores along several dimensions into a unidimensional scale is either feasible or sensible. However, the important thing about the work of Rosser and others is that the trade-offs between dimensions are made explicit, based on applied research on preferred combinations of trade-offs. Unfortunately, the application of the QALY technique is currently restricted to a fairly narrow range of acute health care procedures and it is as yet of limited value in the learning difficulty field (Donaldson *et al.* 1988).

The time dimension

We saw above that one major type of outcomes is a measurement of changes between two or more points of time, for example before, during and after the service intervention (times 1, 2 and 3, typically referred to as T1, T2 and T3). A longitudinal evaluation assesses these changes. A typical example is the evaluation of the shift from hospital to community care (dehospitalization).

The start date should precede the policy or service intervention under examination, or at least be as soon after the intervention as possible. This provides the baseline against which outcomes will be measured. The ideal, of course, would be continuously to study outcomes over the full lifespan of the people involved, on the reasonable assumption that interventions impact upon all life experiences and qualities thereafter. However, this is clearly impractical. The best pragmatic approaches would ensure that the length and intensity of the evaluation are sufficient to encompass all the major outcomes.

Design issues

The central issue is whether or not a service intervention produces more of an effect or outcome than would have occurred either with no intervention or with some alternative intervention. Consequently, the ideal research design is one able to demonstrate persuasively that the changes are a function of the intervention and cannot be accounted for in other ways (Rossi and Freeman 1985).

The various options for research design all involve the establishment of controls that attempt to standardize for intervening and confounding factors in the production of outcomes. They fall into two groups (Rossi and Freeman 1985). The first group, comparative designs, includes separate control or comparison groups and uses randomised, constructed and statistical controls. These are discussed below. The second group, single-group designs, does not include a separate control or comparison group, but instead uses weaker reflexive controls (before–after comparisons by themselves), generic controls (comparisons with established, standardized norms about 'typical states/changes') and shadow controls (comparisons with predictions of 'experts').

The classic comparative design is an experimental design. This consists of experimental and control groups that receive different treatments (e.g. 'movers' and 'stayers') and are constructed through randomization. Such a design is able to distinguish between gross effects – the overall impact, only part of which might be caused by the intervention – and net effects – those results attributable solely to the intervention (see Butterfield 1987). Randomized designs are common and effective in the natural sciences, where laboratory conditions make randomization easy.

Close (1977), MacEachron (1983) and Landesman (1987) are three of the very few learning difficulty studies to use randomization to select experimental and control groups. The Landesman study has a particularly powerful design, based on random assignment of matched trios of users to community group homes, new duplexes added to institutions and institutional (control) units.

By way of contrast, nearly every study (for example, Knapp *et al.* 1989; Leedham 1989) has been unable to use an experimental design. There are at least four principal reasons for this:

1 The selection of people for different types of service intervention is mainly a non-random process, often involving 'creaming'.
2 Although a number of people stay in existing services, they do not constitute a control group from which the intervention is withheld because service rundown has various effects on users. We cannot say what would have happened in the absence of interventions.
3 Bias is introduced via key personnel becoming aware of the different treatments or processes and generally learning as they go along (Smith and Cantley 1985a).
4 Random inclusion and omission of users involve various ethical and political dilemmas.

Non-randomized quasi-experiments are typically the only feasible approach. For example, the Personal Social Services Research Unit (PSSRU) studies of Knapp *et al.* (1989) and Leedham (1989) took advantage of a series of semi-natural experiments in which users with similar characteristics end up in different time 2 settings. Furthermore, Leedham (1989) used constructed controls, which involve the matching of 'equivalent' or similar people across experimental and control groups, and statistical controls, which use statistical methods to hold constant differences between the various groups being compared. This may be some way from the experimental design ideal (see Butterfield 1987), but it is generally the nearest we can get.

Recent examples of the surprisingly small number of other quasi-experimental studies (small relative to the total number, and given the intense clamour for such studies) of dehospitalization include those based on hospitals in Derby (Knapp *et al.* 1989), Wessex (Smith *et al.* 1980; Felce *et al.* 1983), South Wales (Hemming 1982, 1986), Darenth Park Hospital near Dartford (MRC SPU 1986) and Pennhurst Hospital in Pennsylvania (Conroy and Bradley 1985). Most longitudinal studies take the form of follow-up investigations with few or no controls. One problem faced by all dehospitalization studies – and especially by those with few or no controls – is the difficulty of comparing like with like. The ideal is to assess hospital and community settings in as 'normal' an operating environment as possible. In practice, the picture is confused by the effects of the hospital rundown process, the transitional nature of many community placements and the user adjustment process. These problems point to the overwhelming need for long(er)-term evaluations.

Sampling

The design considerations discussed above point to the importance of:

1 Getting a broadly representative 'spread' of users in terms of key characteristics and circumstances. The literature on dehospitalization shows that challenging behaviours (especially problematic and conspicuous ones) and mobility problems are major determinants of discharge and of the success of community placements.

2 Maximizing the potential for 'matching' users in or moving to different types of service arrangements.

These aims point to the use of a non-random 'stratified/quota sampling' and 'judgement sampling' methods (Burgess 1984; Mann 1985), selecting subjects according to various key criteria or quotas. This requires fairly detailed prior knowledge of users and settings.

Methodological approaches

Methodological introduction

This section describes the nature of qualitative and quantitative approaches in a somewhat idealized way, with particular attention to their strengths. It also reviews how the methods actually operate in practice. A number of problems and challenges are highlighted. Then, we proceed to consider the complementarity of the two approaches. The next chapter provides a detailed description and discussion, on a dimension-by-dimension basis, of the selection, development, use and quality of specific focuses and instruments.

Methodological approaches embrace both data and methods of collecting data, which are different, although overlapping, subjects. All the main data collection methods – direct researcher experience, direct communication between researcher and user, direct communication between researcher and others, and informant-completed questionnaires – can and do yield both qualitative and quantitative data.

Qualitative approaches

We have seen that user-level accomplishments are tremendously complex. They have lots of constituent elements, which, moreover, interact with one another in many different ways, with both the elements and interactions varying from person to person. Qualitative approaches approximate largely to the set of 'common-sense' approaches that a layperson would adopt, based on personal experience, intuition, speculation, an understanding and appreciation of personal, social and moral values and judgements, and so on (Baumeister 1981). Qualitative approaches have been well described by various writers. The following brief summary draws particularly from Edgerton and Langness (1978), Taylor and Bogdan (1981), Bercovici (1981, 1983), Edgerton (1984a, b), Stainback and Stainback (1984), Walker (1985) and Bryman (1988).

First, qualitative approaches are ways of viewing and understanding human beings and social and cultural phenomena in a naturalistic and holistic fashion. The focus is on the total person, the total living environment (the natural setting), processes of person–environment interaction and adaptation, and the overall social ecological context more generally. The approaches are 'ideographic' in that they generally locate findings in specific time periods and locales, the classic example being the case study. Carefully documented case studies can offer pointers and lessons of general relevance (see Smith and Cantley (1985a, b) in relation to the evaluation of policy initiatives).

Second, social life represents a process that is constantly reforming, reshaping and redirecting itself (Deutscher 1973). 'Because . . . lives change in response to various environmental demands, just as they develop in reaction to maturational changes, we emphasize process not only in an effort to document change but also in a search for causal linkages' (Edgerton 1984a: 1–2). The purpose of process research is to identify important production processes and so contribute to policy and practice development.

Third, within the naturalistic-holistic-process perspective there is a special orientation towards people's subjective experiences, perceptions, opinions and concerns: 'The qualitative researcher views human behaviour as a product of how people interpret their world. The task of the qualitative researcher is to capture this process of interpretation' (Taylor and Bogdan 1981: 73). Hence comes the centrality of Weber's *Verstehen* (understanding) of acts and motives. The researcher attempts to see the subjects' world through their own eyes, using their own frames of reference. This is known in anthropology as an emic as opposed to an etic perspective, and involves a preparedness to empathize with subjects. The emic perspective recognizes that subjects are the most appropriate and valid sources of information, with a unique perspective on their personal experiences (Wyngaarden 1981; Atkinson 1989; Prosser 1989; Wilkinson 1989; Atkinson and Williams 1990). Hence the importance attached to soliciting the views and opinions of various participants about key aspects of life and quality of life.

Furthermore, 'the meanings that people ascribe to their own and others' behaviour have to be set in the context of the values, practices, and underlying structures of the appropriate entity . . . as well as the multiple perceptions that pervade that entity' (Bryman 1988: 64). Qualitative approaches can accommodate a whole host of (often competing) perspectives and data sources. Smith and Cantley (1985a, b) use the term 'pluralistic evaluation' to describe their approach to policy evaluation. The naturalistic-holistic-process perspective usually involves long-term, intimate acquaintance with people and their lives, with researchers 'taking to the trenches'. Both breadth and depth of coverage are emphasized.

Fourth, qualitative approaches are often inductive, with an investigative, exploratory and discovery orientation. The main emphasis is on the discovery and generation of theory, although existing theory is often used as a general starting point. Qualitative researchers develop ideas, concepts, analytical categories, arguments and working hypotheses and theories from the data themselves – and from the processes of collecting data – rather than from preconceived, structured (and perhaps inappropriate) frames of reference based on existing theory. They are thus flexible and open-ended; the researcher is like a craftsperson. Relevant issues, questions and approaches to data collection and analysis emerge from the research process, in which the researcher becomes sensitized to what is meaningful. Inferences or leads drawn from one data source, whether expected or unexpected, can be corroborated or followed up by another. Such flexibility is particularly beneficial when evaluating services that are developing fairly rapidly or are innovative (Smith and Cantley 1985a).

Such inductive methods 'further the formulation and testing of hypotheses and the generation of theory' (Bercovici 1983: 205). Two classic means to these ends are 'analytic induction' and 'grounded theory'. Bryman (1988: 82–3) provides a useful summary of both. Using analytic induction, a rough definition and hypothetical explanation of the problem is followed by examination of cases to determine their fit with the hypothesis. If the fit is poor, either the hypothesis is reformulated or the problem is redefined to exclude negative cases. The procedure continues until no further negative cases have been encountered and a universal relationship has been established. The idea of grounded theory was first formulated by Glaser and Strauss in the mid-1960s as a means of generating theory that is embedded in data. During fieldwork, the researcher develops 'categories', which illuminate and fit the data well. Generalized and abstracted versions of these categories guide the research process and stimulate further theoretical reflection and the development of various hypotheses. A theoretical framework gradually emerges.

Quantitative approaches

Quantitative data are observations that readily lend themselves to numerical representation (Rossi and Freeman 1985). Quantitative approaches have been more widely published, taught, accepted and rewarded in research circles than have their qualitative counterparts (Taylor and Bogdan 1981). Quantitative advocates stress a number of ways in which quantitative approaches are (or could be) superior to qualitative approaches. Their argument is summarized below, drawing particularly from Bryman (1988).

Quantitative approaches are equated with the prestigious 'scientific method' and are typically exemplified by the social survey. They are conventionally believed to be heavily influenced by positivism in conception and orientation. The following simplified summary of what positivism is supposed to comprise builds on that provided by Bryman (1988: 14–15):

1 Positivism entails a fundamental belief that the methods and procedures of the natural sciences are appropriate to the social sciences.
2 Only observable phenomena can validly be warranted as knowledge.
3 Scientific theory and knowledge express and reflect the accumulated findings of empirical research (often labelled the doctrine of inductivism).
4 Scientific theories provide a 'backcloth' to empirical research in that hypotheses are derived from them and are then submitted to empirical test. 'This implies that science is *deductive*, in that it seeks to extract specific propositions from general accounts of reality' (Bryman 1988: 15).
5 There is a general wariness of moral, personal or social values, which may impair scientific objectivity. Thus a sharp distinction is usually made between scientific statements and normative statements, because the latter cannot be observed directly (Bryman 1988).

As in the natural sciences, there are three main stages, with clear boundaries between them. First, complex processes are translated into sets of general concepts and hypotheses. These are derived largely from existing theories, which can be at the macro-theory (or meta-theory, e.g. the production of welfare model) level or micro-theory level. This is the deduction process. The resulting concepts help to make some sense of the complex reality of inputs, outcomes and causal links, and to 'think straight'. Macro-/meta-theories are particularly good at helping to suggest questions and hypotheses, while micro-theories are useful for illuminating causal processes within the macro-/meta-theories.

Second, the concepts (derived from existing theory) are dissected and operationalized by specifying the operations by which they are to be measured. The result is that standardized research instruments – usually pre-coded questionnaires, observational schedules or checklists – are used to gather data. These instruments are usually much quicker to use than qualitative techniques as they usually do not demand close or sustained contact with subjects. The same instruments are generally applied across all cases and all situations, thus aiding comparability and replicability. It is argued that quantitative data are more rigorous or hard or precise, and considerably easier to analyse than qualitative data, which tend to be more voluminous, complex and contradictory.

Third, the data are subjected to various statistical analyses in order that the hypotheses is tested rigorously. The link between quantitative data and mathematics is useful in the complex, multi-factorial reality of outcomes evaluation. Examples concern the concept of statistical significance and the ability to adjust for bias or errors using, for example, validity and reliability tests. Findings help to develop and refine existing theory. This is the induction process.

Quantitative research aims to generalize from the specific to the more general by developing causal propositions and broad predictive models supported by theory and empirical findings. This explains the considerable importance placed on maximizing the degree to which samples are representative of wider populations. This is a key determinant of the predictive power of models and the degree to which they can be applied to various current and future situations.

Quantitative research is usually not as orderly as the idealized model outlined above suggests. For example, it is often messy – 'It tends to involve false trials, blind alleys, serendipity, and hunches to a much greater degree than the idealization implies' (Bryman 1988: 21) – and highly exploratory and unpredictable in outcome. Bryman concludes his review of quantitative approaches by saying that they 'can be seen as linked partly to positivism and partly to a diffuse and general commitment to the practices of the natural scientist' (Bryman 1988: 41).

Critical review: problems and challenges to overcome

One only has to look briefly at the learning difficulty literature to see that research is dominated by the concerns and techniques of quantitative science. However, qualitative studies have become more commonplace in the past decade or so, particularly in the USA. Qualitative approaches have traditionally been used as part of quantitative approaches and/or as supplementary to them. This subsection reflects personal experiences (Leedham 1989) of reviewing *and* using both qualitative and quantitative techniques and data. The major problems and challenges discussed below influence the choice of data collection instruments and techniques (see Chapter 5) and have important implications for data analysis and interpretation.

The underlying problem with qualitative research concerns the generally unknown representativeness and generalizability of data. The impact of the researcher's values, presuppositions and biases are often unknown, and thus data tend to 'remain enmeshed in a broad social, cultural, and personal context' (Edgerton and Langness 1978: 334). Specific snippets of information, examples or anecdotes are or can be used to provide evidence for a particular line of argument. 'There are grounds for disquiet in that the representativeness or generality of these fragments is rarely addressed . . . The reader is rarely given a vantage point from which the formulation of alternative accounts is possible' (Bryman 1988: 77).

An interesting specific example from the learning difficulty field is provided by Ellis *et al.*'s (1981) critique of Blatt and Kaplan's (1966) vivid photographic critique of life in a US mental handicap hospital, *Christmas in Purgatory*. Ellis *et al.* argue that selective demonstrations do not constitute generalizable research, and thus findings may well be idiosyncratic. More specifically, we can 'question the feasibility of seeing through others' eyes if observers themselves are so heavily implicated in what is found' (Bryman 1988: 77).

The generally unknown representativeness and generalizability of data represents a considerable problem and challenge for qualitative research. Even qualitative data that are relatively sound will find that their applicability and usefulness are undermined. Moreover, problems of representativeness and generalizability work in various ways to contaminate data quality by undermining validity, reliability and sensitivity.

Unfortunately, quantitative approaches suffer from a mirror image of this contamination process. Most quantitative approaches in the learning difficulty field yield data that are of dubious, poor or bad quality in terms of validity, reliability and sensitivity. This clearly undermines their representativeness and generalizability. The root of the problem is the distortion of meaning that often occurs in the translation of complex and continuous real-life processes into specific numerical units or categories that can be reliably counted. Qualitative advocates argue that the scientific method does not fully recognize the differences between people and their social reality – the subject matter of the social sciences – and the objects of the natural sciences. There are a number of major and overlapping sets of problems. It is important to note that the following critical review is generally couched in terms of quantitative approaches because of its special relevance for such approaches. Nevertheless, it is also applicable – in different ways and to a lesser degree overall – to qualitative approaches.

The first major problem is that some quantitative approaches, by their very nature, tend to paint unbalanced and biased, rather than holistic, pictures. In practice, they tend to fare worse than qualitative approaches here. One fundamental reason is that some factors and variables receive either much more or much less attention than their importance warrants (problems with operational definitions often play a part). Concepts are often only loosely related to a wider body of theory (Bryman 1988). Many critics of quantitative approaches stress that we are attempting precise quantification of isolated variables 'that are nowhere demonstrated to be the most relevant for prediction or understanding' (Edgerton 1984a: 2).

These problems are compounded by the fact that

an individual's course of adaptation is likely to be masked by dramatic fluctuations, both negative and positive. Unless the course of this adaptation is monitored more or less continuously ... any attempt [at assessment] ... risks producing both false negative and false positive findings, depending on whether assessment occurs during a 'peak' or a 'valley'.

(Edgerton 1984b: 502)

As we have seen, both quantitative and qualitative evaluations can be static cross-sectional or continuous longitudinal in nature. However, in practice most quantitative studies are restricted to one or two specific time periods and thus tend to miss the 'intervening process' and some of the most important links between independent variables, dependent variables and, perhaps most significantly, external variables (Deutscher 1973).

Deutscher proceeds to argue that quantitative research may lead us up a blind alley. Furthermore, 'There are always other variables to consider and so we never discover that it is a dead end' (Deutscher 1973: 40). In the final analysis, there is little way of knowing what the relationships among a restricted range of specific concepts, factors and variables at one or two specific time periods actually mean without having a holistic picture of the phenomenon or process in question. And it is virtually impossible to get a holistic picture without qualitative foundations.

The problem of unbalanced and biased snapshots is compounded by a second major problem, which is that concepts, domains and variables are notoriously difficult to define operationally. This problem is particularly great for quantitative approaches, because concepts are often conceived primarily in terms of the operations developed for their measurement (Bryman 1988). It is often virtually impossible, in practice, to fit many aspects of real people and real life into predetermined, usually arbitrary, concepts, domains and variables. There is usually lots of conflicting evidence and, moreover, operational definitions of items or scoring criteria, if they exist, are generally insufficiently precise for quantification purposes. There are far too many overlaps and grey areas for comfort, and researchers and respondents 'either set a uniquely defined standard or vascillate in their standard setting from item to item' (Stack 1984: 399–400). On top of this, quantitative instruments abound with ambiguous questions, leading questions, double questions and various jargon and technical terms (Mann 1985).

The result of this interpretive nightmare is the kind of reliability criticisms typically reserved for qualitative approaches: data vary according to the researcher, the respondent, the weather and a host of other extraneous factors. The preoccupation with reliability in quantitative research in general and the critique of qualitative approaches in particular is thus somewhat paradoxical. It seems that quantitative research and its advocates are more concerned with precise measurements than with important ones. Deutscher (1973: 41) puts it well:

> We have, in our pursuit of reliability, been absorbed in measuring the amount of error which results from inconsistency among interviewers or inconsistency among items on our instruments. We concentrate on consistency without much concern with what it is we are being consistent about or whether we are consistently right or wrong. As a consequence we may have been learning a great deal about how to pursue an incorrect course with a maximum of precision.

Brooks and Baumeister (1977) argue that we are making a science of missing the point. Deutscher (1973) goes futher by arguing that the enchantment with reliability militates against the discovery and use of new perspectives, new methods and new knowledge.

Problems with individuals' responses to interview situations and questions, especially structured ones, constitute the third major problem area. The two quotations below provide an overview of the problem:

> It appears that people express different opinions depending on who is asking and under what conditions. We have opinions we express in private and they are not necessarily the same as those we express in public. Furthermore, the opinion we express in one public is not necessarily the same as that we express in a different public.
>
> (Deutscher 1973: 219)

> It is a truism in social science that an individual's responses to any kind of interrogation are to a large extent determined by the situation and what that situation means to the respondent. Much questionnaire research appears naive about fundamental principles regarding the relationship between individuals' motivational frameworks and their responses to research questions.
>
> (Bercovici 1983: 15)

These problems apply to all respondents, but tend to be exacerbated when users themselves are interviewed. There are two main and overlapping sets of problems or challenges. Before looking at these, it is important to emphasize that the main culprit is probably the methodological approaches used (Simons *et al.* 1989).

The first problem is that many users have insufficient understanding and communication skills for the pre-coded questionnaire approach commonly adopted in quantitative research. Multiple choice and open-ended questions are often too complex, for example because they tend to include concepts, such as distinctions of degree (never, sometimes, often), that are not intuitively meaningful to many respondents. A number of users, especially those with more severe disabilities, cannot or do not respond meaningfully to even simple verbal questions.

Second, for those who do respond there are at least four major road-blocks to good quality data (especially quantitative data):

1 There is a major problem of acquiescence, i.e. the respondent tending to agree with whatever the interviewer says. Sigelman *et al.* (1981: 121) found that large proportions of respondents would have the researchers believe they are Chinese, school bus drivers, know how to fly an airplane and that it snows (in Arkansas) in summer.
2 In a similar vein, there is a tendency for respondents to attempt to give the right, expected, pleasing or socially desirable answer, and generally to paint an over-rosy picture. Respondents may be self-protective, fearing that voicing a negative opinion could work against them (Gollay *et al.* 1978; Wyngaarden 1981; Edgerton 1984b).
3 For some respondents who do not acquiesce there is a problem of 'nay-saying', i.e. tending to disagree with whatever the interviewer says.
4 Some respondents tend to choose the most recently heard option, regardless of content.

These various 'masks of concealment' mean that what people say they do or feel often bears little resemblance to what they actually do or feel (Deutscher 1973; Edgerton 1984b). This distortion of reality and under-mining of data quality is likely to be most acute in quantitative research where data collection is generally more obtrusive and where subject and researcher are typically strangers. It can also seriously damage rapport between subject and researcher (Edgerton 1984a, b).

Comparing and combining qualitative and quantitative approaches

The differences between qualitative and quantitative approaches are a matter of considerable debate. One school of thought depicts them as mutually exclusive models of the research process, while another school argues that the two approaches each have strengths and weaknesses in relation to any particular research topic or question (Bryman 1988). Over the past 10 to 20 years the latter school seems to have gained ground. There has been growing recognition that a number of the problems and challenges faced by the respective approaches are different in degree rather than in kind. Both the potential *complementarity* (even interdependence) of the two approaches and the argument for a combined approach have recently become fairly strong themes in the literature.

Qualitative and quantitative approaches have considerable scope for helping and complementing each other throughout the research process. Both approaches create and test hypotheses and develop theory. Indeed, most of the best studies are based on qualitative foundations supplemented by diligent use of high-quality quantitative approaches and data.

Much has been written on the various ways in which qualitative data help and complement quantitative data. Qualitative data are especially useful at the preparatory and exploratory stages, where their detailed descriptions can provide firm foundations for more rigorous quantitative analysis. They can throw up general questions, concepts, hunches and hypotheses, and can be of tremendous help in the development of research instruments. An example is provided by Smith and Cantley (1985a: 41): 'frequently a qualitative account . . . must precede any attempt at the quantification of variables and much of the research was designed to isolate those factors which are important, prior to their subsequent and more precise measurement.'

At the analysis and interpretation stages, qualitative data perform a crucial role in informing, illuminating and illustrating, in providing explanatory depth and in helping to understand the limits within which the statistical models provide a basis for understanding and prediction (Davies 1986). Their potential for supplementing quantitative data is particularly marked in relation to an understanding of, first, processes and mechanisms that 'produce' statistical relationships and, second, people's subjective experiences.

Similarly, there are various ways in which quantitative data help and complement qualitative data:

1 Quantitative, like qualitative, data allow a preparatory and exploratory 'mapping' of key issues and can suggest avenues for further investigation.
2 They can help in the selection of cases and subsequently can facilitate a more powerful research design, like a quasi-experimental one.
3 They can, in theory at least, help to establish how representative and generalizable qualitative data are. Lofland (1971: 6) argues that quantitative studies 'serve primarily to firm up and modify knowledge first gained in a fundamentally qualitative fashion'.

Data collection and fieldwork: an introductory review

Overview of data collection techniques

The strategy used for moving towards combined qualitative and quantitative approaches of the kind discussed above has two main thrusts. First, solid qualitative foundations need to be developed. This enables relatively good quality data to be collected on all the key accomplishments and research dimensions. This is especially true when qualitative data are integrated within a theoretical context and when they are used alongside quantitative approaches. Second, quantitative approaches need to be developed – where appropriate – that yield good quality data that can properly be subjected to powerful statistical techniques. This means being highly selective in the selection and development of quantitative instruments.

There are two core sets of specific data collection techniques:

- generally being there as an intelligent observer (direct experience/ observation);
- conducting informal, semi-formal and/or formal depth interviews and group interviews.

Both sets of techniques embrace varying degrees of structure, ranging from 'generally being there' to using highly structured pre-coded research instruments.

Direct experience work can yield quantitative data in addition to masses of qualitative data. The 'observer as participant' approach is the most common (Leedham 1989; Wilkinson 1989). It involves spending large amounts of time – over a long period – in the places where people live and work from day to day, generally getting to know individuals and their everyday lives. Such naturalistic, ethnographic techniques were used by the founding fathers of modern anthropology, such as Boas and Malinowski, and have enabled researchers to achieve at least a partial comprehension of alien circumstances and ways of life (Edgerton and Langness 1978; Edgerton 1984b). It is essential to build up rapport and become, if only relatively so, a 'natural' part of subjects' lives. It should be possible to become a 'psuedo-insider' – or, to use the terminology of Lofland (1971: 97), a 'simultaneous insider–outsider' – while retaining disciplined detachment and researcher status. This is the passport to seeking whatever data seems most appropriate (cf. Edgerton 1984a, b; Simons 1986).

Considerable importance is placed on soliciting the views and opinions of various participants about key issues. Interviews and conversations are typically semi-structured, covering key issues and varying in detail depending on the knowledge and interests of respondents. Interviewing style typically involves a 'good deal of probing, asking respondents to explain and elaborate upon their replies' (Smith and Cantley 1985a: 38). Lofland (1971) provides a useful guide to interviewing techniques and issues.

These approaches enable us to describe most aspects of people's life activities, including some that occur rarely or are ordinarily hidden from view. It also provides some sense of how participants think and feel about their lives.

Finally, combined qualitative–quantitative approaches and techniques are particularly well placed to test data quality by means of a process known as triangulation, the use of multiple indicators to measure a single concept. Lots of information sources, data collection methods and data types are brought together to verify a single phenomenon, thus strengthening data credibility (Stainback and Stainback 1984). Triangulation is a major feature of various studies (for example, see Knapp *et al.* 1989; Leedham 1989).

Overview of the fieldwork process

The everyday mechanics of the fieldwork process are typically neglected in books and reports, usually on the grounds that they are not particularly important and/or not particularly relevant to academia or funding bodies. However, fieldwork and related activities provide essential foundations of applied research. In many respects, the findings are only as good as the fieldwork. This section provides an introductory review of key fieldwork methods and issues.

Access and consent procedures can be complicated, difficult and time-consuming, especially for an external researcher. It is important to get to know people and to emphasize the confidentiality of information. In social service settings there are hierarchies of power and consent. Research sponsorship and access to settings and individuals is defined by senior personnel in the higher reaches of the hierarchy, who act as gatekeepers. Service users – and their families – are typically at the bottom of the hierarchy. The lower an individual's place in the hierarchy, the more difficult it is for them to refuse consent. This has a positive influence on participation rates. Even when individuals are given the option to refuse to be observed or interviewed, it is seldom taken up (Burgess 1984; Leedham 1989).

Despite the hierarchies of power and consent, it is obviously good practice continually to negotiate access and consent with the people actually involved in the research and to attach a high priority to safeguarding the rights of users. It seems that users have traditionally been subjected to research that would have been deemed unacceptable outside the special needs field in general and learning difficulty field in particular (e.g. Conroy and Bradley 1985). This needs to change.

With regard to more severely disabled users, in particular, the principle of informed consent can prove a very thorny area. The fact that it is often extremely difficult to get 'informed consent' can make it all too easy either to ignore the user altogether or to ask for permission while not being too concerned with the actual answer given.

Building up and maintaining good relationships with everybody involved is very time consuming but essential, as is developing an

appreciation of the politics of situations. Research cannot normally suc-
ceed without the good will and, indeed, active support of subjects. It is
important to demonstrate a genuine, supportive interest in the everyday
lives of subjects, although it is obviously impossible to become a real
'insider' (Lofland 1971). Major investments must be made in general
relationship-building. It is crucial to *involve* everyone in the research
process, even if only to allay their fears. This takes a lot of intensive effort
and involves a lot of sitting around and talking, but pays handsome
dividends in terms of cooperation, help and friendship (Leedham 1989).
It is possible to become reasonably integrated into most settings, assuming a lower and lower profile (Smith and Cantley 1985a; Simons 1986;
Leedham 1989). This crucial aspect of research method seems to be undervalued. Unfortunately, it seems that the 'come-and-go' type of research
still dominates.

Leedham (1989) postulated that his fieldwork was enhanced by what
Lofland (1971) terms the 'observer as acceptable incompetent' model:

An observer, almost by definition, is one who does not understand.
He is ignorant and needs to be taught. He has always to be watch-
ing and asking questions . . . In being incompetent (but otherwise
polite and easy to get along with) the observer easily assumes the
role of *one who is to be taught* . . . To be young and to be known as
[a] . . . graduate student at some educational institution is likely the
strongest feature one can have going for one as an observer.

(Lofland 1971: 100–1)

The author's relatively 'ordinary' background, orientation and interests
helped considerably (Leedham 1989).

Collecting data can be far from straightforward. Making arrangements
for staff interviews, in particular, is often a complicated business owing
to too few staff and too much work and stress. Bearing this in mind,
interviewing often proves difficult, particularly when using quantitative
instruments. Interruptions can aggravate the situation.

Direct observation is often exceptionally demanding in terms of both
time and effort (see Chapter 5 for more detail). Leedham (1989) points
out that some staff who were incidental to his research study were,
needless to say, sometimes suspicious, particularly when they saw the
author asking lots of questions, filling countless notebooks and taking
photographs. This underscores the importance of 'selling' the research to
everyone in the setting.

As highlighted by Lofland (1971), Leedham (1989) and Wilkinson (1989),
personal involvement in the situations being researched is sometimes
problematic, especially where there arises a felt necessity to join in and
help.

At the practical level of maintaining the role and one's acceptability to the participants, it is probably necessary for one to perform at least some services in the setting . . . [In] a wide range of emergent circumstances, it will seem highly peculiar if the observer does not volunteer his help.

(Lofland 1971: 97–8)

Feedback in one or two years time is a somewhat distant service – consequently it is often necessary to be a 'swift response information resource' to subjects. Leedham (1989) found that some of the requests for help risked him being drawn into local disputes. A less immediate problem was the often-felt temptation to 'give up the observer-analyst role and to take up the enterprise of doing something, of trying to change things for the particular people involved, or the institutions' (Lofland 1971: 98). The results of this are well summarized by the following quotes from two direct observers, Julie Wilkinson and Ian Leedham:

The impact on the researcher was disturbing. After a month or so the powerlessness that seemed to be experienced by her companions, and therefore indirectly by herself, induced feelings of frustration and occasionally anger.

(Wilkinson 1989: 59)

It was often highly frustrating to continue in the researcher mould, even though faith in the value of the findings and feedback was usually – but by no means always – fairly strong.

(Leedham 1989: 100)

Ethical issues and dilemmas are always present. There can be a very real conflict between the rights of users (and other research participants) and the needs of research, even bearing in mind the contribution of research to service development. For example, does research constitute an invasion of user privacy? On the one hand, much research is, almost by definition, an invasion of privacy (how would *you* feel if your daily life was being observed by an outside researcher?). There are, quite clearly, major moral and ethical dilemmas surrounding detailed research into the user's home and behaviour. Dilemmas like this apply to any residential setting, but are arguably most pertinent with regard to community living (Mansell *et al.* 1984; Leedham 1989). On the other hand, privacy can itself sometimes be questioned on ethical grounds. Privacy can mean secrecy, a very useful weapon in defence of the status quo. When viewed like this, privacy can lose its significance as a cherished privilege (Blatt 1970). More generally, in relation to ethical issues, 'it would be far too easy to pass critical judgements upon the conduct of any investigator' (Burgess 1984: 214).

The politics of research are fascinating. The researcher is in a difficult position politically, a major factor being that she or he can be perceived as an agent or spy of the Department of Health, a service agency (often the 'other side') or 'management' in general. Such perceptions can be reinforced by the isolation felt by many carers and by the inquisitive nature of the research exercise. Consequently, it is essential to be continually aware of the politics of everyday situations – for example, concerning how participants perceive the researcher's stance in relation to local disputes, like conflicts of interest between management and frontline staff, and alliances – in order to avoid getting into deep water (Lofland 1971; Leedham 1989).

However, the researcher is in a powerful position in certain respects, for example through being 'independent' and through possessing lots of detailed and often sensitive information. Three 'essentials' are worth highlighting here (Leedham 1989): first, stressing 100 per cent anonymity and confidentiality and gaining everyone's confidence; second, involving everyone in the research; third, stressing feedback and its value.

Research is often seen as threatening and negative. For example, through highlighting shortcomings, it can put personnel on the defensive. Research is a potential – and perhaps very real – threat. There is a particular fear of the possibility of scandals. The contrasting view is that research is a positive thing. For example, through highlighting shortcomings – and good practice – research can act as a stimulus to improving things. These negative and positive views of research are often held simultaneously. Researchers, especially when they are in the field, must maximize the positive response and minimize the negative response. This is not easy, but is essential if the research is to maximize the quality of its data and, subsequently, maximize its contribution to improving opportunities and services.

5 Outcomes 2: specific research dimensions and their measurement

Introduction

Chapter 4 provided a framework for a set of research dimensions by attempting to specify what it is that policy and service interventions in the learning difficulty field should aim to achieve or produce. It also considered key aspects of research design and methodology in the evaluation of outcomes.

It was noted that the user-level and service/organizational-level accomplishments outlined in Chapter 4 are pitched at a high level of generality and need to be translated into specific research dimensions in order to enable practical evaluation. This chapter shows the results of this translation process.

User-level accomplishments (i.e. final outcomes) are translated into the following research dimensions:

- everyday functioning – adaptive and maladaptive behaviour;
- engagement in activity;
- personal experience of life and life quality;
- personal presentation;
- social relationships, networks and community participation.

A straightforward description of user-level accomplishments, although useful, will tell us little about the processes by which they are produced, and about the role of policy, services, environments and other factors in such processes. There are at least four main sets of services and process dimensions that exert a powerful influence on all the user-level accomplishments:

- physical environment;
- social environment;

- staff;
- frameworks for matching resources to wants and needs.

Finally, effects on other people (i.e. external outcomes) are considered.

Everyday functioning: adaptive and maladaptive behaviour

Definition and importance

One of the most widely used research dimensions is that of adaptive behaviour and maladaptive behaviour. Adaptive behaviour is central to the learning difficulty concept, and is defined as 'the effectiveness or degree with which individuals meet the standards of personal independence and social responsibility expected for age and cultural group' (Grossman 1983: 1).

Adaptive behaviour refers to typical everyday functioning and general independence skills and abilities, and includes both positive and negative adaptation (Leland 1978; Meyers *et al.* 1979; Grossman 1983). Positive adaptation is the development of skills and abilities that enable the individual to cope with environmental cues and demands. Three core elements of coping have been identified: personal independence; personal responsibility or adaptation; and social responsibility or adaptation. Negative adaptation refers to challenging behaviours that are problematic for the individual (personal maladaptation) and/or for other people (social maladaptation). The concept of adaptive behaviour is rooted in actual functioning in everyday environments, most of which can be observed directly (e.g. Bercovici 1983; Humphreys *et al.* 1983).

Adaptive and maladaptive behaviour are important reflections of the competence accomplishment, and thus of self-determination and choice (see Chapter 4). Maladaptive behaviour is extremely important, as there is a well-established association between challenging behaviours, carer difficulties and the individual remaining in or returning to a more restrictive placement, like an institution (Eyman and Call 1977; Gollay *et al.* 1978; Sutter *et al.* 1980; Eyman *et al.* 1981; Schalock *et al.* 1981; Hemming 1982; Borthwick-Duffy *et al.* 1987; Emerson *et al.* 1987b). This applies particularly to destructive and disruptive behaviour, like aggression and self-injury (Morreau (1985) provides a useful behaviour classification schema that considers environmental impact). Challenging behaviours can make the individual highly conspicuous, and thus often militate against community presence, respect and community participation.

Research instruments

The formal beginning of adaptive behaviour measurement can be traced back to Doll's work in developing the Vineland Social Maturity Scale to measure 'social competency'. There are currently numerous instruments for measuring aspects of adaptive behaviour, and some for maladaptive behaviour. Meyers *et al.* (1979: 432–3) refer to a 'confusing abundance' of (according to Spreat *et al.* (1983), well over 200) adaptive behaviour scales, mostly unpublished and in local use only. There seem to be two main sets of reasons for the high volume of activity. First, adaptive behaviour is central to the American Association on Mental Retardation's (AAMR) widely adopted definition of 'mental retardation' as 'significantly sub-average general intellectual functioning existing concurrently with deficits in adaptive behaviour' (Grossman 1983: 1). Second, there has been in-creased emphasis on more formal diagnosis and screening, individual planning, and monitoring and evaluation of user progress. There has, surprisingly, been conspicuously less activity in the field of maladaptive behaviour assessment.

Leedham (1989) reviewed over 50 instruments, mostly American. His basic selection criteria excluded most scales almost immediately (see Table 5.1). The instrument that scored best – or least badly – on these criteria was the latest edition of the well known and widely used American Association on Mental Deficiency Adaptive Behavior Scale (AAMD-ABS: Fogelman 1974, 1975). Other contenders included the Balthazar Scales of Adaptive Behavior (Balthazar 1973, 1976) and the Minnesota Develop-mental Programming System (University of Minnesota Outreach Train-ing Project 1976). The ABS scored better than the best known and most widely used instruments in the UK; for example, the Progress Assessment Chart (PAC), Wessex Behaviour Rating Scales, Disability Assessment Schedule (DAS), Hampshire Assessment for Living with Others (HALO), Social Training Achievement Record (STAR) Profile and Bereweeke Skill Teaching System.

The ABS met all the selection criteria detailed in Table 5.1. In addition, it was well known and had been widely used in research studies, examples being Hemming (1982, 1986), Humphreys *et al.* (1983), Mansell *et al.* (1984) and Felce *et al.* (1985, 1986) in the UK, and O'Connor (1976), Gollay *et al.* (1978), Eyman *et al.* (1979), Kleinberg and Galligan (1983), MacEachron (1983) and Landesman (1987) in the USA. These and other studies showed that validity and reliability were acceptable for the ABS Part 1, the adap-tive behaviour section, but poor for Part 2, the maladaptive behaviour section (Fogelman 1975; Isett and Spreat 1979; Meyers *et al.* 1979; Stack 1984). Leedham (1989) made some significant improvements to both Parts 1 and 2.

Interpretation: actual functioning versus potential abilities

A major threat to validity – and consequently to reliability and sensitivity – emerged from consideration of the ABS Manual (Fogelman 1975) and

Table 5.1 Reviewing and selecting adaptive/maladaptive behaviour instruments: selection criteria and reasons for exclusion

Desired attribute	*Typical reasons for exclusion*
Population covered: adults of all ages; complete range of disability	Children or young adults only. Mild/moderate disability only
Comprehensive domain coverage: adaptive and maladaptive behaviour	No maladaptive behaviour (this excluded the vast majority of instruments)
Acceptable validity; assesses actual functioning or has potential to do so (see below)	Validity poor or suspect; assesses potential abilities and does not have potential to assess actual functioning (see below)
Reasonable reliability	Reliability poor, suspect or unknown
Sufficient detail to be sensitive to changes over time	Too little detail (e.g. because screening or survey tools)
Fairly quick (e.g. under $1\frac{1}{2}$ hours) and easy to use	Too detailed and/or lengthy; 'rater technician' needs training and/or professional supervision; scale/manual not user-friendly
Third party interview assessment method	Direct observation/testing (time-consuming); informant-completed (interpretation and reliability problems etc.)
Easy/quick availability	Availability problems (especially concerning US instruments)

the literature more generally. It became apparent that most adaptive behaviour evaluations – including those using the ABS – confuse actual functioning (what users actually do) and potential abilities (what they could do, given the opportunity).

The ABS Manual refers to 'behaviors that are not possible for some people to perform because the opportunity does not exist', and then states that 'In these instances, you must still complete your rating; give the person credit for the task described in the item if you feel absolutely certain that he or she can and would perform it without additional training had he or she the opportunity to do so' (Fogelman 1975: 9). This also applies to behaviours that are 'against local regulations'.

The evaluation of the NIMROD community care service in Cardiff used a modified ABS Part 1. Humphreys *et al.* (1983: 10) note what the Manual says, but argue that

the practice of crediting skills which clients did not actually perform as part of daily life would not only be a source of great
unreliability, but would also mask any real changes in skill usage
which may become apparent purely as a function of change in living environment. Accordingly, clients are only credited with skills
which they are known to employ.

A core element of adaptive behaviour is the extent to which the individual meets the social expectations of his or her environment. One
key question is: which social expectations, of which environment? If
the 'social expectations' and 'environment' refer to societal expectations
– the 'standards of personal independence and social responsibility
expected for age and cultural group' stressed in the AAMR definition
of adaptive behaviour – then the Mental Handicap in Wales Applied
Research Unit (MHWARU) 'actual functioning' argument appears more
sensible. Such an external, societal reference means that actual functioning rather than the abstract notion of potential abilities is of central importance. Furthermore, looking at what people actually do or don't do
highlights a lack of opportunities – for adaptive *and* maladaptive behaviour – in many areas of living. The fact that people are denied various
opportunities *is* of relevance, and should not be glossed over as it is in
the ABS Manual's recommendations.

If, on the other hand, the 'social expectations' and 'environment' refer
to the social environment of the facility (e.g. the hospital or home), then
the ABS Manual's argument for assuming that, in effect, users *do* have
the opportunities perhaps makes a little more sense. However, there are
at least three major problems with this. First, the social expectations and
environment of hospital wards will probably be very different from those
of ordinary houses, so we will not be comparing like with like. Second,
and following on from this, it is highly likely that changes in potential
abilities will be dwarfed by changes in everyday, actual functioning.
Thus, following the advice of the ABS Manual would tend to minimize
changes over time, while following the MHWARU line would tend to
reveal many more changes over time. Third, the 'potential abilities' argument implies, by default, that adaptive and maladaptive behaviour occur
in an environmental vacuum. This contradicts the definition of adaptive
behaviour. Bercovici (1983: 164) argues that most adaptive behaviour
instruments are based on a clinical as opposed to a social-developmental
model, and thus tend to ignore environmental factors and influences.
She argues that there is consequently far too much emphasis on individual traits and personal deficiency (as was the case with IQ assessment) and on discrete behaviours as assessment variables and targets for
intervention.

In summary, the MHWARU argument much better fits the concept of adaptive behaviour, which is rooted in actual, everyday functioning, most of which can be observed directly.

A related point of relevance to interpretation concerns the different norms and expectations that exist between different settings, for example family homes, staffed group homes and institutions. Holburn (1986: 212), for example, refers to a 'tolerance of deviance bias' with regard to maladaptive behaviour, and proceeds to argue that it is possible – perhaps likely – that staff with prolonged exposure to people with severe maladaptive behaviours become less sensitive to, and more tolerant of, maladaptive behaviour. This will apply particularly to staff in institutional settings, owing to the higher proportion of people with severe maladaptive behaviours in such settings. Furthermore, the smaller scale of family and group homes in the community will almost certainly increase sensitivity to, and decrease tolerance of, maladaptive behaviour. The result will be deflated maladaptive behaviour ratings in institutional settings and inflated ratings in family and group homes.

Maladaptive behaviour

It was widely recognized that the validity and reliability of the ABS Part 2 needed substantial improvement. The crux of the problem is that the scoring procedures consider only behaviour frequency, ignoring its relative severity or impact. Thus 'Frequently prefers to be alone' is weighted the same as 'Frequently attempts suicide', so an individual who displays many mildly inappropriate behaviours can appear more maladaptive than someone who displays a few severely inappropriate acts. The ABS Manual (Fogelman 1975) recognizes this problem.

Leedham (1989) reports that his search for a good quality maladaptive behaviour instrument to be used alongside the ABS Part 1 proved unsuccessful – the Fairview Problem Behavior Record, the most promising contender, had been withdrawn by its authors. A journal article by MacDonald and Barton (1986) on revising the ABS Part 2 and developing a 'Maladaptive Behavior Scale' (MBS) came to the rescue. The MBS had a weighted scoring system that took into account both severity and frequency of behaviour, and had improved operational definitions of items and also definitions of frequencies. The development of the MBS has subsequently been detailed by MacDonald (1988).

A weighted scoring system of the MBS type had been suggested by several previous studies (e.g. McDevitt et al. 1977; Knapp and Salend 1983) and partially attempted by at least one (Taylor et al. (1979) for the 'violent and destructive behaviour' domain), while the need for improved operational definitions had been stressed by Stack (1984) in particular. Leedham (1989) developed a weighted scoring system that would yield weighted item-by-item scores that could be summed into various composite scores.

Table 5.2 Revised Adaptive Behavior Scale

Adaptive behaviour domains	Maladaptive behaviour domains
1 Physical development	1 Violent and destructive
2 Language development	2 Antisocial
3 Numbers and time	3 Rebellious
4 Economic activity	4 Untrustworthy
5 Independent functioning	5 Withdrawal
6 Domestic activity	6 Stereotyped and odd mannerisms
7 Vocational activity	7 Inappropriate interpersonal
8 Self-direction	8 Unacceptable vocal
9 Responsibility	9 Unacceptable or eccentric
10 Socialization	10 Self-abusive
	11 Hyperactive
	12 Sexually aberrant
	13 Psychological disturbances
	14 Substance abuse

This worked very well, thus adding further weight to the embryonic scoring systems developed by Clements *et al.* (1980, 1981), MacDonald and Barton (1986) and MacDonald (1988).

The Revised Adaptive Behavior Scale

The significantly improved version of the ABS developed and used by Leedham (1989) was referred to as the Revised Adaptive Behavior Scale (RABS). The RABS comprises 24 'domains' as shown in Table 5.2, and five 'factors'. The domains are representative of those covered by the overall set of adaptive behaviour instruments (Meyers *et al.* 1979).

These domains can be reduced to the five factors identified by Nihira (1969, 1976, 1977, 1978) and confirmed by subsequent studies (e.g. Guarnaccia 1976; Lambert and Nicoll 1976). The factors are consistent with those identified by several studies using different instruments (Meyers *et al.* 1979):

Adaptive behaviour

1 Personal self-sufficiency (basic skills contributing to meeting immediate personal needs).
2 Community self-sufficiency (skills needed for self-sufficiency beyond immediate personal needs, and as reflected in relationships with other community members).
3 Personal–social responsibility (broad spectrum of motivational attributes).

Maladaptive behaviour

4 Social maladaptation (extrapunitive, aggressive or otherwise antisocial behaviours).
5 Personal maladaptation (intrapunitive, 'autistic behaviour syndrome').

Leedham (1989) used the 'third party' assessment method, with length of interview ranging from about 45 minutes to two hours. The respondent is generally the person who has spent the greatest number of waking hours with the user over the previous six months or so. It is sometimes difficult to identify the 'best' respondent. There is some controversy over the relative suitability of 'senior' frontline staff and 'junior' staff. The former often seem to have a good overall picture of an individual, but sometimes lack knowledge about the details of everyday functioning. The latter often seem to have the detailed everyday knowledge, but a number seem to lack the overall picture. An additional problem with respondent selection concerns staff who have known the user for many years. Such staff often seem to have *less* knowledge about the user's current everyday functioning than, say, a staff member who has known the user and been working with him or her for one or two years.

Once the respondent has been selected, the initial briefing is crucially important. First, the briefing must make it clear that the focus is on actual, everyday functioning rather than on potential abilities, and on what the user actually does rather than what he or she is able or allowed to do. The vast majority of respondents in the Leedham (1989) study felt that this actual functioning approach made considerable sense. Second, respondents are asked to think of the user's everyday functioning over the previous six months. A specific time period like this is necessary if changes over time are to appear; it is important to specify a time period to which time 1 relates and to do likewise for time 2 and so on. The ABS Manual does not refer to this issue. One problem with imposing a definite timescale is that it may be unrepresentative; for example, the picture over the previous six months may be contaminated by an unrepresentative episode of behaviour lasting for, say, two or three months. This problem is particularly acute in relation to people who experience large mood swings and/or major changes in behaviour patterns.

Interpretation and scoring of individual RABS items is often far from straightforward. Some key points and issues are summarized below, while more detail can be found in Leedham (1989: Appendix 5.3). Consistency of interpretation was aided by the RABS being administered by the author alone.

Leedham (1989) found that the issue of prompts and assistance proved very difficult when administering Part 1 (cf. Humphreys *et al.* 1983). The advice of the ABS Manual was followed: items that specify 'with help/assistance' for completion of a task are referring to direct physical assistance or continual verbal prompting; the user is given credit for an item if she or he needs a general verbal prompt or reminder to start the task (unless the item states 'without prompting/reminder'). Another problem concerned the 'check all statements . . .' items. The individual statements are specific examples of the characteristic being assessed, and this can thus lead to a misleading picture, in that the specific examples are often not synonymous with the general characteristic. Finally, the inadequacies of Part 1 were particularly noticeable with users who had very few communication skills, considerable physical disabilities or frailties, and mental ill-health symptoms such as anxiety, stress and obsessional or ritualistic behaviours. The RABS certainly has a 'high-floor' effect in that profoundly disabled users tended to score 0 on many or most items (Humphreys *et al.* 1983).

The maladaptive behaviour section had more than its fair share of problems. Respondents were asked for a rough average frequency of maladaptive behaviours per week, averaged out over the previous six months. Many found this task very difficult. A problem of interpretation concerned the boundary between the 'never/rarely' and 'occasionally' frequencies. Continual probing for more accurate information was helped by relating item content to domain headings and by using the examples of statements given on the questionnaire in order to move towards operational definitions of the item statements (some of which are very vague). However, the examples of statements are themselves problematic in so far as the relative importance of the item statements and the examples is unknown. A final problem with the maladaptive behaviour section is the double-counting of some maladaptive behaviours inherent in considering each item separately. There does not appear to be any workable solution to this problem.

Despite these various difficulties, most respondents in the Leedham (1989) study thought the RABS was the best instrument of this type they had seen. The RABS worked reasonably well.

Engagement in activity

Definition, importance and the personal diary

Engagement in activity is typically taken to mean interaction with people or materials in a manner that is likely to maintain or develop adaptive behaviour. Prolonged inactivity, in contrast, tends to wither the body and mind (Mansell 1987). The 'personal diary' developed and used by Leedham (1989) – and referred to as the 'client diary' in that study – is the product of an extensive critical review of the engagement literature. It covers engagement in activity, care-giver support levels and activity locations.

The personal diary defines 'engagement' as participatory engagement in appropriate and purposeful activity that is goal-oriented in some way, as opposed to being neutral or inappropriate. Engagement codes cover essential functions (personal care etc.), educational activity, work/occupational activity, domestic activity, leisure or recreation activity, preparation for a new activity and reciprocal social interaction with other people. The non-engagement code is used for all activities or behaviours that are neutral or inappropriate. The codes build particularly on those used by Butler and Bjaanes (1977), Felce *et al.* (1980a, 1983), Evans *et al.* (1983), Mansell *et al.* (1984), Thomas *et al.* (1986), Landesman (1987) and Mansell (1987).

The six care-giver support codes build on the distinction between prompted and unprompted activities made by Bennett (1986), and also on work by Bjaanes and Butler (1974) and Butler and Bjaanes (1977), among others. Five prompted-by-person codes comprise a continuum of prompting and support levels, ranging from a general verbal or gestural prompt through to the activity being done for the passive user. The other code is used for an activity that is independent of person prompts. Finally, there are eight activity location codes. Previous studies that have looked at activity locations include Grant and Moores (1976) and Crowell *et al.* (1980).

Engagement in activity is an important consequence of person–environment interactions, and embraces many of the accomplishments. For example, we can say that the service system and environment are appropriate to the extent that they provide a range of real opportunities and generally support the translation of the individual's skills and abilities, however limited, into participatory engagement in appropriate and purposeful activity (Felce *et al.* 1985).

Development of the personal diary

The personal diary developed and extended previous work in at least three main ways. These relate to the primary focus on one individual over a complete day, the development of workable operational definitions and the use of the 'observer as participant' model.

First, following Bennett (1986), the primary focus is on one individual over a complete waking day. This contrasts with the time sampling approach used by most studies, which involves observing one subject for a few seconds and then moving on to others before returning to the original subject, and which is often conducted for specific parts of the day (e.g. Grant and Moores 1976; Berkson and Romer 1980; Crowell *et al.* 1980; Felce *et al.* 1980a, 1983; Landesman-Dwyer *et al.* 1980; Mansell *et al.* 1982, 1984; Evans *et al.* 1983, 1985; Thomas *et al.* 1986; Landesman 1987). The group rather than individual orientation has enabled many studies to cover large numbers of subjects in this way and, often, to collect large amounts of highly structured quantitative data. A major problem is that it is easy to lose contact with a number of users, for example because they leave the house (the current setting) and go elsewhere.

Second, most engagement instruments comprise lists of activity categories and, perhaps, a few additional contextual categories like individual–group context. However, operational definitions are usually lacking or inadequate, giving rise to frequent interpretation nightmares. This criticism can be levelled at the vast majority of engagement studies (see Bjaanes and Butler (1974) for a classic example). By default, the focus tends to be on broad activity contexts and patterns rather than participatory engagement in appropriate and purposeful activity. For example, the TV is always on, but few users – certainly in the experience of Leedham (1989) – actually *watch* it in any remotely purposeful way. The development of workable operational definitions for the personal diary involved a lot of sweat and tears.

Third, Leedham (1989) based his direct experience work on the 'observer as participant' model. The personal diary work followed many months of becoming increasingly integrated into the setting, building up rapport and becoming a relatively natural part of subjects' lives, a simultaneous insider–outsider. This provided a passport to seeking whatever data seemed most appropriate, and to minimizing moral and ethical problems. The result was that the presence of the simultaneous insider–outsider seemed to have a minimal effect on people's behaviour and did not irritate people too much (see McCormack 1979; Wilkinson 1989).

The observer as participant model was chosen ahead of the interview model (e.g. as used by O'Neill *et al.* 1981) and three other direct experience models. With the first direct experience model, the complete observer or bird-watcher model, observation 'is very similar to that of the ornithologist who constructs a "hide" so as to be able to observe birds in their natural habitat without disturbing them in any way' (Mann 1985: 99). No external stimuli are applied to subjects, so all situations and actions are totally natural. However, already being well known to users and staff made 'bird-watching' impossible (Leedham 1989).

Furthermore, the 'bird-watcher' is severely limited in terms of type and amount of data (the birds are easily disturbed). The approach used by Mansell *et al.* (1982) is severely limited in this respect and, in addition, provides a good example of how not to get good quality data. After arguing that the observer should 'avoid eye contact with anyone, stand still and look at the stopwatch until taking the observation', the authors state:

If the observer has been talking to clients or staff before the session starts, they should make clear to everyone that they are going to start observing. Further contacts should then be ignored ... At the end of a session ... put down the clipboard, tell everyone that observations are finished and spend a few minutes socialising.

(Mansell et al. 1982: 4)

The authors have disturbed the natural habitat in all these ways and have consequently undermined the validity of their data. It is thus somewhat ironic that they should express such concern for the reliability of the data. They disturb the natural habitat still further in their quest for reliability data: 'Observations should ... be taken independently, with the reliability observer following the main observer's lead as to where to stand and when to move' (Mansell *et al.* 1982: 3). If the users or carers had wings, they would surely have flown away after all this.

The second model is the participant as observer model. The researcher adopts the role that enables him or her to become a full group member and yet able to be inquisitive without fully disclosing his or her researcher role. Again, the fact that the researcher (Leedham, 1989) was already well known to most participants precluded using this model. Furthermore, there are obvious ethical question marks against it.

The final model, the 'complete participant' model, is 'typified by the spy, who is believed by members of the group to be a genuine member of that group and is not known to be an observer at all' (Mann 1985: 106). The classic example of this approach is provided by Goffman (1961), whose work was based largely on a year working at a Washington DC institution. A more recent example is Alaszewski (1986), who worked in a mental handicap hospital as a nursing assistant. Both Goffman and Alaszewski became socialized into the institution culture. Again, the author's researcher role was already known. Furthermore, rather like the 'bird-watcher', the complete participant 'spy' is somewhat limited in terms of type and amount of data because he or she has a job to do and, moreover, cannot come into the open. 'In being an unknown observer, the range of matters into which one can openly inquire is restricted to those things that to members seem appropriate for someone in his role to ask about' (Lofland 1971: 94). Such an approach would have precluded other forms of data collection, most notably interviewing. And, once again, there are major ethical problems.

Administration of the personal diary

The personal diary is a particularly labour-intensive method of collecting data. For example, Leedham (1989) was only able to complete the personal diary with eight users, while Wilkinson (1989) reports that the equivalent, 'being there', phase of her evaluation lasted for 558 hours over about 126 sessions, implemented over a nine-month period. Selecting a 'reasonably typical' day is difficult. In practice, it is difficult enough to select a 'not completely atypical' day. Most days have some feature, like a special activity, which distinguishes them from other days. The aim is to find a day that provides the best flavour of the whole week.

Using the personal diary is particularly demanding, involving long hours and late nights:

> The diary typically began at about 7 a.m. and ended at about 10 p.m., and the need to be continually ready for changes in client activity meant no breaks (and certainly not at meal times, which were generally the busiest part of the day for many clients). Although it was sometimes hard to keep up with some very active clients, the main problem was one of sheer boredom. However, a few hospital (in particular) and community facilities can be danger-ous places, so the need for maximum alertness is heightened (for example, the author was bitten once, and grabbed hold of and pushed on many occasions). Working for 15 hours or so without a break is, at the best of times, extremely tiring and debilitating. Feeling physically ill with sheer exhaustion, particularly from late after-noon onwards, was a particular problem.
>
> (Leedham 1989: 120–1)

Wilkinson (1989: 59), commenting on her similar work, points out that 'Conducting the research proved to be an exhausting and draining experience.'

Intensive direct observational work is one area where it is particularly easy to come into conflict with staff, typically because they think it is themselves who are being observed. Consequently, particular attention must be paid to 'selling' the personal diary idea. Leedham (1989) found that staff responses were generally good in both hospital and community, although there were some instances of staff 'putting on a good show'. User response varied according to level of awareness and communica-tion abilities.

The personal diary yields good quality quantitative data. Moreover, it yields masses of good quality qualitative data concerning the focal in-dividual, other people in the setting and living environments more generally. Indeed, being forced to spend *complete* waking days in living and working environments is an education in itself (Leedham 1989).

Personal experience of life and life quality

The central importance of this dimension was highlighted in Chapter 4. The focus is on user perceptions of and satisfaction with the life experi-ences embraced by the accomplishments. Personal life experiences have been 'sorely neglected' by research (Emerson and Pretty 1986), although the growth of consumerism is slowly changing this. A useful review of the literature is provided by Sigelman *et al.* (1981), Wyngaarden (1981), Flynn (1986) and Prosser (1989).

The few studies that have interviewed users directly include Gollay *et al.* (1978), McDevitt *et al.* (1978), Birenbaum and Re (1979), Seltzer (1981), Passfield (1983), MRC SPU (1986), Cattermole (1987), Atkinson (1989), Flynn (1989), Knapp *et al.* (1989) and Simons *et al.* (1989).

Examples of recent quantitative instruments are the Lifestyle Satisfaction Scale (Heal and Chadsey Rusch 1985), the Consumer Interviews Questionnaire (Conroy and Bradley 1985), the Life Experiences Checklist (see Raynes 1988), the PSSRU Interview for Morale and Life Satisfaction (see Knapp *et al.* 1989) and the User Interview used in the Rowntree/PSSRU long-term study of community care (see Cambridge *et al.* 1991). The last instrument, the User Interview, covers home environment, structured activities, social contacts and life satisfaction. It makes use of various visual aids in order to improve response rates.

We have already seen (Chapter 4) that there are some major problems with regard to individuals' – and especially users' – responses to interview situations and questions, especially where pre-coded questionnaires are concerned. The two major problems are: (a) some users have limited understanding and communication skills; (b) for those who do respond there are at least four major roadblocks to good quality data (quantitative data in particular) – these can be labelled 'acquiescence', 'right answer', 'nay-saying' and 'last option'.

Many exciting innovations are taking place with direct interviewing of users, although there is a tremendous distance to go, particularly regarding people with few communication skills. A number of studies have successfully applied qualitative inductive techniques by conducting informal, semi-structured and conversational interviews (e.g. Atkinson 1989; Flynn 1989; Simons *et al.* 1989). A variety of media – such as photographs and videos – have proved useful devices for eliciting more information, and in life story case studies more generally. Conroy and Bradley (1985) and Simons *et al.* (1989), among others, have used pictures of people, places and happy, neutral and sad faces. This approach enables us to reach people with few or no verbal skills, for example by asking the question: what sort of face would *you* have if . . .?' (Simons *et al.* 1989).

The life story approach is another exciting area of innovation. Atkinson and Williams (1990) present a collection of life stories by people with learning difficulties, using poetry, art, photography and story-telling. Probably the best known life story in this field is Joseph Deacon's autobiography (Deacon 1982), which was written collaboratively by Deacon and three friends. In a similar vein, the use of life story books is well illustrated by Frost and Taylor (1986), who conclude: 'The life story book group project was a positive and valuable experience which gave the clients a structured and understandable way of talking about themselves and their past, present and future' (p. 29). Their life story work provided the foundation stone for self-advocacy work.

Personal presentation

Pride in personal appearance is an important indicator of many of the accomplishments and, moreover, of the individual's perception of his or her self-concept as a person (Morris 1969; see chapter 3). It has important implications for successful acceptance and integration. Important components include cleanliness and grooming, clothes, posture and general appearance. Unfortunately, the few checklists that exist – for example, the PSSRU Personal Presentation Checklist (see Thomason 1986) – tend to be very basic and overly subjective. Consequently, it is probably best to collect descriptive, qualitative data.

Social relationships, social networks and community participation

The central importance of these dimensions was highlighted in the discussion of the accomplishments, particularly respect and community participation (see Chapter 4). These dimensions have traditionally been somewhat under-researched, but have become more popular in recent years.

Examples of recent evaluations are provided by the Kirklees Relocation Research Project (see Booth *et al.* 1988) and the Bolton CHC (1987) evaluation of the Bolton Neighbourhood Network Scheme. The Kirklees Project used the Index of Community Involvement instrument as part of its 'Staff Schedule'. Coverage includes type and location of service/ facility, frequency of use, organization of staff support and individual– group context. The Staff Schedule also includes a section called 'Relatives and friends'; this records visits, contacts and relationships. The Bolton evaluation allocated a rough set of values to different types of social activities and relationships, with items reflecting real community participation scoring the highest. Activities that are segregated from the local community (for whatever reason) score the lowest. The scoring system provides a solid base from which to analyse community involvement.

Physical environment

Physical environment is important for at least three main sets of reasons. First, architectural forms stand for, communicate and produce cultural expectations; as Wolfensberger (1972: 40) notes, 'Architecture speaks a powerful language'. Architectural forms are manifestations of what a culture deems appropriate, and therefore mirror cultural values (Wolfensberger 1975; Robinson 1987): hence their centrality to normalization principles. Second, physical environment is not just a static shell, but an important determinant of social environment (Gunzburg and Gunzburg 1973, 1987): it can support or hinder goal-directed activity, for instance through the degree of control it gives to residents over everyday choices concerning privacy, comfort and relationships. Third, physical environments can be modified.

The main research focus has been on the external and internal physical and architectural features of facilities and the neighbourhood context in which they are located. The Built Environment Rating Scale or BERS (for residential provisions) developed and used by Leedham (1989) uses a five-point scale to rate how appropriate specific aspects of the physical environment are by the standards of a 'desirable ordinary residence' that most people do live in or would like to live in. It considers, where applicable, a rating of homelike versus institutional, and a subjective impression of pleasant and attractive versus unpleasant and unattractive. For each room or area of the residence specific items include size, furniture, decoration, doors and windows, signs, lighting, heating, environmental personalization, personal possessions and anti-fire paraphernalia. There are various additional items relating to the living unit as a whole.

The BERS draws particularly on the design principles of the excellent 236-item Architectural Checklist – based on the institutional versus homelike continuum – developed by Robinson *et al.* (1984). It also builds on the Questionnaire on Quality of Life (Birmingham CPMH 1986), the PSSRU Environment Checklist (see Thomason 1986), the 69-item Index of the Physical Environment (see Raynes *et al.* 1979; Pratt *et al.* 1980), the 36-item Physical Environment Index (see MacEachron 1983), the Multiphasic Environmental Assessment Procedure and various other instruments. Leedham (1989) also developed and used a general descriptive checklist as an *aide-mémoire* in the collection of descriptive qualitative data on physical environments. A number of photographs were also taken.

Social environment

There are at least three main streams of work on the social environment of service provisions.

The human management practices model

The first stream of work is sociological in nature and based on the work of Erving Goffman (1961). Goffman identified four classic features of the total institution. These features, which together comprise the human management practices model, are well described by Bercovici (1983: 34):

1 Rigidity of routine, the extent to which practices are inflexible from day to day and from one user to another; neither individual differences among users nor unique circumstances are taken into account.
2 Block treatment, the degree to which users are regimented, i.e. dealt with as a group or en masse, as opposed to more individually.
3 Depersonalization, the extent to which users are allowed personal possessions, provided privacy or given opportunity for self-expression and personal initiative.
4 Social distance, the degree of integration or separation between staff and users.

Goffman's work has been developed and refined by researchers like King, Raynes and Tizard, whose work over the years has been directed towards comparing the characteristics of different institutions. The resulting instruments – for example, the Inmate Management Scale (King and Raynes 1968) and the Child Management Scale (King *et al.* 1971) – measure the degree to which staff practices are institution-oriented or user-oriented. Subsequent scales in this tradition include the Revised Resident Management Practices Scale and Group Home Management Schedule (see Raynes *et al.* 1979; Pratt *et al.* 1980).

These instruments had been successfully used in a number of previous studies, for example King and Raynes (1968), King *et al.* (1971), McLain *et al.* (1975, 1977), Raynes *et al.* (1979) and Pratt *et al.* (1980). However, the scales are short and basic, typically consisting of 16 to 28 items. Moreover, there is a confusing abundance of them (at least nine) and no publication which pulls them all together. They are also difficult to get hold of. Consequently, it is probably best to look for alternative social environment instruments and to collect general qualitative data on human management practices.

Normalization-based approaches

The *second stream* of work is based explicitly on the normalization philosophy, and particularly on the Program Analysis of Service Systems (PASS) and PASS Implementation of Normalization Goals (PASSING) evaluation perspective. A PASS-based approach assesses at least five major and overlapping aspects of the living environment (see Bercovici 1983):

1 Physical and social integration into the community.
2 The human management practices model, explicitly or implicitly employed. The main models are the medical, social-developmental, detentive-corrective, warehousing (physical maintenance) and custodial-control models.
3 The age and culture appropriateness of human management practices, and the messages that flow from them (mainly via labelling). These

factors are important determinants of self-perception and the perceptions of others.

4 The quality of the environment, both physical and social, and the degree of control users have over it.

5 (Closely related to items 1–4). The attitudes that staff have towards users in general and working practices and the staff–user relationship in particular.

The latest version of the PASS evaluation instrument, PASS-3 (Wolfensberger and Glenn 1975a, b; Wolfensberger 1983b), contains 50 items and has been widely used, examples being Eyman *et al.* (1979) and the Eyman *et al.* (1987) foster care placements study. An 18-item Short Form of PASS-3 (Flynn and Heal 1981) has been used by Conroy and Bradley (1985), among others. It apparently has very satisfactory validity and reliability (Heal and Laidlaw 1980: 144). PASSING (Wolfensberger and Thomas 1983; Wolfensberger 1983b) is a 43-item, more user-friendly development of PASS. Pilling (1990) reports on the first stages of a comprehensive evaluation of PASS being undertaken at the City University, London.

In a similar vein to the PASS-based approach, the Accreditation Council on Services for People with Developmental Disabilities (USA), the National Development Group for Mentally Handicapped People and MENCAP, among others, have developed normalization-based standards or checklists to aid service evaluation (see Raynes 1988, for a review). Most promisingly of all, Evans (1988) reports on the development and use of a 'Standards Matrix' based on the user-level accomplishments discussed in Chapter 4.

The PASS and PASSING instruments can be very difficult to use. The following reasons draw particularly from Haycox (undated) and Renshaw (1986).

1 The weighted scoring system is based on the authors' opinion of each item's importance, rather than on empirical evidence.

2 There are problems with the 1 to 5 rating scale, which is heavily biased towards the bottom scores. 'Five' is scored where it is difficult to conceive of any possible improvements – the 'best of all possible worlds' – while '1' represents a wide range of possibilities from the worst conceivable service, doing substantial harm to users, through to services which approximate to the 'norm' of currently available services. Score '1' represents a high security prison: massive improvements have to be made if the service is to escape to a score of '2' or higher. This militates against sensitive measurement of progress (the rating scale and/or items need to be adapted in order to 'catch the effect'). A related problem is that nearly all (current) services will score badly and, moreover, may be demoralized by subsequent criticisms.

3 The ratings are based on a lengthy and difficult process of 'team-reconciliation' involving a number of evaluators, who have to endure extremely demanding workshop sessions. Conroy and Bradley (1985) point out that about six to fifteen person days are needed for a complete 50-item PASS-3 rating.

4 The language is highly inaccessible and the manuals are difficult to use. Each item, for example 'service neighbourhood assimilation potential', is followed by many pages of long-winded and jargon-laden explanation (Renshaw 1986).

Closely related to the Goffman-based and normalization-based streams is the Learning Opportunities Coordination (LOCO) tool developed by Gunzburg and Gunzburg (1987) and the Questionnaire on Quality of Life developed by Birmingham CPMH (1986). LOCO assesses the contribution of the physical and social environment to social and personal development. It is the successor to Gunzburg's '39 Steps leading towards normalized living practices' (Gunzburg 1973). The Birmingham CPMH questionnaire provides a fairly comprehensive organizing framework. It contains eight sections, entitled physical details, access to community, integration, staff behaviour, decision making, routines, education and training, and leisure. It has been used by James and Jeffes (1984), among others. Unfortunately, it suffers from interpretation problems resulting from a lack of operational definitions of items.

The social-ecological model and social climate

The third stream of work is social-psychological in nature and exemplified by the work of Rudolf Moos and colleagues at the Social Ecology Laboratory, Stanford University, California. Moos and colleagues have developed a social-ecological model of human adaptation:

> the model specifies the existence of two systems – the personal and environmental – each of which helps to shape the other. That is, some of the characteristics of environments reflect the personal resources of the individual functioning in them, whereas individual qualities (such as personality traits, attitudes and expectations, and personal resources) are affected by the environmental context. The personal and environmental systems combine to influence ... adaptation both directly and indirectly via mediating factors.
>
> (Cronkite *et al.* 1984: 190)

This model has spawned the Multiphasic Environmental Assessment Procedure (MEAP; Moos and Lemke 1982, 1984; Lemke and Moos 1984; Lemke *et al.* 1984; Moos 1984), which evaluates physical environment, user and staff characteristics, organizational structure and social environment.

Moos and colleagues argue that there are underlying patterns which characterize a wide variety of environments, and have developed the 'social climate' concept based upon an assumption that environments have unique 'personalities' just as people do. They view the social climate as the key mechanism – or mediator – by which the influences of physical and social environment are translated into final outcomes (Moos 1974a; Cronkite *et al.* 1984). The resulting battery of social climate scales has been used in a wide variety of settings, particularly in the care of people with mental health problems and elderly people. Social climate is central to the MEAP.

A set of social environment scales (SES) was developed and used by Leedham (1989). The SES comprise revised versions of two widely known social climate scales – the Ward Atmosphere Scale (WAS) and Community Oriented Programs Environment Scale (COPES) – and Characteristics of the Treatment Environment (CTE), which is not one of the social climate scales but comes from a similar tradition. The WAS and COPES – and social climate scales more generally – contain three sets of dimensions (see Moos 1974a, b, c):

1 Relationship dimensions assess how involved people are in the environment, the degree to which they support one another and the extent to which they express themselves freely and openly.
2 Personal growth or goal orientation dimensions measure the attainment of basic goals like personal and social development.
3 System maintenance and change dimensions deal with the extent to which an environment if orderly and clear in its expectations, maintains control and responds to change.

The CTE has two factors (see Sutter and Mayeda 1979):

1 The autonomy factor measures the degree to which users are encouraged and enabled to exercise independence, choice and self-determination in everyday living.
2 The activity factor measures opportunities for users to engage in purposeful activities.

Development and use of the social environment scales

The WAS/COPES were originally designed for the care of people with mental health problems, and have been used extensively in that field. There are only a few examples of the WAS/COPES being used in the learning difficulty field, but those that do exist – most notably the McGee and Woods (1978) study of a residential vocational training centre for adolescents, which used the WAS, and the Pankratz (1975) study of two halfway houses, which used the COPES – point to adequate validity and reliability, and recommend their wider employment. Shinn (1982: 128), although criticizing certain aspects of the scales, argues that they 'remain the standard against which other measures of perceived treatment environments must be compared. Evaluators would do well to select either the appropriate (full length) Moos scale or a modification of it.'

The CTE was also designed originally for the mental health field, but the 1970s saw the specific development of learning difficulty versions. First, Silverstein *et al.* (1977) translated the original 72-item CTE into a 59-item 'CTE: MR/DD Institutional Version', yielding the Autonomy and Activity factors referred to above. Second, McLain *et al.* (1977) developed a 48-item 'CTE: MR/DD Community Home Version'. All three versions of the CTE contributed to the development of the SES. Studies that have used the CTE: MR/DD include the McLain *et al.* (1977) study of various residential settings, the Eyman *et al.* (1977) study of hospitals and community residences in California and Colorado, and Rotegard *et al.* (1983), who used a questionnaire comprising nine CTE items in their national survey of 236 US residential facilities. All of the evidence points to adequate validity and reliability.

The SES built on the WAS/COPES and the CTE in a number of ways (see Leedham 1989, for full details):

- the WAS and COPES were combined into one scale, with the CTE following the combined WAS/COPES;
- various modifications (simplifications) were made to item wording and scoring;
- the rating scale (true/false) was made more precise by using the CTE's 11-point rating scale instead.

Four versions of the SES were developed:

1 Residential provisions – real social environment.
2 Day provisions – real social environment.
3 Residential provisions – conceptions of ideal social environment.
4 Day provisions – conceptions of ideal social environment.

The real–ideal distinction follows that used in the WAS/COPES. The idea is to compare the real with the ideal and to identify where progress has been made and/or needs to be made. The residential–day facility distinction is necessitated by the fact that residential and day provisions are often separate, with separate sets of personnel.

Leedham (1989) found that the SES were not particularly easy to administer or respond to. First, it proved essential to become highly familiar with the scales. Second, it was crucial to select respondents who would be honest and open. Fortunately, it did not prove too difficult to find such people. Third, it was essential to brief the respondent in a clear and comprehensive way. The key briefing points were reinforced throughout the interview.

A lot is being asked of the respondent. He or she has to consider each of 152 items in some detail, weighing up all the conflicting evidence and eventually coming to some kind of numerical conclusion. Certainly, the lack of operational definitions for items makes administering and responding to the SES extremely difficult. At the end of the 80 minute-or-so interview, the respondent and the author were often very weary and, indeed, somewhat disillusioned with quantitative instruments of this kind.

A fair amount of the item-by-item SES data collected by Leedham (1989) is of questionable or poor quality. In addition, the SES domain structure is problematic. Most of the domains measure aspects of the social environment that are virtually impossible to distinguish from one another. Some of the WAS/COPES domains also mix positive and negative aspects of the social environment. Unlike the other domains, which focus on positive social environment, these tend to produce a mixed rank order of 'better' and 'worse' provisions that seems to be somewhat divorced from reality. Furthermore, these data are redundant in terms of policy and practice utility because they do not relate specifically to intervention objectives. Thus if we find important links between mixed domains and aspects of user welfare, it is difficult to know how the social environmental attribute should be manipulated by policy-makers and practitioners. Is it the positive or negative aspects of the domain that are important determinants of user welfare?

The approach to rescuing some good quality data was to choose certain items from each domain to form a small number of 'global' indicators. Items were chosen in a way that minimized the problems discussed in this and previous subsections. Full details are provided in Leedham (1989).

Staff

Staff at all levels are the most important resource input into services. Staff numbers, training and experience, organization, working practices and experiences, responsibilities, management, attitudes, job satisfaction and opinions are all important research foci, especially bearing in mind their close relationship with social environment. Examples of instruments are the PSSRU Staff Record Forms (see Thomason 1986) and the detailed questionnaires used by Haycox (1989) in his evaluation of the Maidstone Community Care Programme.

A number of studies – including Haycox (1989), Knapp *et al*. (1989) and Leedham (1989) – have collected large amounts of qualitative data and have analysed staffing issues in some detail.

Frameworks for matching resources to wants and needs

A focus on frameworks for matching resources to wants and needs – for example, 'service brokerage' or 'case management' frameworks –

supplements the key 'user' and 'services and process' dimensions considered above in at least three important ways:

1 It provides essential information on all the user-level and service/organizational-level accomplishments discussed in Chapter 4, and helps to cement together the individual and service/process dimensions.
2 It provides a bridge between objectives and outcomes at two levels: 'bottom-up' objectives and outcomes revolving around accomplishments (Chapter 4), and 'top-down' objectives stemming from the overall service system and policy levels.
3 It is a rich source of evidence on the relationships between needs, resources and outcomes at both the micro and macro levels.

Effects on other people (external outcomes)

We noted in Chapter 4 that an analysis of final and intermediate outcomes needs to be supplemented by consideration of the effects of policy and service interventions on other people, most notably the costs and benefits experienced by carers and by society at large. The best methodological approach is undoubtedly to collect qualitative data on the key issues involved (see Chapter 4 for a review).

An extremely good qualitative interview schedule is the Adult Placement/Home Carer Interview (see Cambridge *et al.* 1991). The schedule uses open-ended questions with comprehensive 'probes' (probing statements acting as an *aide-mémoire*) in order to collect information on experiences and feelings about *caring*. It covers the following topics:

- background details (e.g. composition of household);
- history (of the particular caring relationship);
- routines (support, activities);
- physical support.
- functional support.
- Help for the carer (from family, friends, neighbours, services – actual and needed help);
- immediate social and health costs and benefits (carer's physical and mental health, social/family/community life, carer–person relationship).
- economic costs and benefits (financial benefits, costs of caring, financial situation, paid employment, opportunity costs, purchase of services);
- experience (extent to which expectations are met, best and worst features, needs etc.).

Notes on the analysis and interpretation of data

This section concludes the chapter by offering some pointers with regard to the analysis and interpretation of outcomes data. The pointers are overlapping and interrelated.

First, as explained in Chapter 2, we need to use the *production of welfare framework* in order to address the key questions of efficiency and equity.

Second, it is essential to be absolutely clear about what policy and service interventions should be aiming to achieve or produce. Consequently, we need to use the idealistic *accomplishments framework* as a frame of reference for defining and evaluating 'quality of life', needs and outcomes (see Chapter 4). Thus the accomplishments framework is an essential part of the production of welfare framework.

Third, we need to consider all three main *types of outcomes*, as follows:

- final outcomes;
- intermediate outcomes;
- external outcomes.

Fourth, we should be aware of the opportunities and constraints posed by the research design and methodological approaches used (see Chapters 4 and 5). In particular, we should aim to paint 'the whole picture' using good quality data.

Fifth, we should realize the complexity of relationships between variables. The distinction between statistical analyses using two (bivariate) or more than two (multivariate) variables illustrates the point. Relationships between dependent variables and independent variables are obscured and generally complicated by a plethora of intervening variables. Consequently, even the most sophisticated cross-tabular comparisons are unable to tease out the main interdependencies, not to mention causal direction. Hence there is an overwhelming need for multivariate analyses.

Sixth, this points once again to the need to incorporate our work within the production of welfare framework.

6 Outcomes 3: evidence and issues

Introduction

In the previous two chapters we have defined outcomes and considered methodologies for evaluating and measuring them in practical ways. There has been a special emphasis on final/user outcomes. We have also looked at the processes by which final outcomes are produced.

So, what are the realities for people with learning difficulties? In this chapter we attempt to provide a 'position statement' of the current situation. We describe and discuss key aspects of the lives of people with learning difficulties, and attempt to work out *why* things are like they are. We consider a range of issues and concerns relating to policy, services and practice, with a special emphasis on implications and ways forward.

Final outcomes 1: position statement on user-level accomplishments

Overview

There are perhaps 100,000 specialists, and many other professionals and administrators, managing a vast range of resources. In addition to operating the services, these workers have spent time in countless conferences and training courses. They have written and read a whole library of textbooks and journals. They have endlessly debated policy and studied its implementation. And the net result? In terms of real difference to people with learning difficulties, as opposed to the changes in salaries for workers or the volume of jargon, not very much. Some of them – by no means all – now live in smaller groups than they would have in 1971. The regime is likely to be rather more permissive. They are more likely to be living in an ordinary house, in an ordinary street. But they almost certainly have little to do with the community.

(Dowson 1991: 15)

In general people are still being offered services which happen to be available, rather than having services created to meet their individual requirements.

(Welsh Office 1991b: 13)

Most people in the UK live in families. Family living is a good thing; it is considered by many to be a foundation-stone of our society. Most people grow up in families and then move on when they are aged between 16 and their mid-twenties. After a period of establishing themselves as individual adults, with unique characters and experiences, most people subsequently get married and have families of their own.

Most people with learning difficulties also live in families. However, the situation is very different. Most people with learning difficulties continue to live in the parental home, with their parents, well beyond their twenties or even thirties. They are generally denied the opportunity to move on and to establish themselves in the adult world, let alone to create their own family situations. Indeed, most adults with learning difficulties face many years of reliance upon their parents, often until the parents become elderly and are no longer able to cope with the situation.

Furthermore, services for people with learning difficulties are generally inappropriate to their needs. Most current services are organized and provided in a very much top-down and paternalistic way, with a considerable reliance on expert judgements made by professionals and managers. Prescription, funding decisions and provision are performed by the same agency, even the same people. This encourages block-funding, block-provision and fitting people in to the best (least bad) alternative. Most services are based upon segregation, congregation and institutionalization, obvious examples being long-stay hospitals (which account for over half of the combined local/health authority budget for adults with learning difficulties), hostels, training centres and large private homes (see below for a description and discussion of these services). The result is that people with learning difficulties have few rights, few choices and no real power as consumers. They become 'clientized', passive and dependent on the services offered.

On a more positive note, there are some isolated examples of people with learning difficulties living and participating in their local communities. The services that support and enable these positive outcomes are based explicitly on the accomplishments model. Hardly surprisingly, there is clear evidence to suggest that these kinds of services generally perform best in terms of effectiveness and, moreover, cost-effectiveness and external benefits.

However, the experiences of the great majority of people with learning difficulties and their families fall significantly short of the modest aspirations – such as ordinary domestic life; worthwhile work or daytime occupation; skilled support with learning – which these achievements have encouraged.

(Towell and Beardshaw 1991: 14)

The challenge is to make services based on good practices the rule rather than the exception.

Community presence

Community presence is the sharing of the ordinary places that define community life.

Most people with learning difficulties live with their parents, in an ordinary house in an ordinary street. Some others live in a variety of ordinary living arrangements, with whatever staff support is necessary. Some people share a range of ordinary places, such as homes, workplaces, shops and community resources.

However, it is widely recognized that most people with learning difficulties are not sufficiently present in their local communities. This is particularly true for people who use services, the majority of whom have to use services that segregate them from ordinary life and congregate them with other people with learning difficulties. It is also true for many people living with their families (see below).

Informed choice

Informed choice boils down to having the autonomy and freedom to define who we are and what we value. It relies in part on being aware (informed) of opportunities and constraints. In general, opportunities for making choices and decisions are highly limited for most people with learning difficulties, although there have been some major improvements for some people. This is true for autonomy in everyday life and, in particular, for choices concerning life-defining matters.

Competence

Competence is the opportunity to perform functional and meaningful activities, with whatever encouragement, support and help is needed. In research terms, there has been considerable interest in adaptive behaviour and engagement in activity.

Most research work has focused on the move from hospital to community care. The general picture is that the move from hospital to community – and especially the move to more normalized environments – is often associated with significant improvements in adaptive behaviour and, to a lesser extent, engagement in activity. However, a number of studies have found small or no improvements – or even a worsening – in adaptive behaviour and engagement in activity despite quite considerable environmental improvements. Furthermore, most studies report that maladaptive behaviour (challenging behaviour) remains broadly constant or else worsens. More details can be found below.

Self-determination

Self-determination means being self-determining in terms of lifestyle; it is associated with ownership of one's own life and with positive self-identity. As above, there has been considerable research interest in adaptive behaviour and engagement in activity, particularly with regard to people moving from hospital to community care. In recent years there has been increased awareness of people's right and need for self-determination. However, there is widespread concern about lack of freedom and about parents and staff 'owning' people and their lives.

Participation: valued participation in community life

Valued participation in community life revolves around being part of a wide-ranging network of two-way relationships with ordinary people (family, friends, colleagues) and ordinary places (home, work, shops and so on). It reflects our deep needs to love and to be loved, to give, to receive and to share. This is what 'community' is really all about.

Overall, there has definitely been progress towards the goal of valued participation in community life, and the progress is ongoing. However, progress has generally been slow and disappointing and there is certainly a tremendous distance to go. Most people with learning difficulties still lead a marginalized existence with relatively little integration in ordinary community settings and with ordinary community members. There are generally few opportunities for integrated work, education and leisure. Moreover, friendship, ties and connections are lacking for most people, most of the time.

Personal continuity

Personal continuity means the experience of ongoing relationships with people, places and possessions. Although boredom and a lack of change are undoubtedly a major problem for a number of people with learning difficulties, lack of continuity is an equally big problem. The main factor is that people are expected to move from service to service as their needs change, rather than the services being purpose-built around the person's evolving needs and wants.

Personal experience of life and life quality

There has been a limited, though growing, interest in the morale and life satisfaction of people with learning difficulties. Most of the limited available evidence concerns users' perceptions of the move from hospital to community care. The general picture is that, hardly surprisingly, people want to maximize their personal experience of the accomplishments discussed in Chapter 2. Consequently, they prefer ordinary living in ordinary communities, particularly where they have freedom to make their own decisions and choices. Some more details can be found in the next section.

Final outcomes 2: families, institutions, supported ordinary living and 'moving'

Families

The vast majority of people with learning difficulties live with their families. Families are and always have been the main service providers and yet have always been neglected by services. Despite some shining examples of good practice and positive outcomes, it is still the case that most families throughout the UK are expected to struggle on with little or no appropriate help. The problems are exacerbated once the person approaches, reaches and passes school-leaving age, owing to the major inadequacies of opportunities and services for adults. There are often considerable worries about who will care in the future, especially when the parents are no longer able to do so.

Many families and people with learning difficulties are being placed under intolerable stresses and strains. The situation is bad for all concerned:

- Bad for the people with learning difficulties and their families, who are denied an ordinary family life and often face social isolation. Furthermore, the care-giving family members often face physical and/or mental breakdown.
- Bad for service agencies, who have to pick up the pieces in the end. This often takes the form of crisis management, which is a notoriously inefficient and unjust way of going about things.
- Bad for the community as a whole, which has to live with all the social problems that are part and parcel of the above picture. Examples include the breakdown of families, social marginalization, problems of physical and mental health, and reduced economic productivity.

Institutions 1: long-stay hospitals

There are at least four good reasons for briefly describing and discussing long-stay mental handicap hospitals:

1 Approximately 27,000 people live in such places.
2 Long-stay hospitals account for a vastly disproportionate amount of resources. A report by the Audit Commission (1989) showed that almost 60 per cent of the combined local and health authority budget for adults with learning difficulties was still locked in hospital provision. These resources are desperately needed for the development of community provision.
3 Most services for people with learning difficulties – whether hospital- or community-based – are institutional.
4 There is still a fierce debate between advocates of 'reformed hospitals and institutions' and the ordinary life/accomplishments model.

Institutions have various classic features. This is especially true of residential institutions in general and long-stay mental handicap hospitals in particular. This section summarizes a case study of a hospital. Haycox (forthcoming), who also focused on Hospital X, concluded as follows: 'The "quality of life" of residents within [Hospital X] . . . was, upon any measure, exceptionally poor . . . like other "institutions" the impact upon residents was largely one of "standardisation" and "de-humanisation"' (Haycox forthcoming: 41 and 42). More detail from the Leedham (1989) case study is provided below.

Hospital X had all the classic physical features of a long-stay institution (see Morris 1969; Robinson 1987). The vast grounds were beautifully maintained. The buildings were big, grey, spartan, barrack-like and generally uninviting. Using the language of Rivera (1972: 16), 'It's as if a group spent all its savings to buy choice land for a country club, but then ran out of money and could afford to erect only army barracks.' There were wrought iron fire escapes, rows of massive dustbins, iron fences, laundry trolleys, a tall chimney and massive verandas. The numerous signs stressed that this was no ordinary residence and that the residents were 'different'.

The wards were worse inside than outside. The environment was extremely institutional and left discerning visitors (of whom, perhaps, there were very few) in no doubt that this was a third class service for third class 'patients'. Various signs and labels advertised the fact that most equipment and furniture had been either donated charitably or provided by the Health Authority. There were lots of wheelchairs, Kirton chairs and anti-fire paraphernalia. Corridors, rooms, furniture, decoration, lights, radiators, doors and windows were of the classic institutional

design. There was little variation between rooms, still less personalization of the environment and little or no opportunity for privacy. The
toilet and bathroom areas were particularly appalling in this and other
respects (see Morris 1969). The wards did not look lived-in; they were
just institutional shells. Not surprisingly, the staff had their own, considerably better quality, canteen and toilets.

Staff–user ratios – and the ratio of trained to untrained staff – were
inadequate. There were typically three staff on duty for a ward of about
18 highly dependent residents. The views and practices of many staff
were reactionary in relation to current philosophies and values. An earlier
study of Hospital X by another of the authors (see Haycox 1989; Haycox
and Brand 1990) found that attitudes tended towards authoritarianism
and paternalism. Staff morale was at rock-bottom. Absentee rates reached
the stage where the continued operation of the wards was threatened.
There was a heavy reliance on agency and bank staff. Staff were stretched
to the limits, and the work became more dangerous and less rewarding.
Staff became increasingly apathetic. Bad practices went unchallenged and,
indeed, flourished.

Everyday life in Hospital X was dominated by Goffman's (1961) four
classic features of the 'total institution' – rigidity of routine, block treatment, depersonalization and social distance. There was a general atmosphere of decay and few signs of substantial upgrading of physical plant, let
alone of service ideologies. There was no active keyworker system, and
even the move away from hospital-issued clothing had been reversed.

The entire day was based upon fixed and rigid routines, and revolved
around mealtimes and basic personal care (see also Haycox forthcoming;
cf. Morris 1969; Alaszewski 1986). Most of the time was spent merely
'passing time'. The Leedham (1989) case study paper described a typical
day using the following headings:

• So begins another weary day
• Food
• Drugs
• Toilet
• Temporary diversion for some
• The dayroom
• Bathtime
• Bedtime (one more day out of the way)

Temporary diversion was in the form of the Occupational Therapy
Department, which had better staff–user ratios and offered a more
stimulating environment than the wards. The dayroom, as the staff called
it, was the place where residents awaited their next meal or personal care
need. The atmosphere of decay was compounded by the smell, which
was often terrible.

The totally inadequate staff–resident ratios meant block as opposed to individual treatment. 'Tea mixed with milk and sugar to save time, mess and trouble. How many lumps, say when with the milk? You must be joking' (Ryan and Thomas 1980: 35). Feeding, toileting, bathing and waiting were typically conducted on a group basis. It was common to see a staff member feeding two or more residents simultaneously. A similarly dehumanizing practice was that a number of residents were transported from the wards to the OT Department in an open trailer attached to a motorized truck. It was as if the residents were not sufficiently human to have the right to individual care, privacy, and personal dignity.

> Being in the institution was bad . . . I didn't have any clothes of my own and no privacy . . . The real pain came from always being part of a group. I was never a person. I was part of a group to eat, sleep, and everything. As a kid, I couldn't figure out who I was. I was part of a group. It was sad.
> (Young resident, in another institution, quoted by Shearer 1981: 91)

The principal aim at mealtimes and toilet times was to get the job over with as soon as possible and with the minimum of fuss. Alaszewski (1986: 158) calls this 'sequential body servicing'. Ambulant residents were often wheeled around in wheelchairs for convenience, while the lifting of people was often done clumsily. Some residents were wheeled around – sometimes semi-naked – in their Kirton chairs. Conveyor belts in the dining rooms and toilet/bathrooms would have been handy. Staff had to work like this because it was the only way to get all the basics done. Residents simply had passively to wait their turn (often for a long time).

It was extremely difficult to think of Hospital X as a 'hospital home'. It was more like the places described by various Committees of Inquiry in the late 1960s and early 1970s and in the 'critique of institutions' literature more generally. Hospital X was undoubtedly similar to most other long-stay mental handicap hospitals, which have been labelled by Shearer (1986: 8) as 'monuments to lack of thought and attention to individuals'. As Spencer (1981: 305), reporting her experience of living for a week in a mental handicap hospital, points out: 'It is in the common values of humanity that I found the institutional experience most lacking'.

Institutions 2: 'community facilities'

Most people with learning difficulties live in the community, and most of them lead a marginalized existence with relatively little integration in ordinary settings and with ordinary people. Friendships, ties and connections are lacking for most people most of the time.

'Community facilities' are often part of the problem rather than part of the solution. They are typically institutional in nature. Obvious examples include day centres and residential provisions like hostels and large homes. These are based on principles of congregation and segregation. Even services that include elements of good practice are constrained by a number of institutional, non-normalized features and practices. Many of the difficulties and barriers revolve around the top-down planning approach, with its focus on providing block services to groups of people as opposed to starting from the needs and wants of individual people.

There are well-known problems with the morale and motivation of staff in both residential and day centre settings, with high levels of frustration, disillusionment, stress and burnout. These problems are evidenced by high levels of staff sickness and turnover. And these problems persist *despite* the generally high levels of initial dedication, expectations and enthusiasm on the part of most staff (see Leedham (1989) for more detail on residential staff).

The difficulties and constraints in relation to staff can be summarized as follows:

- staff recruitment (delays, conditions of service, bureaucratic restrictions, low pay);
- staff–user ratios (underestimated, e.g. with regard to demands of 1:1 working, staffing flexibility and user dependency levels, challenging behaviours, one person sleep-ins, jack-of-all-trades, rostering and lack of cover, basic care and containment model);
- staff training and development (not enough of it, where are we going?, no real training emphasis, low status and remuneration, inadequate career structures);
- staff support, supervision and teamwork (often lacking, undervalued, isolated and trapped, lack of consistency, self-help tactics);
- organizational and management influences (top-down hierarchical systems and decision-making, bureaucratic empires).

Supported ordinary living

A growing minority of people with learning difficulties have been fortunate enough to participate in one of various state-of-the-art developments.

A leading example in the UK is the Wells Road service in South Bristol (see Ward 1989), which has successfully catered for people with severe learning difficulties and various additional special needs. Ward (1989) reports improved quality of life for users, compared with (a) individuals' past experience and (b) other residential alternatives in the Bristol area at the time. 'Measured against the yardstick of the Five Accomplishments . . . residents at Wells Road were certainly "better off" in every respect' (Ward 1989: 190). In addition, 'the new service brought enormous relief and satisfaction to individuals and families who in the past had received very little and for whom the future had promised little but

uncertainty and concern' (Ward 1989: 193). However, a number of difficulties were also experienced by the Wells Road service, including:

* incompatible groups and the problems caused by this;
* inconsistencies in staff behaviour;
* the poor quality of the local ATC;
* 'the sheer social impoverishment and lack of relationships in most
  residents' lives' (Ward 1989: 191).

Other good practice developments also report positive outcomes. For
example, a service in Eastern Nebraska (see Crowhurst 1991) provides a
wide range of community services to approximately 1,100 users – over a
third of whom have profound learning difficulties – and employs some
650 staff in the process (Crowhurst 1991).

Moving from institutional living to community living

Many studies have provided empirical support for the superiority of
community care over hospital care, especially when the former revolves
around normalization-based approaches (Conroy and Bradley 1985; Davies
1988; Knapp *et al.* 1989; Leedham 1989; Haycox forthcoming; Booth *et al.*
1991).

The move from hospital to 'the community' has enabled many people
with learning difficulties to experience major gains in community presence (Leedham 1989; Haycox forthcoming; SSI 1990). Integration in ordinary residential settings is, hardly surprisingly, most marked for users
in the smaller and more normalized staffed group homes. People have
often experienced major gains in privacy and in comfort and personalization of the environment, and for some people real progress has been
made towards the goal of living in a place that can genuinely be called
their own home. However, a number of movers still live in settings where
various non-normalized, institutional features dominate. The traditional
congregate facilities provide the best examples of this (see above and
Leedham 1989: Chapter 9).

Dehospitalization is often associated with significant improvements in
adaptive behaviour (e.g. Close 1977; Eyman *et al.* 1979; Smith *et al.* 1980;
Thompson and Carey 1980; Conroy *et al.* 1982; Witt 1981; Kleinberg and
Galligan 1983; MacEachron 1983; Conroy and Bradley 1985; Felce *et al.*
1985; Turner and Turner 1985; Hemming 1986; Shaw *et al.* 1986; Davies
1987; Eastwood and Fisher 1988; Knapp *et al.* 1989; Leedham 1989; Haycox
forthcoming). Domestic skills, social behaviour and self-help skills are
the most frequently identified areas in which gains are most likely after
transfer to more normalized placements (e.g. Rotegard *et al.* 1985).
However, a number of findings paint a considerably less positive picture.
Many studies have found that quite considerable environmental improvements are associated with small or no improvements in adaptive

behaviour (e.g. Aanes and Moen 1976; Birenbaum and Re 1979; MRC SPU 1986; Landesman 1987; Wing 1989). In addition, some studies provide apparently paradoxical evidence to suggest that individuals living in less normalized settings gain relatively more in terms of adaptive behaviour growth (e.g. Conroy and Bradley 1985), while Zigler and Balla (1977), among others, suggest that institutional living has positive influences on user functioning and development.

Dehospitalization is also associated, to a lesser extent, with improvements in engagement in activity (Felce *et al.* 1980a, 1985, 1986; O'Neill *et al.* 1981; Thomas *et al.* 1986; Sperlinger 1987; *Twenty Two* 1988). *However*, as with adaptive behaviour, various studies have found small or no improvements in engagement in activity despite quite considerable environmental improvements (Birenbaum and Re 1979; MRC SPU 1986; Landesman 1987; Leedham 1989).

The classic example of a negative final outcome finding – and one that is of major concern – is that of maladaptive or challenging behaviour and the apparent link with certain important losses of freedom that have been incurred in some cases. Most studies report that maladaptive behaviour remains broadly constant (e.g. Conroy and Bradley 1985) or worsens (e.g. Landesman 1987; Knapp *et al.* 1989; Leedham 1989; Haycox forthcoming). As we saw above, maladaptive behaviour is the primary reason for placement breakdown and readmission to less normalized settings (see Blunden (1989) for a vivid case study). *Despite* this generally negative picture, a small number of studies have found dehospitalization to be associated with improvements in maladaptive behaviour (e.g. Thompson and Carey 1980; Turner and Turner 1985).

Leedham (1989), among others, has reported widespread concern that people have incurred some important losses of freedom following dehospitalization. Staff in some of the staffed group homes, in particular, felt that some users were 'prisoners in their own home', lacking the space and freedom to wander that they used to have in hospital. Furthermore, the presence of staff 24 hours a day is much more intrusive in the (smaller) community settings than in hospital. In hospital, residents had a certain amount of personal privacy owing to the scale of the place and the relative scarcity of staff. It was easy to avoid staff. There was also a choice of audiences: put crudely, residents could find situations where they could dominate or else be dominated by other people. An ordinary house is much more restrictive in these senses, because there are only a handful of rooms and other people.

These factors help to explain the negative findings often associated with maladaptive behaviour (and the other negative findings). However, although freedom and opportunities for self-determination are often highly limited for many people, it is important to remember that people moving from hospital to community care generally seem to have increased opportunities for personal decision-making (e.g. Knapp *et al.* 1989; Leedham 1989).

Overall, there has definitely been progress towards the goal of participation in community life, and the progress is ongoing. However, the achievements have been coupled with some negative outcomes and, moreover, numerous problems and constraints. Research studies that have reported negative and/or disappointing outcomes include Birenbaum and Re (1979), James and Jeffes (1984), MRC SPU (1986), Schalock and Lilley (1986), Bolton CHC (1987), Cattermole (1987), Knapp *et al.* (1989), Leedham (1989) and Wing (1989). Thus Leedham (1989) found that despite marked improvements for some users, most still led a marginalized existence with relatively little integration in ordinary community settings and with ordinary community members. Friendships, ties and connections were lacking for most people most of the time. Marginalization was especially prevalent in the congregate settings. Similarly,

> The under-developed daytime activities were a most depressing aspect of the inspection findings. Many users missed the hospital activities whilst acknowledging that they would never return permanently to hospital from choice. However, too many of them were insufficiently stimulated or occupied, and whilst some were happy to live through unstructured days they had few realistic alternatives. More and different day care services were needed.
>
> (SSI 1990: 17)

The limited evidence suggests that moving from hospital to the community is associated with significant improvements in users' morale and life satisfaction (e.g. Edgerton *et al.* 1984; Conroy and Bradley 1985; Cattermole 1987; Knapp *et al.* 1989; Wing 1989). Gollay *et al.* (1978) and Passfield (1983) stress users' general satisfaction with their new lives in the community, especially with regard to freedom to make decisions and choices. 'Given the experience of alternative lifestyles [the movers] registered a clear and consistent preference for options and environments that maximised their independence and for life in the less restrictive and more normal setting' (Booth *et al.* 1991).

The production of final outcomes

The normalization effect

Considerable research attention has been focused on relationships between environments and final outcomes. This is hardly surprising given that the normalization principles (a) have exerted a major influence on service development and (b) embrace both user-level and service/ organization-level accomplishments (see Chapter 4).

Normalization principles postulate a strong positive causal link between the normalization of physical and social environments and improvements in final outcomes. For example, they suggest that, *ceteris paribus*, the fostering of one individual by a fairly typical family or placement in a four-place group home in an ordinary house and street will be more normalized (and will thus lead to better outcomes) than will placement in a hostel or residential home with, say, ten or more places. It is postulated that greater physical and social integration into the community and a more user-centred social environment will lead to improved social relationships and community participation, which are themselves key facets of quality of life and are likely to be leading determinants of improvements in personal experience of life quality.

A number of studies have provided evidence of a strong 'normalized environments effect'. For example, the PSSRU studies of Knapp *et al.* (1989) and Leedham (1989) concluded that effectiveness and cost-effectiveness were generally best for the more normalized living environments (they were only slightly more expensive than equivalent T1 costs and the costs of other T2 arrangements, but they were associated with better accomplishments and outcomes) and worst for the least normalized, segregated and congregate settings.

Individual characteristics and the normalization effect

It is important to note that the 'normalized environments effect' is not the only force at work. For example, many studies have found that quite considerable environmental improvements have been associated with small or no improvements in user-level accomplishments.

The body of theory and empirical findings contains a plethora of conflicting evidence on causal relationships between the individual characteristics of users (quasi-inputs, using the production of welfare terminology), environmental factors and final outcomes. Such relationships are, quite clearly, immensely complex. Many studies (e.g. Eyman *et al.* 1979; MacEachron 1983; Seltzer *et al.* 1983) echo the conclusion of Conroy and Bradley (1985: 150): 'Compared to unchangeable individual characteristics ... program and environmental variables appeared to be relatively weak in predicting, or explaining, variations in individual growth.' A particularly important individual characteristic (quasi-input) is maladaptive behaviour (e.g. Landesman 1987; Leedham 1989). For example, it is well known that maladaptive behaviour is by far the best individual predictor of the user returning to a less normalized placement, such as a hospital or hostel (see Chapter 5).

Conroy and Bradley (1985: 158) point out that their five years of research and analysis 'did not produce any final list of things that "really matter"', while Sandler and Thurman (1981) are among many who stress that research has failed to specify environmental factors that are important determinants of the growth and development of users. Type and size of living arrangements are particularly good examples of variables that, in themselves, have little impact on final outcomes. Their impact and thus importance are mediated through other variables, especially social environment (see King *et al.* (1971) and virtually any study since then).

Relatively few studies have used a coherent conceptual framework of the production of welfare type for identifying aspects of environments, individual user characteristics and other things – in specific circumstances and combinations – that 'really matter' (from whatever perspective). Examples of studies that have evaluated the combined importance of individual characteristics and environmental factors include Hull and Thompson (1980), Knapp *et al.* (1989) and Leedham (1989). By way of contrast, most longitudinal studies have explored the effects of pre-placement user characteristics (quasi-inputs) on the success of service interventions, but have failed to look simultaneously at environmental factors. Not surprisingly, little progress has been made. No consistent relationship has been found between final outcomes and any personal attributes. The exceptions are adaptive and, in particular, maladaptive behaviour, but even these factors are dependent to a large degree on environmental conditions.

Policy issues and concerns

> Too little attention was paid to clarifying the philosophical value base and service principles from which the quality and style of services were to be provided . . . Too many journeys were started without having agreed the desired destination.
>
> (SSI 1990: 22)

A radical restructuring of the service system is needed if real and lasting improvements in outcomes – and, linked to this, in cost-effectiveness and equity – are to be achieved. There is no escaping from this. The implication, of course, is that central and local policies need to be reformed radically in terms of vision, commitment, frameworks and mechanisms.

As highlighted in earlier chapters, the policy and practice situation is generally grim and is hardly the ideal backcloth to the development of an idealistic needs-based and user-led system. It is widely accepted that services for people with learning difficulties have always been characterized by severely inadequate resource levels and that there are extremely large and serious amounts of unmet need. Ultimately, there is a distinct lack of a committed and coherent central policy backed up by adequate resources.

The NHS and Community Care Act 1990 has some laudable objectives for the social care sector, for example enabling people to live in their own homes, caring for the carers, clarifying responsibilities and accountability, and improving value for money. However, it does not address the real issues, that is the need for user empowerment and service brokerage as a way of achieving the objectives. Instead, the reforms concentrate on improving relationships between the people in the household – the stakeholders in the existing, top-down service system – while neglecting the fact that the house is built on sand. Some progress will undoubtedly be made, but more fundamental improvements are desperately needed if more widespread and lasting improvements are to be achieved.

As the pressure group Values into Action (VIA) put it, the Caring for People proposals (the community care reforms embodied in the 1990 Act), and much of the commentary on them,

> indicate a continuing belief that the service machine can deliver, if only it can be put together in the right way. The evidence would suggest that's either a deception or a gross conceit . . . Where in the UK has there been any large scale success in helping people with learning difficulties to achieve a socially valued, integrated lifestyle? As far as we know, nowhere.
>
> (VIA 1989)

The underlying problem with the new legislation is that it does not attempt a fundamental separation of prescription and provision, or of prescription and funding. Case/care management combines these conflicting functions, and consequently is likely to lead to 'more of the same'. It is a weak mechanism for achieving the radical change that is needed.

The lack of a coherent set of aims, objectives and responsibilities based on a sound philosophical base of the kind presented in Chapter 4 is particularly worrying (e.g. Shearer 1986; Mansell 1988; Leedham 1989; Towell and Beardshaw 1991). Fundamentally, central policy still revolves around the 1971 White Paper, *Better Services for the Mentally Handicapped*, which was equivocal and contradictory in that it attempted to accelerate the shift from hospital towards community care while simultaneously encouraging the development of existing and new institutional services. Central policy has always involved 'half-hearted stabs at reform within an outdated . . . system' (Campaign for People with a Mental Handicap 1972: 30). There is still no central policy for the development of ordinary life opportunities and services for all people with learning difficulties. Controversy about the future role of segregated, institutional services continues, with the Government's stance being ambivalent. As Mansell (1988) argues, muddle and dispute dominate, with progressive development paralysed.

The lack of direction in central policy goes hand in hand with other bulwarks of the status quo. In particular, powerful political and professional interests – not least jobs, careers, status and the medical model – are vested in maintaining the status quo, whereas support for change generally has no comparable base. A number of people associated with traditional services tend to feel devalued and threatened. Furthermore, the legal basis of service provision in the UK remains weak, especially in comparison with the establishment of clear legal rights in some American states and Scandinavia. These legal rights have been powerful levers for change in those countries. The most notable legal advance in the UK, the Disabled Persons Act 1986, which places specific obligations on service agencies, still appears to face a long wait for anything like full implementation. Given this bleak climate, it is hardly surprising that the status quo – the institutional inheritance – has proved immensely tenacious and that needs-based and user-led community services have generally developed slowly and unevenly, in a piecemeal, *ad hoc* fashion.

Implications and ways forward

The purpose of this final section is to assess the implications of the issues discussed above for the development of policy, services and practice, and thus to suggest various ways forward.

Frameworks and mechanisms that promote and support accomplishments: empowerment and service brokerage

People with learning difficulties have the same basic needs and wants as everyone else. Consequently, there is no reason why the process of achieving needs and wants should be any different from that applying to the general population. 'That means becoming more compatible with communities, and valuing the ways in which ordinary people and communities operate' (Dowson 1991: 26). As stated in Chapter 2, the general idea of empowerment and brokerage is tremendously 'natural' and simple.

Examples of good practice developments: core services

Service brokerage provides coherent frameworks and powerful mechanisms for improving opportunities and supports. This will facilitate and support the development of a number of core services. These are described and discussed below, under the headings of:

• supported ordinary housing;
• flexible staff teams;
• family and carer support services;
• advocacy;
• the 'fixed point' of action;
• enabling and supporting valued participation in community life.

These services will be very different from most existing services. They will be more flexible and, as part of this, more labour-intensive (and much less facility-based). Furthermore, they will build on the activities and processes of ordinary people and communities. They will play a major part in improving opportunities and supports – and subsequently outcomes – for people with learning difficulties.

Supported ordinary housing
The home is 'the place of our security and the base of our exploration . . . [and] our stake in our own community' (Shearer 1986). People have a right and a need to live in their own home and neighbourhood, whether with relatives or with partners of their choice, and to receive appropriate supports to enable them to use the home as a base from which to explore all aspects of community living. Housing options include:

- the parental home;
- family placement/fostering;
- staffed group home;
- co-residence arrangement in which one or more users share a flat or house with one or more other people who provide agreed supports;
- unstaffed group home in which two or more users share their own flat or house, with visiting support as needed;
- independent living in which the user lives unassisted, with visiting support as needed.

Flexible staff teams
Good services are labour-intensive rather than building-intensive. People are the key element of an enabling and supportive service. Staff will work in people's own homes and in a variety of community resources and facilities. They will enable and support people to participate in the community in valued ways. Examples of services to be provided include:

- practical 'how to . . .' information and support (supplementing that provided by the service broker);
- home care and respite provision (including increased night-time support);
- 'getting alongside' support, for example enabling the person to go to the pub or to get and keep a job;
- health education;
- specialist help, such as speech therapy, physiotherapy and psychology input.

Another type of flexible staff team is illustrated by various innovative responses to the demands posed by severe challenging behaviour. Most of the approaches that are presently being implemented and evaluated revolve around specialist peripatetic teams working alongside local staff to support people in their everyday living environments (Blunden and Allen 1987; Emerson *et al.* 1987b; Maher and Russell 1988). One of the most innovative and promising responses is provided by the South East Thames Regional Health Authority Special Development Team (SDT), which provides additional expertise and resources to assist services to develop their ability to support people with severe challenging behaviours locally (Emerson *et al.* 1987b; Mansell 1993). Emerson *et al.* (1987b) and Blunden and Allen (1987) draw the following main conclusions from their experiences of the Special Development Team and specialist teams more generally. Teams should (in relation to people with severe challenging behaviours):

• work intensively with people who present the greatest challenges to local services; they should have tightly controlled and restricted caseloads negotiated with local services;
• have a clear commitment to providing a time-limited service that focuses on adding to, rather than replacing, local carers and personnel;
• have the power and resources to fund individually tailored packages;
• have the ability to recruit staff with the necessary skills and experience;
• identify and work proactively with people in need of support before a crisis occurs;
• have a mandated commitment to, and responsibility for, service development as well as to working with individuals.

The model being developed in Bristol and Weston DHA by Maher and Russell (1988) and others includes alternative respite care facilities as an additional resource available to teams.

Family and carer support services
As emphasized many times in this book, human resources are the most important input into services in that they are typically the primary enablers of accomplishments. Consequently, it is essential to invest in networks of support. This means giving a high priority to caring for the carers and for families more generally.

We need to ensure adequate opportunities for the training, development, support and supervision of carers and families. Flexible staff teams (as discussed above) will be the main service providers. We also need to invest in and care for the service providers, for example the members of the flexible staff teams. As Taylor *et al.* (1987: 70) report,

One of the most common threads in . . . programs demonstrating model practices was the importance of letting staff know they are valued. Common themes included respecting staff, involving staff in decision-making, instilling ownership, trusting staff decisions, giving staff responsibility and providing staff with needed supports.

Advocacy

Advocacy is central to the new core services and is concerned with:

- being a member of the community, living an ordinary life, with equal opportunities;
- getting your voice heard and getting your needs, wants, opinions and hopes taken seriously and acted upon (Calderdale Advocacy 1991).

It generally takes two forms: self-advocacy and advocacy partnerships. Self-advocacy means pursuing both the points by speaking up for yourself (in the same ways that the general population does), individually and/or in groups such as People First. Advocacy partnerships – often referred to as citizen advocacy – are based on friendship and on doing the ordinary things that friends do. From this basis of friendship, the advocate is able to represent the partner's interests as if they were his or her own.

The 'fixed point' of action

It is essential to have a base – a 'fixed point' – from which the core tasks of service brokerage will be organized, performed and reviewed. The 'fixed point' will provide a base for service brokers and, possibly, for organizations such as user groups. There will be a base in each locality, for example in a community centre or some sort of 'shop-window' place. Users will have access to their service broker – or a member of the brokerage team – at all times.

A key service provided from the fixed point will be an information and advisory service. The broker will get alongside users and families in order to help them through the maze of needs and resources. This will involve helping users to secure individualized funding and/or to get access to needed services, and to press service providers to make the services more relevant to users' needs and wants. Community development work, including outreach and public education, will also be emphasized.

Enabling and supporting valued participation in community life

The primary aim of services should be to enable and support people to take advantage of community resources and opportunities, from going to the pub with friends to full-time employment. The core services considered above have this as a major objective in that they are enabling people to develop their own friendships and support networks where they can receive, give and share. 'What is needed to help people to do these things [the range of ordinary activities that most people take for granted] is not sophistication, training or complicated programmes – but support. Just simple practical help' (Puddicombe 1991: 12). Meaningful and valued work, education, leisure and community participation inside and outside the home are central needs in our culture. Taking user-level accomplishments seriously necessitates a fundamental shift away from facility-based provision towards flexible individual packages of opportunities for work, education, leisure and community participation based on individual needs and wishes and organized around individual plans.

There is quite clearly a virtually unlimited breadth and depth of potential opportunities for work, education, leisure and community participation in the home and via various community resources used by the general population, such as factories, offices, shops, banks, colleges, churches, leisure centres, cafes, clubs and pubs. The home should be used as a base from which to explore all aspects of community living, both home-based and community-based. The maximization of mainstream integration and community participation offers massive potential benefits for users and could help to remove attitudinal barriers in society as a whole.

Services should avoid the establishment of permanent, facility-based services that inhibit flexible service packaging. The new needs-based system 'releases staff to be out in the streets, in community resources or training in the home' (Bender 1986: 15). The roles of residential and day staffs will thus tend to merge into each other. This will improve the coherence and integration of individual plans. It will also lessen some of the excessive staffing and transport constraints experienced under the current facility-based system.

Needs-based models have obvious benefits for users, carers, staff and the community in general. As with service development more generally, there is a very considerable potential for major gains in cost-effectiveness and equity, especially in the longer term. However, large injections of extra resources will almost certainly be needed, particularly in the short term.

Meaningful employment is central to our culture and is thus a primary determinant of anyone's quality of life. This implies a very considerable challenge for services, particularly with regard to more severely disabled or people with challenging behaviour. But it can be done; there are big reservoirs of untapped potential (Shearer 1986; Porterfield 1988; Puddicombe 1991). Severely disabled people 'can be productive in integrated, profit-oriented businesses and industries and should not be restricted to non competitive, segregated, stigmatised environments' (Brandon 1988: 20).

There is a need for increased provision of normal workplaces where it is recognized that some people may not be able to work as productively as others and will need to be supported and subsidized accordingly. Training should take place where skills are to be used rather than in segregated training projects (Brandon 1988; Feinmann 1988). There are numerous small-scale work experience, job finding and supported employment schemes, placements and ideas (Wertheimer 1985; Porterfield 1988) in the UK and the USA, which provide some particularly interesting schemes and ideas.

First, various schemes involve creating opportunities by seeking out ideas for new services and products, developing business plans and seeking out relevant grants and contracts (Brandon 1988). Growth areas like leisure, 'caring' and catering – in addition to local 'neighbourhood' services in general – seem to be particularly promising (e.g. Wertheimer 1987; Emery 1988). Second, jobs are found through selling the concept of employing a user to employers, examples being 'job finders' staff and 'shop-window' workshops. The small but increasing number of specialist employment agencies – such as Excel Employment – are making particularly exciting progress in this respect. Third, 'pathway' schemes involve an existing employee acting as a support to the user (who receives the general wage rate), a well-known example being the MENCAP Pathway Scheme (Gray 1985; Shearer 1986).

There are many examples of sheltered employment and training schemes, many of which provide a springboard to mainstream employment. Among the better known examples are the Applejacks training cafe in Camden, the Gillygate Wholefood Bakery in York (Shearer 1986), Project Intowork in Sheffield (Feinmann 1988), outreach programmes at Camperdown ATC in Newcastle (Emery 1988) and various sheltered industrial workplaces in Eastern Nebraska (ENCOR) and Minnesota (Williams and Salomon 1980). Pountney (1987) describes the Birmingham Employment Preparation Unit (EPU), which offers occupational training in building, general engineering, office, catering and cleaning skills, supported by an academic, social and life skills programme. The EPU makes use of both in-house and community resources, and sells products commercially, EPU users have moved on to a range of jobs and work placements.

Education has a crucial role to play, for both children and adults.

Children should be educated in ordinary schools in ordinary ways (i.e. using the National Curriculum), with whatever specialist help is needed. Maximum integration is essential if 'special needs ghettos' are to be avoided. Towell and Beardshaw (1991), among others, point to the importance of pre-school provision (e.g. mother and baby groups, nurseries, playgroups and clubs), clear specification of educational objectives and effective home–school communication.

Similarly, adults should be educated in integrated ways. Classes should at least be based in a non-segregated, mainstream setting, probably a college. This allows integration in terms of the 'hidden curriculum', particularly via (a) contacts with other students, and (b) having similar rules and expectations applied to general behaviour. Gray (1985), among others, stresses the importance of positive role models. An example of integrating adults with severe learning difficulties is provided by

Kingsway-Princeton FE College in central London and its 'Gateway 2' course (Shearer 1986).

For any given topic, full integration in mainstream classes is ideal, but probably only desirable where the user can participate meaningfully (with any support needed) in some way. Griffiths *et al.* (1985), among others, point to a large reservoir of untapped potential. At some point decisions are needed on what constitutes the minimum acceptable level of functioning or maturity for any given user and mainstream class. The fallback position is, of course, special needs classes in mainstream settings. Severe challenging behaviour, in particular, represents a major barrier and challenge. Service providers also face very considerable challenges with regard to users with the most severe learning difficulties. Some exciting innovations are taking place in practical areas like cooking, music therapy, music, movement and art therapy, but there is a tremendous distance to go.

Leisure and recreation are important to everyone. As with work and education, the aim should be to take advantage of the massive range of community leisure resources and opportunities available to the general population. There is a big need for leisure enablers with developmental roles, as employed in the Warwick MENCAP Care in the Community project, for instance. Some exciting developments, for example the 'Outreach' scheme in Manchester and the Islington adult education 'Links' scheme, are described by Shearer (1986).

Moving forward

People with learning difficulties – like the vast majority of people – want and need to participate in community life in valued ways. Approaches revolving around empowerment and service brokerage as set out in Chapter 3 enable people to achieve this in basically the same way the general population does.

The pioneers of empowerment and service brokerage are attempting to develop one or more small-scale demonstration projects to develop the case and offer practical pointers. The aim is to demonstrate that empowerment and brokerage are not just idealistic but also offer potential gains in cost-effectiveness, equity and external benefits (e.g. helping other social policies). The projects are likely to involve a re-allocation of existing blocks of resources, probably focusing initially on people who are particularly badly served by existing arrangements. Such projects would be powerful levers for change, both directly – through their impact on people's lives – and indirectly – through their impact on public attitudes and the political climate.

7 Cost measurement in theory

Introduction

This chapter is concerned with the principles of measuring costs. It is, therefore, rather theoretical, although points are illustrated with relevant examples. The application of these principles to policies for the care of people with learning difficulties is exemplified in Chapter 8.

As far as this chapter is concerned, a distinction is drawn between financial and economic concepts of cost. In no sense is one concept superior to another: they usually serve different purposes. Financial costs are used in ensuring that money is spent legally in public institutions and to keep public agencies within their agreed spending limits. This is important for both the stewardship of public money and the planning and control of the economy as a whole. Most public agencies work to cash-limited budgets approved by Parliament or local councils. These limits are set from the point of view of both 'reasonable' tax burdens and the need to control public expenditure within the economy as a whole. The economic concept of cost is concerned with the efficient allocation of resources as a whole but not necessarily with the distribution of costs across different agencies and individuals. At times, there will be a tension and choices will need to be made about which is the most appropriate definition of costs to use. These points are demonstrated within this chapter but it has to be remembered that the difference between the two notions of cost is one of purpose of use, not superiority of approach.

Concepts of costs

As stated in the previous section, it is important first of all to distinguish between financial and economic concepts of costs. Financial costs are related to cash flows. In the narrowest sense, financial costs are related to agencies that have to expend the cash on goods and services. It is usual in policies for people with learning difficulties for there to be several agencies (e.g. National Health Service, local authority departments, voluntary societies, housing associations, as well as many individuals) concerned with developing and administering services. Since most of these will be operating within fixed cash-limited budgets, they will naturally be concerned with their own cash flows, financial probity and efficiency. The cost of a resource in financial terms is the amount of cash paid for its use.

The economic approach is more agnostic than this. There is an underlying questioning as to whether or not the cash paid for a resource is an accurate valuation of its use. The economic concept of cost is based on the axiom that resources are scarce and the use of a resource in one way denies its use in alternative ways. In deriving benefits from using resources in one way, people sacrifice the benefits from using resources in alternative ways. The notion of scarcity, the need for choice and the inevitable sacrifice of forgoing alternative choices that is implied by scarcity underlies the fundamental economic concept of opportunity cost. The opportunity cost of a resource is the value of the benefits of consuming that resource in its next most valuable use. The basic question that the economic approach poses in costing resource use relates to whether the cash paid for its use reflects its opportunity cost or value forgone in alternative uses. The answer to this question depends on how far competition between resource users leads to the most efficient allocation of resources in the economy as a whole.

Generally, if there is a considerable amount of competition for resources, they will tend to be used to the point where the cash paid for the use of one extra unit of a resource is equal to the value of the extra benefit produced. In a commercial context, a firm would hire labour costing £10,000 per year up to the point where it just added £10,000 to revenue. Any other firm that wanted to employ this labour would have to pay more than £10,000 per year to attract it away from such use. Clearly, it would not do this unless it envisaged that labour adding more than £10,000 to its revenue. For their part, the people supplying this labour would offer their services to firms paying the highest wage. Competition between buyers and sellers ensures, in theory at least, that resources are allocated in such a way that their market price is equal to the value of the goods and services they produce.

The key to this way of allocating resources is competition between buyers and sellers. Many factors intervene to lessen competitive forces. Governments impose taxes on goods, services and incomes. Firms merge to reduce competition, one firm becomes a monopoly supplier of a specific commodity, some services do not lend themselves well to a competitive form of organization (e.g. policing), workers form trade unions to fix wages. Some resources are used freely because it is difficult to charge for their use (e.g. firms consume air, water and land where no property rights exist and no cost is imposed on them). These are the social costs or externalities described in Chapter 2.

Thus, if the idealized form of a competitive economy is not achieved, the price or cash received for a resource may well not reflect its opportunity cost. The task of economic evaluation is to estimate the adjustments that have to be made to resource prices so that they reflect their opportunity costs.

Measuring costs

Economic costs are concerned with all the resources used in the pursuit of a policy objective. While financial costs refer to the cash paid by different agencies, economic costs concentrate on resources used, irrespective of cash flow. The implication of this comprehensive approach for economic appraisals is the adoption of the following routine for all the policies evaluated:

- identify all changes in all the resources used;
- quantify all these changes in resource use;
- evaluate (i.e. put money values) on all these changes in resource use.

The emphasis in these steps is on changes in resource use. Economic appraisals are concerned with comparison between different ways of achieving policy objectives. Typically this might be the development of one service at the expense of another (for example, the substitution of community-based residential homes for hospital care), or it might be concerned with the development of a completely new service (e.g. a new day care service) or with existing services where the alternative might be to discontinue one or all of them. Since each appraisal is concerned with comparing one thing with another, there will usually be increased use of one set of resources compared with decreased use of another set. Changes in resource use will therefore be positive and negative.

The identification of resource use and the subsequent qualification and evaluation are very dependent on the decision-making context. The extent of the changes in resource use varies according to several circumstances, such as whether services are currently in operation, the scale at which they are operating and the transferability of resources between alternative users. From an economic perspective it is meaningless to ask 'what does this service cost?' without detailing the decision context. Thus, economic costs are often difficult to generalize since it will often not be possible to estimate costs as the decision context changes. There is no economic equivalent to the 'statement of standard practice' used in accountancy. Economic costing practices can be set out in principle but they have to be related to examples in order to prevent the exposition from becoming too cumbersome and detailed.

The first step of identifying or enumerating resource change illustrates the need for the decision context. One general rule is to ensure that economic appraisals cover a checklist of agencies and individuals that are likely to be affected by the policy change under appraisal. Typical checklists include the following items:

1 Public agencies
   (a) NHS authorities, e.g. hospital inpatient, outpatient, community services; residential facilities.
   (b) Family health services, e.g. general practitioner services, dentistry, dispensing, ophthalmology.
   (c) Local authority departments, e.g. social services, housing, education.
   (d) Other public agencies, e.g. transport.
2 Voluntary agencies, e.g. housing associations, voluntary societies.
3 Private sector, e.g. residential and nursing home care.
4 People with learning difficulties.
5 Families, friends and relatives of people with learning difficulties.

All these different organizations and individuals may not be affected by all policy changes or developments, but it is useful to use this list as a starting point and explicitly to identify nil changes in resource use. At this stage, too, it is important not to delete items from the checklist because it will be difficult or impossible to quantify or put money values on the identified changes. Certain changes, such as the use of time spent caring by the family of a person with learning difficulties, will be extremely difficult to evaluate, but they may be very important considerations within the appraisal. The list is also important in ensuring that costs which sometimes become hidden or forgotten are taken into account. For example, in costing residential care the services residents receive, for example physiotherapy or psychology, or their use of external facilities, such as day centres, need to be included (Wright and Haycox 1992).

The main problem involved in quantifying changes in resource use is the need to identify how changes in the scale of provision affect costs. For example, it is possible that some services are operating below full capacity and therefore increased usage imposes no or very low extra costs. It may be possible to use some leisure facilities during off-peak hours, when there is spare capacity available and therefore such increased usage could be treated as a zero cost. On the other hand, an increase in the demand for residential care based on small housing units will increase the demand for housing accommodation, and all the costs of such housing have to be taken into account. In quantifying and evaluating costs it is important to identify the extra costs or cost savings that occur over the scale of the proposed policy options. These charges, which vary with the scale of provision, are termed marginal costs. Only in exceptional cases

Figure 7.1   Average and marginal costs

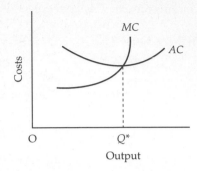

are these marginal costs equal to the average cost of existing provision. Thus, although on average it may cost £20,000 per year to care for someone in a residential home, costs will not increase by £20,000 if an additional person is admitted, nor will £20,000 be saved if one person is discharged and the place is left vacant.

In effect, the distinction between average and marginal costs demonstrates the relevance of the decision context, the specification of the alternative courses of action open to decision-makers and the *changes* in resource use that these alternatives would produce. Figure 7.1 depicts the stylized relationship assumed to exist between costs and the quantity of output. Initially, average costs (*AC*) fall as production (*Q*) increases because fixed costs are shared over more units of output. However, at some point over a fixed period of time, diseconomies of scale begin to set in and average costs then rise as production continues to increase.

The marginal cost (*MC*) curve shows the *change* in total costs brought about by an additional unit of output: that is, the actual cost of increasing output by one unit or, alternatively, the actual savings that could be made if output were to be reduced by one unit. By definition, if average costs are falling then marginal costs must always be lower than average costs, and if they are rising marginal costs must always be higher.

Applying this to a day centre where *Q* would represent the actual number of users, it can be seen that at only one point (*Q**) is the average cost of the centre equal to the marginal cost. In estimating the costs of increased or decreased use, it is the marginal and not the average cost that is relevant.

Evaluating resource use changes involves ensuring that any actual or potential cash outlay associated with the use of a resource accurately reflects its opportunity cost. In general, the workings of labour and commodity markets ensure that this is the case, but where it is not so, it may be necessary to impute a notional value based on an estimate of the value of the resource in its most favoured alternative use. For example, before the introduction of capital charging, many health authorities used surplus property to provide new residential units by adapting ex-staff accommodation or council housing stock or by constructing purpose-built accommodation on what is usually health authority owned land. This represented a common example of resource use without an associated cash flow. The practice reduced the financial costs of capital investment (in some cases to zero), but not the economic costs, which depend on the value of any alternative use to which the property could otherwise be put. Most property has other uses, either within the service or outside it, and its value in the most favoured of these alternatives must be taken into account in the economic appraisal. The replacement cost of property that has alternative in-service uses or the potential market value of other property, with planning permission if appropriate, provide ready indicators of the alternative use values. In most circumstances the potential market value of property provides a useful indicator of its alternative use value.

Two refinements

Costing exercises need to take account of the different times at which payments have to be made and of the assumptions that have to be made in estimating the value of resource use charges.

Allowance for differential timing

Given a choice between settling a debt today or in a number of years time, most people would prefer to delay payment. At the very least this allows funds to be invested to earn interest and reduce the real burden of the cost. The existence of positive real interest rates reflects this 'time-preference', providing evidence that costs of the same nominal magnitude occurring at different points in time cannot be treated as equal in value. It is therefore necessary to take account of differences in the time at which costs are incurred.

The process by which this can be done is called discounting. This involves applying a weighting factor, determined by a discount rate, to costs occurring in the future so that they may be compared as if they had all been incurred at the same time. For example, the value of £100 to be paid in 12 amounts rather than immediately with a discount rate of 5 per cent is just over £95. An alternative approach, applicable where the capital costs can be spread constantly over a period of time, is to convert the capital costs into a notional, annual equivalent. For example, a building with a capital cost of £60,000 and a life of 60 years has an annual equivalent value of £3,168 per year when a discount rate of 5 per cent is applied. This practice is intuitively more appealing given its resemblance to mortgage repayments or rents. In either case, the transformation is simply an exercise in arithmetic made easier by the use of tables that contain discount factors and annual equivalent values.

While it is fair to say that there is no agreement among economists as to what the appropriate discount rate should be, for practical purposes, the Treasury usually recommends a real rate for economic appraisals in health and social services.

Allowance for uncertainty

As a costing exercise is concerned with the resource consequences of different courses of action, it will inevitably be affected by uncertainty about some of the estimates it makes. The results of the costing may be sensitive to the assumptions made to overcome this uncertainty and therefore a thorough appraisal should also assess the robustness of its conclusions. This can be done through a sensitivity analysis, which involves altering the values of key assumptions across a feasible range and examining the differences this makes to the final results. The conclusions of the appraisal are held to be robust if they are not influenced to any great extent by this process. Sensitivity analysis is particularly appropriate to the use of discount rates and the length of life of projects, and most cost studies use varying rates and lengths to life to see how the cost estimates change. Changes in relative prices also affect the results of costing exercises and economic appraisals where one option may involve heavy use of one resource (e.g. staff) compared to another that uses a different resource (e.g. buildings). Studies usually look at the effects of wages rising at a different rate from rents or capital.

Financial effects

An appraisal of the economic costs and benefits of different policy options will help to determine which method of delivering services makes the most efficient use of scarce resources. However, before implementation of the preferred option, consideration often needs to be given to the financial costs of schemes as well. A cash flow analysis should aim to indicate the distribution of expenditure, both over time and between participating agencies, to ensure that budgetary constraints are not seriously breached. Table 7.1 shows the range of agencies that might be involved in the funding or supply of resources used by different forms of residential provision, and demonstrates the potential complexity of a financial appraisal. Economic appraisals emphasize the need to look across all these agencies, whereas more narrow financial appraisals may only look at costs falling on one agency or on the public sector. The diverse sources of resource use emphasize the need to set out all the components of a costing exercise rather than just to give gross costs.

Table 7.1 Possible distribution of financial costs for residential homes

Funding agency and budget	NHS hospital	NHS group home	Local authority hostel	Local authority group home	Private and voluntary nursing home	Private and voluntary group home
National Health Service						
Health and community services	+	+	+	+	+	+
Family health services	–	+	+	+	+	+
Local authority social services departments						
Residential	–	–	+	+	–	–
Day	–	+	+	+	+	+
Domiciliary	–	+	+	+	+	+
*Department of Social Security**						
Income Support	–	–	+	+	+	+
Housing Benefit	–	+	–	+	–	+
SDA/Mobility Allowance	+	+	+	+	+	+
Department of the Environment						
Housing association grants	–	–	–	–	–	+
Others						
Employment training	+	+	+	+	+	+
Informal	+	+	+	+	+	+
Others	+	+	+	+	+	+

* Entitlement to some social security benefits is dependent on the discretion of local social security officers, and their judgement about the type of facility in which the person resides.
+ Probably involved.
– Probably not involved.

The range of funding agencies also complicates the delivery of cost-effective care because of the financial incentives generated by each individual source of public finance. For example, it may be more efficient to support someone at home with a range of suitable domiciliary and day services than in hospital, but if the local authority budgets are not adequate for these purposes, that person may be kept in the less efficient form of care.

Combining an economic evaluation with an appraisal of the financial implications should at least indicate the circumstances where the delivery of more cost-effective care is being hindered by the incentives resulting from different public expenditure regulations.

Disaggregating costs

Aggregating and disaggregating costs

There is often a lack of costing information on specific services (e.g. day services) and on the costs of caring for individuals in specific settings (e.g. at home versus in residential care), or the costs that are available are often aggregated over many different types of service (e.g. for hospital care), localities or even regions. Therefore, planning and monitoring services have to be carried out with minimal knowledge of resource effects and costs. In addition, as explained in the previous section, agencies are often narrowly concerned with expenditure of their own budgets, so the total costs of care for some services are not collected at all.

The purpose of this section is to illustrate the importance of gathering and reporting cost information in a way that helps discussions on policy appraisal and development.

Hospital costs

Average costs for hospitals are good examples of failures to address policy questions, unless the costs are disaggregated to wards or groups of patients. When the resource effects of switching care from hospitals to small, locally based residential units were needed to show how savings in hospital expenditure could be used to finance the new forms of care, the relevant information was only available from specially designed studies of relative costs, as detailed in the next chapter.

It has been known for some time (Wright and Haycox 1992) that the costs of care in hospitals for people with learning disabilities vary from ward to ward where different wards cater for patients with various characteristics (e.g. different age groups or dependency levels). However, it is not possible to determine costs by wards without using a specially designed costing exercise. The results reported in the next chapter were determined in exercises whose main aim was to trace as high a proportion of costs as possible to individual wards or groups of patients. The results show a wide variation in costs from the hospital average.

Costs of residential care

Several problems occur with answering a question such as how much it costs to care for someone in a residential home. First, published data are usually only available at the aggregated level (e.g. local authority), not for individual units. However, each agency usually keeps accounts for each residential home. Second, the costs of residential care are restricted to the services provided within that unit. No account is taken of services delivered into the unit by other staff, e.g. nurses, paramedical or medical staff. Nor is account taken of the services residents use outside that unit, such as educational, training or leisure facilities. Third, no allowance is made for people who use the unit but reside elsewhere. Thus, the costs of residential care that relate to the living unit only, and not the totality of services used, can be misleading in making comparisons with either other residential homes or other forms of care.

New developments in community care are producing many different forms of residential care, provided by the NHS, local authorities, voluntary agencies and the private sector. Each organization has its own method of accounting for expenditure and producing cost information. At present, detailed cost information by unit is scarce. Consequently, most cost information is gathered as part of specialized research rather than as an operational activity. It is little wonder, then, that there is a continual complaint that very little is known in health and personal social services about the resource effects of new or existing policies. The provision of residential care is also becoming more complex in many areas because units are being developed to meet several objectives of long-stay, short-stay and day care. Unless accounting systems develop ways of disaggregating costs over these different objectives from the outset, it will be possible to continue to cost these units only in specialized research projects. In these days of rapid data analysis and presentation, it should not be difficult to devise ways of allocating the costs of a unit between the different functions it is serving and to keep records of usage, so that average cost per day, stay or other unit of activity is readily available.

Day services

Cost information on day services exhibits many of the same problems that affect residential care. In addition, some units, such as social education centres, provide different types of care for different groups of people. Thus, in costing day services it is necessary to develop an information system that includes all the elements involved and that can then disaggregate costs to specific aspects of care. As in the case of residential care, it is essential to make the costs of day services comprehensively reflect the total resource use of the individuals concerned.

The main disaggregation of costs in day care that is of managerial interest is the split between special needs or special care units and general aspects of day care. Staffing costs are worth disaggregating between these major functions and, as shown in the next chapter, special care units have quite an effect on staffing costs.

As in the case of residential care, day services are also changing to meet the challenge of 'ordinary life' policies. Social services departments are moving more towards small resource centres and away from large social education centres. Day services are based on helping people to use the facilities that are part and parcel of the community's general pattern of living. These moves will tend to substitute staff resources for buildings. The costing of different aspects of staff time will raise challenges for routine costing information, and so will the growing use of the community's facilities. As with residential care, the costing systems need to be developed at an early stage in policy development, so that cost and activity information is available on a routine basis.

Disaggregating costs to the individuals

The focus of many costing systems is a service that is appropriate for the way in which budgets are allocated and managers are held responsible for keeping expenditure within agreed limits. However, for planning purposes, information is needed on the relative cost of maintaining an individual in alternative setting X against the cost of maintenance in alternative setting Y. Service-based costs do not answer this question. Instead it is necessary to log the services used by individuals in alternative settings X and Y and to multiply service usage by the appropriate unit cost. This method is particularly needed where people are cared for in their own or parental homes, as illustrated in the next chapter. Usually, it will not be possible to collect this type of information on a routine basis and special sample-based studies will be needed to disaggregate costs to this level.

There is one level of cost disaggregation that is particularly difficult to achieve. This is the cost of looking after one specific resident in hospital or a residential home. It would be necessary to allocate all resource use within an establishment to each individual in the place to assess an accurate cost. Many resources, such as lighting, heating, cleaning, portering and supervisory staff, are available to all residents simultaneously. It is usually possible to allocate such resource use by sharing out the cost over the number of residents being accommodated. Staff time devoted to the direct care of individuals is in a sense identifiable with accurate time and motion studies, but there are many instances where staff are directly working with one resident while generally keeping an eye on one or more of the other residents. There is no straightforward way of allocating costs in these instances. Moreover, indirect care (e.g. report writing or staff meetings) may affect groups as well as individuals and will again pose problems of accurate cost allocation. Finally, there are problems about the generalizability of results. Care routines are often specific to certain groups of residents: if one resident leaves, the staffing is unlikely to change, but routines may well alter for the remaining residents. Thus the cost allocation to these individuals before the change in residents also changes, although their characteristics remain the same. Thus, the vari-ation of costs between residents with various characteristics is probably easier to measure by the use of statistical techniques that analyse costs across different types of care and residents with different personal char-acteristics, as illustrated in the next chapter (Knapp *et al.* 1992; Shiell *et al.* 1993), than by single, observation studies.

Conclusions

An economic appraisal is principally an aid to decision-making and, as such, is both a technical exercise and a way of thinking about questions of resource allocation and priority setting. In summary, five features should be emphasized:

1 *Alternative options.* The precise form of any service development is a matter of choice. Options may differ according to size, location and staffing. To ensure efficient use of resources the alternatives must be made explicit.
2 *Opportunity cost.* Costs are equivalent to forgone benefits and arise because resources have alternative uses. An economic appraisal is concerned with comparing the benefits of doing one thing rather than doing another.
3 *The margin.* Economic costs are context-specific and the resource impli-cations of changes in the scale of provision rarely correspond to the average costs of maintaining it at its current level.
4 *Discounting.* Costs (and benefits) of the same nominal magnitude can-not usually be considered equal in value. Consideration must therefore be given to the time horizon over which costs are incurred.

5 *Sensitivity analysis.* Appraisals, by their nature, are clouded with uncertainty and value judgements. Sensitivity analysis is useful in indicating the degree of risk associated with some policy options.

Whether or not a formal evaluation is undertaken, resource allocation decisions still have to be made. Whatever the technicalities, the very process of identifying alternative means of meeting pre-specified objectives and weighing up their respective resource costs and benefits is in itself a valuable managerial exercise. The approach outlined in this chapter provides a systematic framework in which all relevant factors can be considered, thus allowing the decisions to be made in a rational manner.

8 Cost measurement in practice

Introduction

Now is the time to move from the theory of costing to its practical aspects. This chapter is concerned in the first instance with the costing of community-based services for people with learning difficulties. The main debate throughout the 1980s focused on the costs of the transition from hospital to community care. The main purpose of studies on the relative costs of hospital and community-based care was to identify the resources that would be needed to ensure that the closure programme was carried out effectively and efficiently. However, a controversy arose over the relative costs of the alternative forms of residential and associated services that were provided to accommodate the people moving into the community. Thus, before we examine the issue of the cost of the transition to community care, a review of the costs of different forms of residential, day and short-term care services would be helpful in understanding the debate.

The costs of alternative forms of residential care

There is considerable variety in the provision of residential care for people with learning difficulties. Size of unit varies, the characteristics of residents differ from one unit to another, units are provided by agencies in the public, private and voluntary sectors and the quality of care will tend to vary from one unit to another. How and why do these various factors affect costs?

The relationship between size of unit and costs per resident

Theoretically, costs per resident over a period of time vary with the number of residents accommodated because it is sometimes not possible

Figure 8.1   Costs following a step function

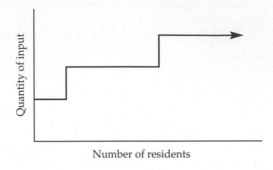

to adjust quickly the quantity of inputs used to the number of residents accommodated. Although occupancy levels are a straightforward explanation of this, there are other more complicated factors at work. A unit that is designed, equipped and staffed to accommodate eight people, for example, would find it difficult, especially over short periods of time, to adjust fuel and cleaning components of costs as well as staffing levels. Thus expenditure will tend to remain constant at times when the number of residents accommodated has decreased. Cost per resident, therefore, will increase. In practice, there are units operating a full capacity accommodating between three and thirty residents. A considerable amount of discussion has arisen over the way in which costs vary with different sizes of residential homes. It is quite easy to imagine that the costs of some inputs do not vary in direct proportion to the number of people accommodated. For example, it may not cost twice as much to heat a unit with eight residents compared to one with four residents. It may be necessary at times to have two staff on duty in a residential home and they could care for between three and five people. In these circumstances the cost per resident would decrease as the size of units increased from four to eight or three to five places.

It is also easy to envisage that if inputs are not easily adjusted to the number of residents accommodated, the costs might rise in a kind of step function, with each 'riser' occurring where the quantity of input has to be increased and each 'tread' stretching over the number of residents that can be cared for within the capacity of that input, as illustrated in Figure 8.1. A cost function with this shape would generate falling costs per resident over the flat or tread section of the function, but steeply rising costs per resident at each riser.

The empirical evidence on the effects of size of unit on costs is difficult to interpret because so many other factors cause costs to vary. The best evidence, although even this may be complicated by other factors, using an analysis of costs per resident over 150 residential homes with a variety of agencies accommodating people with varying degrees of disability, is that cost per resident is fairly constant over a large range of capacity (six to thirty places), but that there appears to be a sharp rise in the cost per resident for units with a capacity of between four and six places (Raynes *et al.* 1990).

The effects of disability on costs per resident

It is logical to believe that there is a direct relationship between increasing costs of residential care and increasing disability levels among residents. Staffing requirements hold the key to this relationship. The less that residents are able to do for themselves or the more they exhibit behavioural characteristics that require staff supervision to avoid harm to staff or others, the greater are the number of staff hours needed to ensure adequate care. Thus, throughout the cost literature there is general agreement that costs increase as levels of disability among residents increase.

Costs of residential homes in the public and independent sectors

The provision of residential homes for people with learning difficulties over the past ten years has been characterized by the mixed economy of supply, especially the growth of the independent sector. There are great difficulties in establishing the costs of homes provided by private owners or registered companies, and very few reliable cost accounts of private residential care have been published. Consequently, costs in independent homes are usually taken to be the fees that are charged to individual residents. There is a theoretical justification for such an approach in the private sector, since charges reflect the prices that cover all the costs of the home, including the reward for owners' risk-bearing and enterprise in providing the capital for the home and taking the responsibility for organizing all the other inputs used. There is less justification for using charges in the voluntary sector because different methods are used to finance and manage voluntary residential homes (Darton *et al.* forthcoming). It is possible that charges do not cover costs of homes, since voluntary funds may be made available to cover losses.

On the whole, the charges made to residents in homes in the independent sector were closely related to the income support levels allowed under social security regulations, and these are generally less than the costs per resident in public sector homes. However, no conclusions about relative efficiency of independent and public sector provision should be drawn without examining all the factors that might be affecting these costs, including size of units, characteristics of residents and quality of care provided.

Costs and quality of residential care

Quality of residential care will vary with the same sorts of things that cause costs to vary. Size of unit, ownership and characteristics of residents are factors affecting quality of care. Thus, relating costs to quality of care presents considerable problems of making like-with-like comparisons. As with costing studies, a considerable amount of attention has been centred on the relative quality of hospital and community-based care. There are relatively few examples of studies that have made cost and quality comparisons of different forms of community-based residential care. However, the 1988–9 survey of 150 residential homes provided by the NHS, local authorities, voluntary societies and private owners in England, carried out by the Universities of Manchester and York, was a useful basis for studying this issue (Raynes *et al.* 1990).

There was a wide variation in costs across the different agencies providing residential care, with NHS-administered homes costing on average £49 per resident day, local authority homes £37, voluntary homes £32 and private homes £28. However, the NHS and local authority homes in the sample had on average a more disabled set of residents than the private or voluntary sector.

Quality of care was measured on four main dimensions: an index of participation in daily living; an index of adult autonomy; an index of community involvement (all Raynes and Sumpton 1987); and a group home management scale (Pratt *et al.* 1980). These indices were supplemented by the use of a measure of environmental quality using a scale of six items concerned with the attractiveness of the building, its surroundings and individual residents' rooms, and by taking account of the proportion of staff with a recognized, relevant nursing or residential care work qualification. There was some variation in the scores on the quality indicators, particularly in environmental quality, where homes in the independent sector had higher scores than in the public sector, and in participation in daily living, where voluntary, local authority and NHS homes scored better than private homes.

The relationship between costs and quality was investigated by the use of multivariate regression analysis, since this allowed for analysis of the variation in costs with variation in another variable (e.g. a quality index), while all the other variables being considered (e.g. size of unit, disability of residents or other quality variables) were held constant. The analysis revealed some interesting correlations and cast doubt on others. First, there was no significant relationship between costs and the environmental quality indicator. There also was no relationship between costs and the size of homes. The relationship between costs and the ages of residents was interesting, showing high cost per resident for the youngest and the oldest residents. Costs tended to fall as length of stay increased and tended to rise with increased disability of residents.

The relationship between costs and the proportion of qualified staff was negative, indicating that the greater presence of qualified staff reduced costs. Generally for quality of care, though, the analysis showed higher costs to be associated with higher quality scores. One of the most interesting, if somewhat tentative, results was that even allowing for the lower disability levels among their residents, homes from the independent sector had relatively lower costs than the public sector homes. The cautious interpretation sprang from the relatively poor rate of response to the questionnaire obtained from private homes (only 50 per cent of home owners approached agreed to participate in the survey) and the use of charges made to residents, rather than actual costs. Thus, it was possible that the homes included in the survey were not representative and there may have been a bias towards the better quality homes whose owners would have shown more willingness to cooperate than owners of poor quality homes. This is, of course, only one survey, and it needs to be replicated on a larger scale, possibly across Great Britain and to include homes in the London area. Nevertheless, it gives important pointers to the need to invest in quality, to use qualified staff effectively and possibly to encourage or confirm the mixed economy approach to residential care.

Day services

As pointed out in Chapter 2, day services have been attempting to meet the objective of providing services within the model of 'ordinary living'. This means that social services officers and members have had to give considerable thought to the existing and future use of existing personnel, buildings and equipment in social education and special needs centres (formerly known as adult training centres), which comprised the bulk of day care in the mid-1980s (Social Services Inspectorate 1989). Since local authorities will be attempting to develop new-style services within existing budgets, the costs of the more 'traditional' services continue to be very relevant.

The costs of local authority day services for people with learning difficulties are conventionally reported in the annual expenditure and cost data on local authority personal social services (Chartered Institute of Public Finance and Accountancy 1992). Care has to be taken with these figures because they may not always include all aspects of day services. For example, costs of transport for people attending different facilities or costs of using different types of recreation facilities or managerial overheads may not be included in some authorities' returns.

Some of these elements may not be important for comparing average cost per person because they form only a small proportion of total cost. Managerial overheads, for example, may form less than 1 per cent of the average cost per person served. However, if the expansion of day services of one type or another involves increasing the establishment of managerial staff, the extra expenditure involved could well be important to the budgetary calculations for the present and future fiscal years.

The most important revenue or current costs of day services are as follows (Social Services Inspectorate 1989):

• staff, either specifically employed in day services, or from other organizations or departments (e.g. physiotherapists, psychologists, sports instructors, teachers);
• transport;
• general goods and services;
• use of community facilities.

The main capital costs are buildings, land, fixtures and equipment, all with varying lengths of life and possible alternative uses.

In 1986, in social education centres containing a special care or special needs unit, social services staff comprised 52 per cent of total costs, while outside agency staff comprised only 4 per cent of total costs. General goods and services accounted for 18 per cent, transport for 14 per cent and capital costs for 10 per cent of total costs. The use of community facilities made up the remaining 2 per cent of costs. In future, there will be a tendency for staff costs to form an increasing proportion of costs along with, possibly, the use of community facilities. The contribution of capital costs is likely to decrease as older and less suitable buildings are disposed of as usage decreases. Transport costs may also decrease if public transport can be substituted for specific social services vehicles.

The development of employment services is becoming an important aspect of day services and the integration of people with learning difficulties into the life of the community in which they live. In the Social Services Inspectorate Report (1989) there was little evidence of such a move, only three out of 48 centres being classified as 'work training', with a weekly cost of £57 per attendance (1986 prices). More recently, an illustrative budget for the development of a 'pathways' employment scheme in a metropolitan district suggests the need for a total annual expenditure of £109,863 for the scheme (MENCAP 1991).

Short-term care

There are several approaches to respite care, which can be based in a residential home provided by a public, private or voluntary agency, in foster homes, in family-based services or in the house occupied by the

person with learning difficulties and his or her family. Different forms
of provision will generate a variety of costs. Where respite care facilities
are provided as part of general residential care, the cost per place provided will be close to that of the cost of providing long-term care. The
costs of providing specialized homes or services that cater solely for
short-term or respite care give a good indication of the resource consequences of this aspect of policy. No routine data on the costs of respite
care are published.

The costs of family-based respite or short-term care vary from one
local authority to another. Rates of pay in 1989–90 for carers depended
on the service that was offered. Some authorities paid by the hour, others
by the week, some by the day, others by 12-hour sessions. The average
payment to carers was £13.69 per session of 12 hours and £129.78 per
week in authorities paying by this period of time. Where carers went into
people's own homes, the average rate of pay was £20–30 for twelve hours
(where evening work was included). A few schemes paid retaining fees
of £25–30 per week to carers when no one was placed with them (Orlik
et al. 1991).

The costs of residential-based short-term care again vary by locality.
At 1986–7 prices, a ten-place specialist unit for children in West Yorkshire was costed at £13,429 per year per place. A smaller unit (with five
places) was costed at £15,796 per year per place (Gerard and Wright
1988). The revenue costs of respite care in units administered by the NHS
and local authorities for 1986–7 worked out at £21,535 and £15,104 per
place per year respectively (Gerard 1990).

Family-based schemes offer a substantial saving on residential units
and there is considerable evidence that families find them equally, if not
more, satisfactory than residential care (Robinson and Stalker 1989).
The costs of this care in 1984–5 were estimated at £9.33 per session plus
£20.35 overhead cost (Robinson 1986).

The transition to community care

Armed with knowledge about the way in which costs of residential homes,
day services, short-term or respite care and social support vary according to factors such as providing agency, user disability, quality of care
and number of people served, we can now easily follow the recent debate on the costs of community-based relative to hospital care for people
with learning difficulties. In effect, hospitals provided (and still provide
for around 25,000 people in England and Wales) residential, day and
respite care services for patients of all ages with differing degrees of
disability. Thus, an important consideration when comparing hospital
with community-based care is to ensure that this variety in patient
characteristics and service provision is fully taken into account. The costs

of residential care have to be adjusted to ensure that all resources used by residents, especially those who attend day services in other locations, are costed.

The Wessex experience of developing community care provided the earliest evidence of the relative costs of hospital and community care. Both capital and revenue costs of hospital provision were compared for large hospitals and 25-place residential homes in the community (Felce *et al.* 1980b). Although there was no difference in capital cost per place provided, revenue costs of the 25-place community units were greater than hospital costs. These comparisons were extended in a later study (Felce 1986) to include a costing of two small houses for adults. In this latter case, the revenue costs of hospitals were greater than the costs of the 25-place community units but less than those of the small houses.

In these studies the cost of hospital care was based on the average cost per patient. One study that tried to relate hospital costs to different characteristics of the patients being accommodated (Wright and Haycox 1992) showed that there was a wide variation in costs between wards that cared for patients from different age groups or with varying degrees of disability. For example, the cost of caring for the most dependent patients was nearly three time the average cost for all patients, while the cost of caring for the least dependent patients was 18 per cent below the average cost. There was nearly a four-fold difference between the costs of caring for the most and least dependent patients. The costs of community-based care were also found to vary by a similar margin, from £15 to £55 per resident day. The study came to the tentative conclusion that the revenue costs of community care were greater than those of hospital care for more disabled people. Capital costs were excluded from this study.

Further studies reinforced this conclusion. A project concerned with the costs of alternative forms of care in South-West England indicated that the costs of providing residential care in ordinary housing accommodation were around 10 per cent higher than the costs of hospital care. However, the costs of providing care in private hostels were lower than those of hospital care. Quality of care was higher in the ordinary housing accommodation than in hospital or private hostels, and the quality of care in the private hostels was better than in hospitals. Thus, care in the private hostels was more cost-effective than hospital care, but the extra quality of care in the ordinary housing accommodation required extra expenditure (Davies 1987).

The closure of Darenth Park Hospital provided a good opportunity to gather further evidence on this issue. Again, the general conclusion was that community-based residential care was on average 57 per cent more costly than hospital care (Korman and Glennerster 1990).

Evidence from these studies indicated that community-based residential care was more costly than the hospital care it was replacing. However, when the evidence was examined more closely, several doubts arose as to whether or not the case had been proven. The doubts centred on the major question of whether like had been compared with like. For example, are the costs of caring in the community for all groups of people with learning difficulties greater than corresponding hospital costs? What effect does size of unit have on these comparisons? How does quality of care affect costs? Although there was evidence that costs and quality were higher in community-based facilities than in hospitals, and that domestic-scale facilities were more expensive than larger homes, few of the studies listed above attempted to answer all of these questions. In addition, they gave no indication of the relative costs of caring for the same group of people in different care settings. The evaluation of the Care in the Community initiative provided the opportunity to tackle this last issue.

The Care in the Community initiative contained a number of projects concerned with the settlement in the community of people with learning difficulties (Knapp *et al.* 1992). In summary, it was found that the costs of the community options were greater than those of hospital care for people who were moved into hostels, group homes, independent living facilities and foster care schemes. Costs of care in the community were lower than those of hospital care for people who were moved into residential homes or into sheltered accommodation. Overall, the average cost of caring for people in community-based facilities was 17 per cent higher than the cost of caring for them in hospital. Thus, there is considerable evidence that, on average, costs of care and quality of care in community-based settings are higher than in hospital care.

The costs of professional services

People with learning difficulties are helped by staff from a wide variety of professions, including psychiatry, general medicine and surgery, psychology, speech therapy, occupational therapy, physiotherapy, social work and general and specialized nursing. The costs of some of these services will be contained in different care settings, for example, hospital outpatient visits, some residential and day care services and general practice. However, some professional services are delivered into family and residential homes on an individual basis, which means that the cost of a visit by any of the aforementioned staff has to be calculated individually. This need becomes more pressing with the development of multi-professional community teams and care management.

The cost of professional services is not always easy to establish from published material; for example, the costs of a social work visit or a home nursing visit are not routinely available. This is partly because 'a visit' is not a homogeneous unit, but varies in length of time, by grade of staff and with different travel arrangements. In addition, behind each visit are other aspects of resource use, and therefore, cost. These include office accommodation, supervisory input, coordination with other staff, telephone calls and postage, nursing and medical supplies, vehicles and clerical or secretarial support. Thus, costs of professional staff can be divided into two elements: *direct costs*, mostly the time of the professional staff involved, transport costs, supplies and equipment; and *indirect costs*, office accommodation, telephone and mail costs, supervisory input, secretarial and clerical support.

In the costing of visits by professionals, the main component of cost will be the salary and employment costs of the staff involved. These can be adjusted to hourly rates by dividing total annual salary and employment costs by the number of hours worked in a year, as follows:

$$\text{cost per hour} = \frac{\text{gross salary and employers' national insurance and superannuations contribution}}{\text{number of hours per week} \times (52 - \text{annual leave entitlement})}$$

It is important to ensure that the time of a visit includes not just the time spent face-to-face with the service user, but also all the time spent travelling, writing up records and consulting other staff. Since visits may vary in duration, costs of professional staff are quoted per hour and per visit. This is because the time factor is very important and because some costs, such as travelling and supplies, vary by the number of visits rather than by the time spent on the visit. Community nursing provides a good example of this: the time spent visiting is weighted by a factor according to the amount of extra clerical, consulting and advisory time each visit produces. If a nurse spends 50 per cent of her time on non-direct care, each hour of visiting produces another hour of non-direct care, and the time of a visit is doubled for costing purposes. Similarly if a nurse spends 20 per cent of time on indirect care and 80 per cent on direct care, the weighting factor will be 20/80 or 0.25. Each hour of direct contact will be augmented to one and a quarter hours for costing purposes. In practice, the problem with professional staff is to identify the proportion of time spent on direct versus indirect care.

Estimating overhead costs for visits by professionals is also quite difficult. How far into the administrative hierarchy it is necessary to go depends on the scale of operations and the purpose of the costing exercise. If, for example, it is aimed at looking at the costs of expanding an activity, it may be possible that only a small proportion of overhead expenses, such as extra supervisory capacity, and a small amount of office furniture and expenses would be involved. The marginal cost of a small increase in provision would be quite low. If, however, the aim is to cost a whole service for contract purposes, it will be necessary to allocate all the administrative overheads, which involve not just the immediate supervisory staff but also service, third-, second- and even top-tier managerial staff. Office expenses and clerical and secretarial support will also need to be costed. The allocation of large chunks of administrative expenses to various services is not an easy task and specific allocative rules have to be devised to explain the methods used. For example, the cost of third-tier managerial staff might be allocated pro-rata to the total expenditure on each main client group. Thus, if expenditure on people with learning difficulties accounts for 20 per cent of social services expenditure in one authority, 20 per cent of the relevant managerial salaries are allocated to the learning difficulties programme. Given these difficulties it is not surprising that examples of the costs of professional staff are only recently emerging in the literature (Netten and Smart 1993). Fortunately, most evaluative studies are concerned with fairly small changes in the scale of professional service, and only minor expenses for overheads need to be costed.

The costs of care at home

Caring at home for any person who has chronic disabilities imposes a number of costs and benefits on the family concerned. Some of these costs arise out of extra financial burdens that sometimes occur in terms of adaptation of living accommodation, heating costs, special diets, specialized or extra clothing needs, special transport requirements and extra sitting-in services. Another set of costs can be imposed by the loss of employment opportunities caused by the need to maintain daily and nightly care or surveillance. Caring may also impose the sacrifice of social and recreational opportunities. When care is provided for long periods of any day over many years, carers can suffer psychological strain and stress, fatigue and a major loss of life satisfaction. Despite these financial burdens and psychological effects, carers often receive some satisfaction or benefit from their labours, in the relationship with the child or adult being cared for, in providing a caring domestic environment and in helping the disabled person to develop physically, socially and intellectually to his or her full potential. It is a major aim of many health and social care services to ensure that these families reap the benefits of caring without having to suffer unendurable costs and burdens. As set out in Chapter 3, many different services in cash and kind exist to meet these aims. The problem is to identify the service mix that optimizes the welfare of the disabled person and carer(s) at a minimum cost. This is not an easy task, partly because of budget constraints, partly because of the nature and range of services available and partly because of the conflict

Figure 8.2   Costs and benefits of informal care

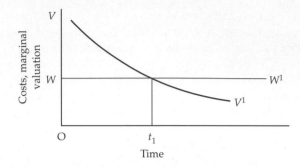

that can occur at times, between meeting the needs of one person while not meeting the needs of the others.

Generally, with the development of care management more attention will be focused on finding ways of ensuring that costs of care do not fall too heavily on family carers. There is considerable talk in the literature about the partnership between statutory services and family carers in providing help for all people with chronic disabilities, physical or intellectual.

The economic approach to this partnership is to find ways of maximizing carers' welfare. Many carers face choices about using their time, for family care, personal enjoyment and work. Different choices produce different sets of costs and benefits. For example, people may choose between work and leisure: the benefit gained from choosing to work is the wage that is earned and the cost is the loss of welfare gained by pursuing leisure activities. Theoretically, it is held that people choose to work until the satisfaction they get from working is just equal to the loss of satisfaction from leisure pursuits. To argue the other way, people will enjoy leisure time until they feel that the cost in lost wages just compensates for not working. This relationship is set out in Figure 8.2.

The line V^1V is the satisfaction gained from each successive hour of leisure. It is a major assumption in economics that successive hours of leisure increase satisfaction, but at a diminishing rate. In other words, enjoying five hours per day leisure time increases total satisfaction with leisure, but the increase in satisfaction in moving from four to five hours is not as great as the satisfaction gained in moving from three to four hours. Similarly, the increase in satisfaction in increasing leisure to six from five hours per day will be less than the increase gained in moving from four to five hours of leisure. The line W^1W is the cost of leisure, or the hourly earnings from work. In this case, no overtime earnings are included so the line is parallel with the horizontal axis. If hourly wages increased after some point, the line W^1W would begin to curve upwards from its present path, but the general argument can be made without using the complications of overtime earnings. If the value of extra hours of leisure (V^1V) and the wage costs (W^1W) are as set out in the diagram, a person who wishes to gain the highest net satisfaction in benefit from the choice between work and leisure will choose Ot_1 hours of leisure per day and $24 - Ot_1$ hours of work. If the person chooses more hours of leisure than Ot_1, he or she would be losing a greater value of earnings than the satisfaction gained from leisure. The choice of leisure time of less than Ot_1 means that the person will be receiving a wage that does not fully compensate for the value of leisure time lost.

Carers of people with long-term disabilities have a more complicated set of choices to make. Their working and leisure opportunities are restricted by having to spare time for caring. However, it is still possible to use the point illustrated above. Assume V^1V is the value of time spent caring. The slope of that time again uses the idea that carers obtain some satisfaction from the time given to their responsibilities, but each successive hour produces diminishing increments of satisfaction. The time W^1W is the value of working and leisure opportunities lost. Again, the net benefit or gain from caring is obtained where the value of the last hour spent caring is equal to the value of the working and leisure time lost.

The implication of this example is that the carer would wish to devote Ot_1 hours to caring. This may only be possible if the formal service system could provide any extra hours of care needed beyond Ot_1. For example, a carer may be able to provide weekday morning, evening and night care, but would like the statutory services to take over in the weekday afternoons. If that is not possible, the carer has to provide more hours of care and suffers a corresponding loss of welfare. These are issues to be addressed by any partnership between statutory and family carers or between care managers and clients. Most of the existing evidence is that carers are paying heavy costs in terms of lost leisure and work opportunities because statutory services are in too short supply to meet all carers' needs (Twigg 1992).

Although these examples sketch out the bare essentials of what is rather complex decision-making, they serve to illustrate some of the main problems that occur in valuing the inputs of family carers. The W^1W line, for example, includes not only the costs of lost earnings, which are easy to evaluate, but also the costs of lost leisure time, which are extremely difficult to evaluate. Many writers, for example, have shown how the sacrifice of leisure time, with its consequent losses of recreational and social activities, places great psychological stress and strain on carers. Thus, although economic appraisals in other public services (especially transport facilities) have developed methods of valuing leisure time, there are doubts as to whether or not these values can validly be applied to caring services (Wright 1986).

Conclusion

The costing studies presented in this chapter cover a wide variety of provision, from full-time residential care to family care. The evaluation of the costs and cost-effectiveness of services for people with learning difficulties is still underdeveloped. Evidence on effectiveness has been built up from specially developed schemes, such as the early Wessex innovations and the All-Wales Strategy, from special schemes for residential care, day services, respite care and community teams or from demonstration projects stemming from the Care in the Community initiative. This evidence generally demonstrates that care in the community and ordinary living models can produce good quality, cost-effective services for people with learning difficulties. The challenge facing the new style management of care in the community is to ensure that the purchasers insist that providers deliver to the standards set by the pioneering or demonstration projects.

9 Conclusion: policy development and evaluation in the 1990s

Purpose of the chapter

Although there had been a recognition of the benefits of community-based care in the 1960s, very few steps had been taken by the end of the 1980s to realize them in practice. Even after the 1971 White Paper (DHSS 1971), progress was very slow. It was the Care in the Community initiative of the 1980s and the special funding arrangements it introduced that really gave the policy a much needed impetus. The Audit Commission's complaints about the still rather pedestrian pace of the hospital closure programme (Audit Commission 1986) led eventually to the present community care arrangements, embodied in the National Health Service and Community Care Act of 1990. The verdict on these changes, from the evidence of policy review and evaluation covered in the previous chapters of this book, is that despite the fact that the transition to community care has not occurred as quickly as many advocates of this policy would wish, there is no denying that substantial progress has been made.

Of course, there is no cause for us to be complacent about further progress with the development of community care: there are still more than 20,000 people waiting to move from hospital to community care. A considerable amount of unmet need still exists among people with learning difficulties who are cared for by their families in their own homes. There is still a need to develop more residential care that promotes independent living within the local community, to provide modernized day services based on the use of general community facilities, to provide better employment opportunities and more emotional, material and financial support to carers. The purpose of this chapter is to take stock of the progress made towards the objectives of effective community care and to discuss the development of initiatives in the next few years.

Policy achievements

Primary prevention policies

The reduction of conditions that cause learning difficulties is closely associated with good maternal health and effective antenatal and obstetric care. Good maternal health is based on good health in general, which depends upon good housing, a healthy diet, abstinence from smoking, alcohol and drug abuse and avoidance of infections such as rubella and HIV. Most of these factors are a matter of mothers choosing healthy lifestyles, not just during a pregnancy but also for a whole lifetime. One major achievement, at least, has been the increasing proportion of adolescent females who have been vaccinated against rubella. Currently the take-up rate is 86 per cent (Department of Health 1992).

Secondary prevention

Antenatal screening methods have played an important role in preventing conditions that cause learning difficulties. As explained in Chapter 3, without these facilities and without potential parents choosing to terminate affected pregnancies, the trends towards greater maternal age would have increased the incidence of the birth of babies with Down's syndrome. For those who disagree with termination of pregnancies such developments are less than welcome, but there is no doubt that many parents have chosen termination and this opportunity is now accepted by many people. The policy dilemma here has become one of whether or not to offer the screening tests to younger mothers-to-be. As discussed in Chapter 3, the costs of screening for Down's syndrome have restricted it to women over 35 years of age. The personal dilemma for couples is whether or not to opt for termination when an affected fetus is detected. New techniques are increasing the possibility of early identification of disabling conditions, not just for learning difficulties but also for a number of physical disabilities, such as cystic fibrosis.

Despite these advances, there will still be an increasing number of people with learning difficulties because of advances in health care. This is to be welcomed, but it means that services must be aimed at caring for a greater proportion of older people with learning difficulties, and health services in particular must become aware of the special risks that affect such people. People with Down's syndrome, for example, suffer a greater than average risk of suffering from the early onset of Alzheimer's Disease (Alberman *et al.* 1992). A growing menace could also be the effect of the increased prevalence of HIV. In the United States, for example, HIV is likely to become the largest infectious cause of developmental delay in the new-born (Felce *et al.* 1993).

General health care

It is becoming increasingly recognized that a number of people with learning difficulties suffer medical conditions that could be treated but often remain undetected. The reorganization of the NHS following the purchaser–provider split, particularly with its emphasis on purchasers identifying the health needs of local populations, should ensure that greater attention is given to specifying the benefits that can be obtained from recognizing the needs of sub-groups of the population who are at special risk. The Welsh Health Planning Forum (1991), for example, has made a detailed list of health gains that can be obtained from identifying and treating conditions for which people with learning disabilities are at special risk. On the providers' side, Department of Health advice has recommended that relevant health services should ensure easy access for people with learning difficulties and their carers, and that a member of the staff with specialized knowledge of learning difficulties should be available to offer appropriate advice to medical, nursing or other professional staff.

Over recent years both the social and health care of people with learning difficulties have benefited from the work of community teams, with their membership comprising both health and social services professionals. The composition of these teams in the future remains unsettled, because the responsibility for care management may or may not be allocated to the whole team rather than to an individual. The service provision role may also be re-allocated to the staff of provider units. Whatever organizational structures and responsibilities emerge in the future, the tasks of the teams and their specialized knowledge of the health needs of people with learning difficulties need to be preserved.

Social care

Achievements in social care have centred on the transition to community care following the closing down of long-stay hospital accommodation, the development of good quality residential care, the recognition of the need to provide day services using general community facilities (including general employment services) and the expansion of services to support carers. The evidence from evaluative studies suggests that progress is being made to develop social care services that recognize the importance of 'ordinary living' models and the main principles of normalization, as set out in the basic accomplishments approach (see Chapter 3).

The general move towards ordinary living principles can be seen in the development of domestic-scale residential care, and evaluative studies have pointed out that the quality of residential care tends to improve as the size of the homes decreases. Some health and local authorities are convinced that the best quality of care will be provided in homes using the generally available housing stock, with three or four places. They have accepted this decision despite the evidence that costs also tend to rise as the number of places in homes decreases; as seen in Chapter 8, costs per place tend to rise quite steeply for homes with fewer than six places. The main cause of this cost increase is staffing levels, since homes with four to six places often require the same number of staff. The total expenditure on homes does not increase very much apart from the purchase of consumables, and the division of this fairly constant total by four, five or six places obviously makes a considerable difference to average cost per place. This has led to the development of more imaginative staffing policies, for example using a mix of peripatetic and core staff to provide care at particularly busy times instead of having fixed staffing levels in one home. It is also possible that after a while the people receiving residential care may become more able and independent and need less intensive staff levels. However, there is no evidence to suggest that this has occurred up to the present time.

The relationships between costs, quality of care and the capacity of homes are confounded by other variables, such as the disability of residents, staff attitudes and home ownership. There is some evidence, for example, that homes in the private residential care sector provide good quality care at reasonable levels of charges (Raynes *et al.* 1990). One conclusion emerging from current studies, which is admittedly very debatable, is that there is no need to be dogmatic about the capacity of residential homes, but there is a need to accept the principles of good quality of care, such as providing residents with choice over the running of their lives and their daily routines, ensuring privacy and dignity, both in the accommodation provided and in the process of care, and promoting the integration of the homes and the residents in their local communities. It is quite possible for the size of homes to vary, but for the principles to be kept firmly in place. This conclusion may not be acceptable to those people who believe that residential care must be provided in ordinary housing stock.

The residential care of people with learning difficulties who also suffer behavioural disorders has raised a number of controversial issues. The recommendations from current practice cover a variety of residential homes or care situations, from secure hospital places (Day 1991) through to domestic-scale ordinary housing accommodation (Mansell 1993). In the pilot projects carried out under the Care in the Community initiative, the group of people with learning difficulties who also had a behavioural disorder found it most difficult to adjust to the transition from hospital to community care (Knapp *et al.* 1992). These different forms of care have been studied by government officials (Department of Health 1989), by influential voluntary agencies (Blunden and Allen 1987) and, more recently, by an *ad hoc* project group whose report (Mansell 1993) set out guidance for service commissioners as well as recommendations on the models of care to be provided. In these models it is recommended that commissioners should consider purchasing residential care in small community-based dwellings.

Day services have also been changing to meet the ordinary living principles. The Department of Health's Social Services Inspectorate (1989) carried out a review of local authority day services and issued a number of recommendations for change, focusing in the main on the replacement of traditional social education, special needs and special care services by general community facilities.

The social education centres often provided a substitute for sheltered workshops or employment. However, if ordinary living principles apply, employment opportunities for people with learning difficulties will move to the ordinary workplace. This is not easy during a time of high unemployment but the principle has grown in favour and it is hoped that there will be an increase in the number of schemes like the Pathway project operated by MENCAP in partnership with local authorities.

Caring for carers has become a slogan in recent years, in recognition of the importance of improving their well-being as well as the well-being of people with learning difficulties. Day services obviously play an important role in providing day-to-day care and giving carers time off from their responsibilities, as well as giving people with learning difficulties opportunities to enjoy local educational, recreational or employment facilities. Short-stay facilities are also important in this respect, and progress has been made in providing family-based care, which is regarded by professionals, carers and people with learning disabilities as preferable to residential respite care. The All Wales Strategy for Mental Handicap [*sic*] has also been influential in developing community care workers and family aide services to give practical support to caring families. The work of the community teams has been instrumental in organizing, coordinating and providing support to these families. Thus, there is a good breadth of service support available to carers of people with learning difficulties. The next stage is to increase their depth and coverage.

Two general considerations are affecting the development of social care services. One of these is finance, the other is staff training. The main drag on progress in replacing hospital by community care has been the lack of a flexible finance policy that would facilitate the transfer of funds from the NHS to social services authorities. In recent years the use of bridging finance has increased, in recognition of the need to cover the double financing of new and existing services before the resources can be freed from the gradual closure of hospitals. Nevertheless, there is still a need to cover this double funding and meet the higher costs of providing care in the community. To some extent these higher costs have been met from social security payments, but since April 1993 local authorities have been responsible for dispensing the care costs that were contained within the social security budget. The financial problem has hindered the development of community care, as originally pointed out by the Audit Commission (1986), whose main complaint related to the slow progress in closing long-stay wards; but later there have been worries about the lack of general community care facilities. The worrying implication of these problems is the development of a two-tier service, where priority is given to services for people leaving hospital while those people who have always lived in the community have, at times, to wait for new services to be developed (Audit Commission 1989). The new community care arrangements, with their emphasis on care management for all people 'with a community care need' and on the involvement of users in the design of packages of care, should help to redress this imbalance.

As stated in our discussion of the development of residential care, the staffing of services has a major effect on both costs and quality. Investment in human resources and capital is of great importance to the provision of cost-effective services for people with learning difficulties. There is growing evidence of the importance of training to the quality of care of all services. In Chapter 8 it was shown how the presence of qualified staff tended to increase the quality of residential care without increasing costs. The recommendations for improved day services (Social Services Inspectorate 1989) emphasized the importance of staff training. In addition, the care of people with challenging behaviour has emphasized the need for special training, either for staff in specialized units or for staff in more general care settings who have people with challenging behaviour using their services. Quality of care is also likely to improve according to the way in which staff are deployed within care settings. For example, setting individual members of staff to work with individuals or groups of users appears to provide better care than when staff and users all work in one large group (Felce *et al.* 1991).

Achievements awaited

The previous section has summarized the progress made, especially over the past ten or so years, in developing better health, housing and social care for people with learning difficulties. The focus of attention is now on the agenda for improvements in the next ten years. Given that in many areas a solid foundation has been laid for the development of services that recognize the five main accomplishments, the major objective must be to widen and deepen the existing service provision. From the available evidence this is a task that is much easier said than done, because there is still a considerable amount of unmet need in services for people with learning disabilities. Increasing the coverage of services raises problems about horizontal and vertical equity. Horizontal equity is measured by the proportion of people needing the services and receiving them. Vertical equity is more difficult to measure, since it is concerned with providing services according to individual need. For example, all other things being equal, the people with the most severe learning difficulties might be expected to receive the most services, but individual problems may be affected by the housing accommodation occupied, by the health and ability of carers to cope with a family member with severe learning difficulties and by family income. Thus, the level of learning difficulty may not in itself be the major indicator of need. In some areas there may be a deliberate decision to trade off vertical equity for horizontal equity, in that services may be spread thinly over as many people as possible rather than concentrated according to intensity of need. Although it is difficult to measure vertical equity target achievement, there is interesting evidence available from the All Wales Strategy to suggest that there is a considerable need to increase horizontal equity (Welsh Office 1991a). For example, a survey of community social services estimated that their coverage was quite low, varying from 18 per cent in the case of short-term care in domestic settings to 63 per cent in residential care in ordinary housing. And this is in Wales, where a considerable amount of extra resources has been allocated to the development of services for people with learning difficulties. The position in the rest of Britain is likely to be more pressing.

From the available evidence, it appears that most service provision needs to be widened to take in those who receive no help at all at present. Family aide services provide a good example. This coverage in Wales is still rather thin, but very few authorities in the rest of Britain have developed analogous services. Community-based residential care is also in relatively short supply, both for people awaiting transfer from hospital and for people living with parents who would like more independent accommodation. We also expect 'ordinary employment' schemes to spread over the next few years but the pace of this spread will depend upon the general employment situation as well as the availability of the necessary financial support. Day services provide a good example of the need to deepen service provision as well as widen it. People do not always receive the quality of service required and its coverage is still partial. There is also the extra consideration that the nature of this service is changing to promote greater integration of users into their local communities.

Care management, with its attendant support of user-involvement, service brokerage and advocacy, is as yet an unknown quantity in services for people with a learning difficulty. The work of community teams for people with learning difficulties has given some insight into how the new arrangements will work. Key components of care management, such as assessment of need, service prescriptions and monitoring of progress, have been part of the everyday work of the teams. Theoretically, the key difference between the work of these teams and new-style care management is the separation of the purchaser and provider roles. The members of the team played both roles, while care managers will be expected to be purchasers – making assessments, purchasing services, monitoring progress – but the provision of services will be the responsibility of the present statutory health and social services, in partnership with the independent sector. Again, the pace of the application of this new system will depend on the economic situation, the total resource effects and the required finance being available.

The targeting of persons at special risk may provide better health care in terms of both the prevention of learning difficulties and the treatment of people with learning difficulties in the primary, acute hospital and community health services. As explained earlier, people with some conditions that promote learning difficulties are often at special risk from other medical complaints that can remain undetected, especially if the person affected has difficulty in communicating or articulating the symptoms being suffered. If parents are articulate they may be able to point out the problems to their family doctors, but again, some parents may not have this ability or may themselves be unaware of the condition and its symptoms. If care management is carried out by an individual rather than a team and if that person is not a health professional, special training or access to health advice may be necessary to ensure that diseases are detected and the person is referred for appropriate treatment. This aspect of the multi-disciplinary nature of community teams needs to be incorporated into the new arrangements.

Brave new world

The brave new world of the introduction of the community care changes and the reorganization of the health services will set a number of puzzles for everyone involved with the care of people with a learning difficulty, including multi-agency collaboration in purchasing and providing services, financial planning and control, and the development of user and carer involvement in service management and delivery. There are likely to be many local variations on each of these themes. Policies for the care of people with learning difficulties have to some extent been facing similar problems for many years now, and joint planning arrangements at the strategic level and the work of community mental handicap teams at the managerial level have provided a solid base for further developments. There are, however, some new pressures to face, including the changing financial scene, the creation of the various 'trusts' in the NHS, the increased demand for user involvement, the application of the Citizens' Charter principles, changes in the local tax base (from community charge to council tax) and (possibly) further changes in local government boundaries.

New principles of budgeting practice will be a very new aspect. Current budgetary practices are based on functions or services, for example residential care, community nursing and home care services, with each service manager being allocated a budget constraint for each financial year. In the new scheme of things, budgets as presently understood are held by purchasers, who allocate their expenditures by contracting for the services they wish to buy. A service's budget is earned through the winning of contracts rather than received as a budget allocation. Previously, service managers received their annual allocation from the organization to which they belonged, primarily the local council or the local health authority. Now there are three sets of purchasers who can contract for these services: health authorities, local authorities and fund-holding general practitioners. Negotiating inside this complex purchasing system is very new for all service managers and, of course, the purchasing role is new to all the aforementioned agencies. Thus, although the experience gained in the core practices of care management by community mental handicap teams has provided such a valuable initial learning experience, they did not have a budget and the consequent purchasing power to buy in the services they needed. They relied on a personally built network of contacts and friendly persuasion to obtain the services their users needed.

The fragmentation of service delivery has tended to be a major drag on the progress of community care. The multiplicity of agencies involved (as demonstrated in Chapter 3), together with their different financing sources, budgetary constraints and other controls, has provided incentives to shunt costs across organizational boundaries (especially on to the social security budget) and to minimize costs within organizations rather than to maximize efficiency within the whole care system. This fragmentation continues under the new arrangements and is exacerbated by the purchaser–provider split because of the three purchasing organizations and a mix of service providers, not only in the public sector but also in the private and voluntary sectors. If providers, for example, seek to minimize their own costs in order to win contracts, there is no guarantee that this will be efficient for the system as a whole.

The mixed economy of welfare approach is still in its infancy. The little evidence that is available, as pointed out in Chapter 8, suggests that competition between the public, private and voluntary sectors is a factor in providing good value for money. Care is needed with regard to how competition operates, especially at the local level. A considerable impetus for community care reorganization came from concern about the rapid growth of private residential and nursing home care for elderly people and its effect on the social security budget. One major objective of the new arrangements is to discourage the admission of elderly people to residential care and to accommodate them in their own homes. The objectives for caring for people with learning difficulties have a different emphasis. They are concerned with the transfer of people from hospital to community-based care as well as with promoting the well-being of these people and those who are now living in the community. In Chapter 3 it was shown that the mixed economy of care is already present in the residential care of people with learning difficulties, with a variety of facilities provided by the NHS, social services departments, private owners and voluntary organizations. All sectors have pioneered innovatory practices. There is, therefore, a strong argument to allow these providers to continue their work, to compete on equal terms and not to apply rigidly rules about the proportion of care that is to be provided outside the public sector or to discriminate against the use of public sector units.

Competition in the mixed economy should be based on quality as well as costs of care. The roles of quality assurance, regulation and inspection are therefore vital to the healthy life of the new arrangements. Many of the quality of care issues are not new. Local authority staff have inspected residential homes and health authority staff have inspected nursing homes for many years now. Consequently, a whole set of useful measures have been developed for assessing quality of care. However, these measures concentrate heavily on the structure or the environment of residential and nursing home care, for example on the ratio of single to shared rooms, the availability of toilets and bathrooms, adherence to precautions against fire and provision of common rooms (Centre for Policy on Ageing 1984). Some measures relate to staffing levels, qualifications of owners or managers of homes and the ratio of qualified to unqualified staff. There are a number of guidelines to ensure that residents have some control or choice over their living routines, over preserving their dignity and maintaining independence.

However, if we are to assess how well the new arrangements are meeting the objectives concerning improvement in the well-being of people with learning disabilities and their carers, we need to start measuring what are termed 'final outcomes' in Chapter 2. In Chapter 4 we explored the methodology of these measures, and no pretence was made that this is an easy process. Nevertheless, case records over the years have been concerned with setting goals for improving the well-being of people with learning difficulties and their carers and noting progress in meeting these goals. Informally, then, a considerable amount of outcome measurement occurs in daily practice. We can expect that care managers will continue this process. The problem becomes one of converting these individualized, informal measurements into generally reported indicators of goal achievements for individuals with a community care need. A simple, if crude, approach for community services that echoes the guidelines for residential care has been set out (Centre for Policy on Ageing 1990).

Evaluation and dissemination

The excitement of working in the brave new world will bring out the innovatory talents in many people working in services for people with learning difficulties. A common thread throughout this chapter has been the lack of general prescription about the means of achieving the ends of the new arrangements, and the variety of approaches we can expect to experience over the next few years. Everyone will be eager to learn about the progress being made in the different methods used in the new purchasing arrangements, as well as in the service innovations developed by providers. Evaluation of these experiences and the dissemination of results will be highly important in informing and educating us all, so that we can profit from the successes as well as learn from the failures that are likely to occur. The key lessons of the evaluation methodology discussed in Chapter 2 are essential features of this learning process. If the correct conclusions are to be drawn from service evaluations, we need to know the exact details of the methodology employed, including the detailed specification of objectives and therefore the measures of outcome used to test whether or not they were achieved, the full range of alternatives evaluated and the costs of each alternative, as well as the outcomes achieved and the methods of collecting the required data. It is also important that the results of these evaluations are placed in the public domain, since one would expect that progress will depend on the steady accumulation of evidence rather than on spectacular, one-off, fully evaluated research projects.

References

Aanes, D. and Moen, M. (1976) Adaptive behaviour changes of group home residents. *Mental Retardation*, 14(4), 36–40.

Alaszewski, A. (1986) *Institutional Care and the Mentally Handicapped. The Mental Handicap Hospital*. London: Croom Helm.

Alberman, E., Nicholson, A. and Wald, K. (1992) *Severe Learning Disability in Young Children: Likely Future Trends*. London: Wolfson Institute of Preventive Medicine.

Apolloni, T. (1980) Key issues and challenges before us. In Apolloni, T., Cappuccilli, J. and Cooke, T.P. (eds), *Achievements in Residential Services for Persons with Disabilities. Toward Excellence*. Baltimore: University Park Press.

Atkinson, D. (1989) Research interviews with people with mental handicaps. In Brechin, A. and Walmsley, J. (eds), *Making Connections. Reflecting on the Lives and Experiences of People with Learning Difficulties*. London: Hodder and Stoughton.

Atkinson, D. and Williams, F. (eds) (1990) *'Know Me as I Am'. An Anthology of Prose, Poetry, and Art by People with Learning Difficulties*. London: Hodder and Stoughton.

Audit Commission (1986) *Making a Reality of Community Care*. London: HMSO.

Audit Commission (1989) *Developing Community Care for Adults with a Mental Handicap*. Occasional Papers No. 9. London: Audit Commission.

Audit Commission (1992) *The Community Care Revolution: Personal Social Services and Community Care*. London: HMSO.

Balthazar, E.E. (1973) *Balthazar Scales of Adaptive Behavior. II: Scales of Social Adaptation*. Palo Alto, CA: Consulting Psychologists Press.

Balthazar, E.E. (1976) *Balthazar Scales of Adaptive Behavior for the Profoundly and Severely Mentally Retarded. I: Scales of Functional Independence. Manual*. Palo Alto, CA: Consulting Psychologists Press.

Baumeister, A.A. (1981) Mental retardation policy and research: the unfulfilled promise. *American Journal of Mental Deficiency*, 85(5), 449–56.

BBC TV (1989) No life of my own. *Open Space*, television documentary, BBC 2, 31 August.

Bender, M. (1986) The inside-out day centre. *Community Care*, 23 October, 14–15.

Bennett, C. (1986) A method of analysis of data collected by continuous observation of activity. Unpublished manuscript.

Bercovici, S. (1981) Qualitative methods and cultural perspectives in the study of deinstitutionalization. In Bruininks, R., Meyers, C.E., Sigford, B. and Lakin, K.C. (eds), *Deinstitutionalization and Community Adjustment of Mentally Retarded People*. Monograph No. 4. Washington DC: American Association on Mental Deficiency.

Bercovici, S. (1983) *Barriers to Normalization. The Restrictive Management of Retarded Persons*. Baltimore: University Park Press.

Berkson, G. and Romer, D. (1980) Social ecology of supervised communal facilities for mentally disabled adults: I. Introduction. *American Journal of Mental Deficiency*, 85(3), 219–28.

Birenbaum, A. and Re, M.A. (1979) Resettling mentally retarded adults in the community – almost 4 years later. *American Journal of Mental Deficiency*, 83(4), 323–9.

Birmingham Campaign for People with a Mental Handicap (1986) Living in a supervised home (staffed or unstaffed): a questionnaire on quality of life. Revised version (Rod Cragg and Jane Harrison).

Bjaanes, A.T. and Butler, E.W. (1974) Environmental variation in community care facilities for mentally retarded persons. *American Journal of Mental Deficiency*, 78(4), 429–39.

Blatt, B. (1970) *Exodus from Pandemonium. Human Abuse and a Reformation of Public Policy*. Boston: Allyn and Bacon.

Blatt, B. and Kaplan, F. (1966) *Christmas in Purgatory. A Photographic Essay on Mental Retardation*. Boston: Allyn and Bacon.

Blunden, R. (1988) Safeguarding quality. In Towell, D. (ed.), *An Ordinary Life In Practice: Developing Comprehensive Community-based Services for People with Learning Disabilities*. London: King Edward's Hospital Fund for London.

Blunden, R. (1989) Robert Griffiths. In Brechin, A. and Walmsley, J. (eds) *Making Connections. Reflecting on the Lives and Experiences of People with Learning Difficulties*. London: Hodder and Stoughton.

Blunden, R. and Allen, D. (eds) (1987) *Facing the Challenge. An Ordinary Life for People with Learning Difficulties and Challenging Behaviour*. Project Paper No. 74. London: King's Fund.

Bolton Community Health Council (1987) *Living in Bolton. A Study of the Lives of Mentally Handicapped People Supported by the Bolton Neighbourhood Network Scheme*. Bolton: Bolton CHC.

Booth, T., Simons, K. and Booth, W. (1988) *Kirklees Relocation Project. The Report*. Sheffield: University of Sheffield.

Booth, T., Simons, K. and Booth, W. (1991) Step by step autonomy. *Social Work Today*, 25 July, 16–17.

Borthwick-Duffy, S.A., Eyman, R.C. and White, J.F. (1987) Client characteristics and residential placement patterns. *American Journal of Mental Deficiency*, 92(1), 24–30.

Bradshaw, J. (1972) A taxonomy of social need. In McLachlan, G. (ed.), *Problems and Progress in Medical Care*, 7th Series. London: Oxford University Press.

Brandon, D. (1988) Real work for real money. *Social Work Today*, 28 July, 20.

Brandon, D. (1991) *Direct Power. A Handbook on Service Brokerage*. Preston: TAO.

Brandon, D. and Towe, N. (1989) *Free to Choose. An Introduction to Service Broker- age*. London: Good Impressions Publishing.

Bronston, W. (1980a) The shape of a marathon. In Apolloni, T., Cappuccilli, J. and Cooke, T.P. (eds), *Achievements in Residential Services for Persons with Disabil- ities. Toward Excellence*. Baltimore: University Park Press.

Bronston, W. (1980b) Matters of design. In Appolloni, T., Cappuccilli, J. and Cooke, T.P. (eds), *Achievements in Residential Services for Persons with Dis- abilities. Toward Excellence*. Baltimore: University Park Press.

Brooks, P.H. and Baumeister, A.A. (1977) Are we making a science of missing the point? *American Journal of Mental Deficiency*, 81(6), 543–6.

Brown, S. (1990) Finding a niche in the system: the case of the community mental handicap team. In Brown, S. and Wistow, G. (eds), *The Roles and Tasks of Community Mental Handicap Teams*. Aldershot: Avebury.

Brown, S. and Wistow, G. (eds) (1990) *The Roles and Tasks of Community Mental Handicap Teams*. Aldershot: Avebury.

Bryman, A. (1988) *Quantity and Quality in Social Research*. London: Unwin Hyman.

Buckle, J. (1983) *Mental Handicap Costs More*. London: DIG (Disablement Income Group) Charitable Trust.

Burgess, R.G. (1984) *In the Field. An Introduction to Field Research*. London: George Allen and Unwin.

Butler, E.W. and Bjaanes, A.T. (1977) A typology of community care facilities and differential normalization outcomes. In Mittler, P. (ed.), *Research to Practice in Mental Retardation. Volume I: Care and Intervention*. Baltimore: University Park Press.

Butterfield, E.C. (1987) Why and how to study the influence of living arrange- ments. In Landesman, S. and Vietze, P. (eds), *Living Environments and Mental Retardation*. Washington, DC: American Association on Mental Retardation.

Calderdale Advocacy (1991) *First Annual Report 1990/91*. Halifax: Calderdale Advocacy.

Callan, J. (1988) *The Economics of Prenatal Screening*. Discussion Paper No. 42. York: Centre for Health Economics.

Cambridge, P. (1987). *Risk-taking and the Care in the Community Projects. A Per- spective of Different Types and Levels of Risk*. Discussion Paper 494. Canterbury: Personal Social Services Research Unit, University of Kent.

Cambridge, P., Knapp, M. and Hayes, L. (1991) Framework paper: methodolo- gies and hypotheses for evaluating long-term outcomes and costs of care in the community for people with learning difficulties (draft, confidential). PSSRU Discussion Paper 705. Canterbury: PSSRU, University of Kent.

Campaign for People with a Mental Handicap (CMH) (1972) *Even Better Services for the Mentally Handicapped*. London: CMH Central Action Group.

Campaign for People with a Mental Handicap (1985) *Going to Work: Employment Opportunities for People with Mental Handicaps in Washington State, USA*. London: CMH.

Cattermole, M. (1987) Changes in quality of life perceived by people with a mental handicap moving into the community – a longitudinal study. Paper presented at British Psychological Society Conference, Brighton, 1987.

Cattermole, M., Jahoda, A. and Markova, I. (1987) *Leaving Home: the Experience of*

People with a Mental Handicap. Stirling: University of Stirling, Department of Psychology.

Centre for Policy on Ageing (1984) *Home Life: a Code of Practice for Residential Care. Report of a Working Party Sponsored by the Department of Health and Social Security*, London: Centre for Policy on Ageing.

Centre for Policy on Ageing (1990) *Community Life: a Code of Practice for Community Care*. London: Centre for Policy on Ageing.

Challis, D., Chessum, R., Chesterman, J., Luckett, R. and Traske, K. (1990) *Case Management in Social and Health Care*. University of Kent: PSSRU.

Challis, D. and Davies, B. (1986) *Case Management in Community Care*. Aldershot: Gower.

Chartered Institute of Public Finance and Accountancy (1992) *Personal Social Services Actuals 1990–91*. London: CIPFA.

Clements, P.R., Bost, L., Loujeania, W., Dubois, Y.G. and Turpin, W.B. (1980) Adaptive behavior scale part two: relative severity of maladaptive behavior. *American Journal of Mental Deficiency*, 84(5), 465–9.

Clements, P.R., Dubois, Y., Bost, L. and Bryan, C. (1981) Adaptive behavior scale, part two: predictive efficiency of severity and frequency scores. *American Journal of Mental Deficiency*, 85(4), 433–4.

Close, D.W. (1977) Community living for severely and profoundly retarded adults: a group home study. *Education and Training of the Mentally Retarded*, 12, 256–62.

Committee of Enquiry into Mental Handicap Nursing and Care (1979) *Report of the Committee* (Jay Report). Cmd 7468-I. London: HMSO.

Conroy, J. (1980) *Reliability of the Behaviour Development Survey*. Philadelphia: Temple University Developmental Disabilities Center.

Conroy, J.W. and Bradley, V.J. (1985) *The Pennhurst Longitudinal Study: a Report of Five Years of Research and Analysis*. Philadelphia: Temple University Developmental Disabilities Center.

Conroy, J., Efthimiou, J. and Lemanowicz, J. (1982) A matched comparison of the developmental growth of institutionalized and deinstitutionalized mentally retarded clients. *American Journal of Mental Deficiency*, 86(6), 581–7.

Cronkite, R.C., Moos, R.H. and Finney, J.W. (1984) The context of adaptation: an integrative perspective on community and treatment environments. In O'Connor, W.A. and Lubin, B. (eds), *Ecological Approaches to Clinical and Community Psychology*. New York: John Wiley and Sons.

Crowell, F.A., Weissman-Frisch, N., Lamson, D. and Boomer, J.D. (1980) NOLE: the naturalistic observation of severely retarded vocational trainees in non-vocational leisure time settings. In Horner, R.H. and Bellamy, G.T. (eds), *Habilitation of Severely and Profoundly Retarded Adults: Volume III. Reports from the Specialized Training Program*. Eugene, OR: University of Oregon Rehabilitation Research and Training Center in Mental Retardation/Center on Human Development.

Crowhurst, G. (1991) Report of the international conference on mental handicap and mental health. *Community Living*, 5(2), 18–19.

Culyer, A.J. (1986) *Economics*. Oxford: Blackwell.

Darton, R.A., Sutcliffe, E. and Wright, K. (forthcoming) *Private and Voluntary Residential and Nursing Homes: A Report of a Survey by the Personal Social*

Services Research Unit and the Centre for Health Economics. Canterbury: Personal Social Services Research Unit, University of Kent.

Darton, R.A. and Wright, K.G. (1993) Changes in the provision of long-stay care 1970–1990. *Health and Social Care in the Community*, 1, 11–25.

Davies, B. (1986) American lessons for British policy and research on long-term care of the elderly. *Quarterly Journal of Social Affairs*, 2(3), 321–55.

Davies, B. and Challis, D. (1986) *Matching Resources to Needs in Community Care*. Aldershot: Gower.

Davies, L. (1988) Community care – the costs and quality. *Health Services Management Research*, 1(3), 145–55.

Davies, L. (1987) *Quality, Costs and 'An Ordinary Life'. Comparing the Costs and Quality of Different Residential Services for People with Mental Handicap*. Project Paper No. 67. London: King's Fund.

Day, K. (1991) *Hospital Based Treatment for Mentally Handicapped People who Present Challenging Behaviour, who are Mentally Ill or who Offend*. Seminar Papers No. 1. Kidderminster: British Institute of Mental Handicap.

Deacon, J. (1982) *Tongue Tied: Fifty Years of Friendship in a Subnormality Hospital*. London: Royal Society for Mentally Handicapped Children and Adults.

Department of Health (1989) *Needs and Responses: Services for Adults with Mental Handicap Who Are Mentally Ill, Who Have Behaviour Problems or Who Offend*. Stanmore: Department of Health.

Department of Health (1990) *Developing Districts*. London: HMSO.

Department of Health (1991) *Speech of the Parliamentary Secretary for Health to the MENCAP Week Conference*, 25 June 1991. London: Department of Health.

Department of Health (1992) *Personal Social Services Statistics, 1992*. London: HMSO.

Department of Health (1993) *Implementing Community Care*. Population Needs Assessment Good Practice Guide. London: Department of Health.

Department of Health and Social Security (1971) *Better Services for the Mentally Handicapped*. London: HMSO.

Department of Health and Social Security (1981) *Care in the Community*. London: DHSS.

Department of Health and Social Security (1985) *Personal Social Services Statistics, 1984*. London: DHSS.

Deutscher, I. (1973) *What We Say/What We Do: Sentiments and Acts*. Glenview, IL: Scott, Foresman and Co.

Disability Alliance (1992) *Disability Rights Bulletin*. Spring, 15–23.

Donaldson, C., Atkinson, A., Bond, J. and Wright, K. (1988) Should QALYs be programme-specific? *Journal of Health Economics*, 7, 239–57.

Dowson, S. (1990) *Who Does What? The Process of Enabling People with Learning Difficulties to Achieve What They Need and Want*. Challenge to Consensus Booklet No. 2. London: Values into Action.

Dowson, S. (1991) *Moving to the Dance, or Service Culture and Community Care*. London: Values into Action.

Doyal, L. and Gough, J. (1991) *A Theory of Human Need*. London: Macmillan.

Drummond, M.F. (1981) *Principles of Economic Appraisal in Health Care*. Oxford: Oxford University Press.

Eastwood, E.A. and Fisher, G.A. (1988) Skills acquisition among matched samples of institutionalized and community-based persons with mental retardation. *American Journal of Mental Retardation*, 93(1), 75–83.

Edgerton, R.B. (1984a) Introduction. In Edgerton, R.B. (ed.), *Lives in Process: Mildly Retarded Adults in a Large City*. Monographs of the American Association on Mental Deficiency No. 6. Washington, DC: AAMD.

Edgerton, R.B. (1984b) The participant-observer approach to research in mental retardation. *American Journal of Mental Deficiency*, 88(5), 498–505.

Edgerton, R.B., Bollinger, M. and Herr, B. (1984) The cloak of competence: after two decades. *American Journal of Mental Deficiency*, 88(4), 345–51.

Edgerton, R.B. and Langness, L.L. (1978) Observing mentally retarded persons in community settings: an anthropological perspective. In Sackett, G.P. (ed.), *Observing Behavior. Volume I: Theory and Applications in Mental Retardation*. Baltimore: University Park Press.

Ellis, N.R., Balla, D., Estes, O., Warren, S.A., Meyers, C.E., Hollis, J., Isaacson, R.L., Palk, B.E. and Siegel, P.S. (1981) Common sense in the habilitation of mentally retarded persons: a reply to Menolascino and McGee. *Mental Retardation*, 19(5), 221–5.

Emerson, E., Barrett, S., Bell, C., Cummings, R., Hughes, H., McCool, C., Toogood, A. and Mansell, J. (1987a) *Developing Services for People with Severe Learning Difficulties and Challenging Behaviour*. Canterbury: University of Kent, Institute of Social and Applied Psychology.

Emerson, E.B. and Pretty, G.M.H. (1986) From rhetoric to reality: evaluating process and outcome in community-based residential facilities. Draft manuscript.

Emerson, E., Toogood, A., Mansell, J., Barrett, S., Bell, C., Cummings, R. and McCool, C. (1987b) Challenging behaviour and community services. 1: Introduction and overview. *Mental Handicap*, 15, 166–9.

Emery, D. (1988) Outreach: finding and using new opportunities. *Community Living*, 1(5), 14.

Evans, G. (1988) A standards matrix. *Llais*, May/June, 4–5.

Evans, G., Blewitt, E. and Blunden, R. (1983) *A Preliminary Study of Problem Behaviours within a Staffed House for Severely Mentally Handicapped People*. Research Report No. 15. Cardiff: Mental Handicap in Wales Applied Research Unit.

Evans, G., Felce, D. and Hobbs, S. (1991) *Evaluating Service Quality*. Cardiff: SCOVO.

Evans, G., Tood, S., Blunden, R., Porterfield, J. and Ager, A. (1985) *A New Style of Life. The Impact of Moving into an Ordinary House on the Lives of People with a Mental Handicap*. Research Report No. 17. Cardiff: Mental Handicap in Wales Applied Research Unit.

Eyman, R.K., Borthwick, S.A. and Miller, C. (1981) Trends in maladaptive behavior of mentally retarded persons placed in community and institutional settings. *American Journal of Mental Deficiency*, 85(5), 473–7.

Eyman, R.K., Borthwick-Duffy, S.A. and Sheehy, N.L. (1987) A longitudinal study of small family care placement. In Landesman, S. and Vietze, P. (eds), *Living Environments and Mental Retardation*. Washington, DC: American Association on Mental Retardation.

Eyman, R.K. and Call, T. (1977) Maladaptive behavior and community placement of mentally retarded persons. *American Journal of Mental Deficiency*, 82(2), 137–44.

Eyman, R.K., Demaine, G.C. and Lei, T.-J. (1979) Relationship between community environments and resident changes in adaptive behavior: a path model. *American Journal of Mental Deficiency*, 83(4), 330–8.

Eyman, R.K., Silverstein, A.B., McLain, R. and Miller, C. (1977) Effects of residential settings. In Mitler, P. (ed.), *Research to Practice in Mental Retardation. Volume 1, Care and Intervention*. Baltimore: University Park Press.

Fanshel, S. and Bush, J. (1970) A health status index and its application to health services outcomes. *Operations Research*, 18, 1021–66.

Feinmann, M. (1988) Project Intowork – how Sheffield achieved the 'impossible'. *Community Living*, 1(5), 12–13.

Felce, D. (1986) Accommodating adults with severe and profound mental handicaps: comparative revenue costs. *Mental Handicap*, 14, 104–7.

Felce, D., De Kock, U. and Repp, A.C. (1986) An eco-behavioral analysis of small community-based houses and traditional large hospitals for severely and profoundly mentally handicapped adults. *Applied Research in Mental Retardation*, 7, 393–408.

Felce, D., De Kock, U., Saxby, H. and Thomas, M. (1985) *Small Homes for Severely and Profoundly Mentally Handicapped Adults. Final Report: July 1985*. Southampton: Health Care Evaluation Research Team, University of Southampton.

Felce, D., Kushlick, A. and Mansell, J. (1980a) Evaluation of alternative residential facilities for the severely mentally handicapped in Wessex: client engagement. *Advances in Behaviour Research and Therapy*, 3, 13–18.

Felce, D., Kushlick, A. and Smith, J. (1983) Planning and evaluation of community based residences for severely and profoundly mentally handicapped people in the United Kingdom. In Breuning, S.E., Matson, J.L. and Barrett, R.P. (eds), *Advances in Mental Retardation and Developmental Disabilities. A Research Annual (Volume I)*. Greenwich, CT: JAI Press.

Felce, D., Mansell, J. and Kushlick, A. (1980b) Evaluation of alternative residential facilities for the severely mentally handicapped in Wessex: revenue costs. *Advances in Behaviour Research and Therapy*, 3, 43–7.

Felce, D., Repp, A., Thomas, M., Ager, A. and Blunden, R. (1991) The relationship of staff: client ratio, interaction and resident placement. *Research in Developmental Disabilities*, 12, 315–31.

Felce, D., Taylor, D. and Wright, K. (1993) *Epidemiologically-based Needs Assessment People with Learning Disabilities*. London: NHS Management Executive.

Ferguson-Smith, N. (1988) Prenatal diagnosis. *Medicine International*, 55, 2376–80.

Finkelstein, V. (1981) To deny or not to deny disability. In Brechin, A., Liddiard, P. and Swain, J. (eds), *Handicap in a Social World*. Sevenoaks: Hodder and Stoughton Educational, in association with the Open University Press.

Flynn, M.C. (1986) *A Study of Prediction in the Community Placements of Adults who are Mentally Handicapped (1983–1986): a Summary of the Final Report*. Manchester: Hester Adrian Research Centre, University of Manchester.

Flynn, M. (1989) *Independent Living for Adults with a Mental Handicap: a Place of My Own*. London: Cassell.

Flynn, M.C. and Saleem, J.K. (1986) Adults who are mentally handicapped and living with their parents: satisfaction and perceptions regarding their lives and circumstances. *Journal of Mental Deficiency Research*, 30, 379–87.

Flynn, R.J. and Heal, L.W. (1981) A short form of PASS-3 – A study of its structure, interrater reliability, and validity for assessing normalization. *Evaluation Review*, 5(3), 357–76.

Fogelman, C.J. (ed.) (1974) *AAMD Adaptive Behavior Scale Manual. 1975 Revision*. Washington, DC: AAMD.

Fogelman, C.J. (ed.) (1975) *AAMD Adaptive Behavior Scale: 1974 Revision*. Washington, DC: AAMD.

Fraser, W.J. and Green, A.M. (1991) Changing perspectives on mental handicap. In Fraser, S.W.J., MacGillvray, K.C. and Green, A.M. (eds), *Caring for People with Mental Handicaps*, 8th edn. Oxford. Butterworth-Heinemann.

Frost, D. and Taylor, K. (1986) This is my life. *Community Care*, 7 August, 28–9.

Gerard, K. (1990) Economic evaluation of respite care for children with mental handicap. A preliminary analysis of problems. *Mental Handicap*, 18, 150–5.

Gerard, K. and Wright, K. (1988) *The Value of Formal Respite Care for Mentally Handicapped Children and their Carers*. A Report to the Department of Health. York: Centre for Health Economics.

Glover, G.R., Rohde, J. and Farmer, R.D.T. (1993) Is the money following the clients with learning disabilities? *British Medical Journal*, 306, 987–90.

Goffman, E. (1961) *Asylums. Essays on the Social Situation of Mental Patients and Other Inmates*. Harmondsworth: Penguin.

Gollay, E., Freedman, R., Wyngaarden, M. and Kurtz, N.R. (1978) *Coming Back. The Community Experiences of Deinstitutionalized Mentally Retarded People*. Cambridge, MA: Abt Books.

Grant, G.W.B. and Moores, B. (1976) Comparison of patient activities in two hospitals for the mentally handicapped. *APEX*, 4, 27–9.

Gray, B. (1985) Social education centres and employment. In Craft, M., Bicknell, J. and Hollins, S. (eds), *Mental Handicap. A Multi-disciplinary Approach*. Eastbourne: Baillière Tindall.

Griffiths, M., Wyatt, J. and Hersov, J. (1985) Further education, adult education and self-advocacy. In Craft, M., Bickness, J. and Hollins, S. (eds), *Mental Handicap. A Multi-disciplinary Approach*. Eastbourne: Baillière Tindall.

Griffiths, Sir R. (1988) *Community Care: Agenda for Action*. London: HMSO.

Grossman, H.J. (ed.) (1983) *Classification in Mental Retardation*, 1983 revision. Washington, DC: AAMD.

Guarnaccia, V. (1976) Factor structure and correlates of adaptive behavior in non-institutionalized retarded adults. *American Journal of Mental Deficiency*, 80, 543–7.

Gudex, C., Kind, P., Van Dalen, H., Durand, M.-A., Morris, J. and Williams, A. (1993) *Comparing Scaling Methods for Health State Valuations – Rosser Revisited*. Discussion Paper No. 107. York: Centre for Health Economics.

Gunzburg, H.C. (1973) The physical environment of the mentally handicapped. VIII: '39 Steps' leading towards normalized living practices in living units for the mentally handicapped. *British Journal of Mental Subnormality*, 19(2), 91–9.

Gunzburg, H.C. and Gunzburg, A.L. (1973) *Mental Handicap and Physical Environment. The Application of an Operational Philosophy to Planning*. London: Baillière Tindall.

Gunzburg, H.C. and Gunzburg, A.L. (1987) *Learning Opportunities Coordination (LOCO). A Scale for Assessing Coordinated Learning Opportunities in Living Units for People with a Handicap*. Stratford-upon-Avon: SEFA.

Haggard, S. and Carter, F.A. (1976) Preventing the birth of infants with Down's syndrome: a cost benefit analysis. *British Medical Journal*, **i**, 753–6.

Hamnett, C. and Mullings, B. (1992) The distribution of public and private residential homes for elderly persons in England and Wales. *Area*, 24(2), 130–44.

Harris, J. (ed.) (1991) *Service Responses to People with Learning Difficulties and Challenging Behaviour*. BIMH Seminar Paper No. 1. Kidderminster: British Institute of Mental Handicap.

Haycox, A. (1989) The Maidstone Community Care Programme: final evaluation report. Unpublished draft version.

Haycox, A. (forthcoming) *Evaluating Community Care: A Case Study*. Aldershot: Avebury.

Haycox, A. (undated) Evaluation of MCCP utilizing the PASS Methodology. Unpublished paper.

Haycox, A. and Brand, D. (1991) *Evaluating Community Care. A Case Study of Maidstone Community Care Project*. Manchester: North Western Regional Health Authority; London: Social Services Inspectorate.

Haycox, A. and Walsworth-Bell, J. (1988) *Increasing the Effectiveness of Screening for Down's Syndrome*. Manchester: North Western Regional Heath Authority.

Heal, L.W. and Chadsey-Rusch, J. (1985) The Lifestyle Satisfaction Scale (LSS): assessing individuals' satisfaction with residence, community setting, and associated services. *Applied Research in Mental Retardation*, 6, 475–90.

Heal, L.W. and Laidlaw, T.J. (1980) Evaluation of residential alternatives. In Novak, A.R. and Heal, L.W. (eds), *Integration of Developmentally Disabled Individuals into the Community*. Baltimore: Paul H. Brookes Publishing Co.

Hemming, H. (1982) Mentally handicapped adults returned to large institutions after transfers to new small units. *British Journal of Mental Subnormality*, 28(1), 13–28.

Hemming, H. (1986) Follow-up of adults with mental retardation transferred from large institutions to new small units. *Mental Retardation*, 24(4), 229–35.

Heron, A. and Myers, M. (1983) *Intellectual Impairment. The Battle against Handicap*. London: Academic Press.

Holburn, C.S. (1986) Maladaptive behavior merits fair treatment: a response to Seltzer and Krauss. *American Journal of Mental Deficiency*, 91(3), 211–14.

Howells, G. (1986) Are the medical needs of mentally handicapped people being met? *Journal of the Royal College of General Practitioners*, 36, 449–53.

Hull, J.T. and Thompson, J.C. (1980) Predicting adaptive functioning of mentally retarded persons in community settings. *American Journal of Mental Deficiency*, 85(3), 253–61.

Humphreys, S., Lowe, K. and Blunden, R. (1983) *Long Term Evaluation of Services for Mentally Handicapped People in Cardiff. Research Methodology*. Cardiff: Mental Handicap in Wales Applied Research Unit.

Hunter, D.R. and Wistow, G. (1986) *Community Care in Britain*. London: King's Fund.

Isett, R.D. and Spreat, S. (1979) Test retest and interrater reliability of the AAMD adaptive behavior scale. *American Journal of Mental Deficiency*, 84(1), 93–5.

James, G. and Jeffes, E. (1984) *Home Support for People with a Mental Handicap*. Worcester: Joint Research and Information Unit.

King, R.D. and Raynes, N.V. (1968) An operational measure of inmate management in residential institutions. *Social Sciences and Medicine*, 2, 41–53.

King, R.D., Raynes, N.V. and Tizard, J. (1971) *Patterns of Residential Care. Sociological Studies in Institutions for Handicapped Children*. London: Routledge and Kegan Paul.

King's Fund Centre (1980) *An Ordinary Life. Comprehensive Locally-based Residential Services for Mentally Handicapped People*. Project Paper No. 24. London: King's Fund Centre.

King's Fund Centre (1988) *Ties and Connections. An Ordinary Community Life for People with Learning Difficulties*. London: King's Fund Centre.

Kleinberg, J. and Galligan, B. (1983) Effects of deinstitutionalization on adaptive behavior of mentally retarded adults. *American Journal of Mental Deficiency*, 88(1), 21–7.

Knapp, M. (1988) Construction and expectation: themes from the care in the community initiative. In Cambridge, P. and Knapp, M. (eds), *Demonstrating Successful Care in the Community*. Canterbury: Personal Social Services Research Unit, University of Kent.

Knapp, M., Cambridge, P., Darton, R., Thomason, C., Allen, C., Beecham, J. and Leedham, I. (1989) *Care in the Community: Final Report*. Discussion Paper No. 615. Canterbury: Personal Social Services Research Unit, University of Kent.

Knapp, M., Cambridge, P., Thomason, C., Beecham, J., Allen, C. and Darton, R. (1992) *Care in the Community: Challenge and Demonstration*. Aldershot: Ashgate.

Knapp, S. and Salend, S.J. (1983) Adapting the adaptive behavior scale. *Mental Retardation*, 21(2), 63–7.

Korman, N. and Glennerster, H. (1990) *Hospital Closure*. Milton Keynes: Open University Press.

Lakin, K.C. and Bruininks, R.H. (1985) Social integration of developmentally disabled persons. In Lakin, K.C. and Bruininks, R.H. (eds), *Strategies for Achieving Community Integration of Developmentally Disabled Citizens*. Baltimore: Paul H. Brooks Publishing Co.

Lambert, N.M. and Nicoll, R.C. (1976) Dimensions of adaptive behavior of retarded and nonretarded public-school children. *American Journal of Mental Deficiency*, 81(2), 135–46.

Landesman, S. (1987) The changing structure and function of institutions: a search for optimal group care environments. In Landesman, S. and Vietze, P. (eds), *Living Environments and Mental Retardation*. Washington, DC: American Association on Mental Retardation.

Landesman-Dwyer, S., Sackett, G.P. and Kleinman, J.S. (1980) Relationship of size to resident and staff behavior in small community residences. *American Journal of Mental Deficiency*, 85(1), 6–17.

Leedham, I. (1989) From mental handicap hospital to community provisions. Unpublished PhD thesis, PSSRU, University of Kent, Canterbury.

Leedham, I. (1991) Services for people with learning difficulties in Calderdale. Mission statement: foundations, principles, and standards. Unpublished discussion paper.

Leighton, A. (1988) Introduction. In Leighton, A. (ed.), *Mental Handicap in the Community*. London: Woodhead-Faulkner.

Leland, H.W. (1978) Theoretical considerations of adaptive behavior. In Coulter,

W.A. and Morrow, H.W. (eds), *Adaptive Behavior: Concepts and Measurements*. New York: Grune and Stratton.

Lemke, S. and Moos, R.J. (1984) *Multiphasic Environmental Assessment Procedure (MEAP) Handbook for Users*. Palo Alto, CA: Social Ecology Laboratory and Geriatric Research, Education and Clinical Center/Veterans Administration and Stanford University Medical Center.

Lemke, S., Moos, R.H. and Marder, A. (1984) *Multiphasic Environmental Assessment Procedure (MEAP) Hand Scoring Booklet*. Palo Alto, CA: Social Ecology Laboratory and Geriatric Research, Education and Clinical Center/Veterans Administration and Stanford University Medical Center.

Lofland, J. (1971) *Analyzing Social Settings. A Guide to Qualitative Observation and Analysis*. Belmont, CA: Wadsworth Publishing Company.

McCormack, M. (1979) *Away from Home. The Mentally Handicapped in Residential Care*. London: Constable.

McDevitt, S.C., McDevitt, S.C. and Rosen, M. (1977) Adaptive behavior scale, part II: a cautionary note and suggestions for revisions. *American Journal of Mental Deficiency*, 82(2), 210–12.

McDevitt, S.C., Smith, P.M., Schmidt, D.W. and Rosen, M. (1978) The deinstitutionalized citizen: adjustment and quality of life. *Mental Retardation*, February, 22–4.

MacDonald, L. (1988) Improving the reliability of a maladaptive behavior scale. *American Journal of Mental Retardation*, 92(4), 381–4.

MacDonald, L. and Barton, L.E. (1986) Measuring severity of behavior: a revision of part II of the adaptive behavior scale. *American Journal of Mental Deficiency*, 90(4), 418–24.

MacEachron, A.E. (1983) Institutional reform and adaptive functioning of mentally retarded persons: a field experiment. *American Journal of Mental Deficiency*, 88(1), 2–12.

McGee, M.G. and Woods, D.J. (1978) Use of Moos' ward atmosphere scale in a residential setting for mentally retarded adolescents. *Psychological Reports*, 43, 580–2.

McLain, R.E., Silverstein, A.B., Hubbell, M. and Brownlee, L. (1975) The characterization of residential environments within a hospital for the mentally retarded. *Mental Retardation*, 13, 24–7.

McLain, R.E., Silverstein, A.B., Hubbell, M. and Brownlee, L. (1977) Comparison of the residential environment of a state hospital for retarded clients with those of various types of community facilities. *Journal of Community Psychology*, 5, 282–9.

Maher, J. and Russell, O. (1988) Serving people with very challenging behaviour. In Towell, D. (ed.), *An Ordinary Life in Practice: Developing Comprehensive Community-based Services for People with Learning Disabilities*. London: King Edward's Hospital Fund for London.

Mann, P.H. (1985) *Methods of Social Investigation*, 2nd edn. Oxford: Basil Blackwell.

Mansell, J. (1987) Activity patterns of clients in mental handicap hospitals. Paper presented at seminar, Institute of Social and Applied Psychology, University of Kent at Canterbury, 28 May.

Mansell, J. (1988) Training for service development. In Towell, D. (ed.), *An Ordinary Life in Practice: Developing Comprehensive Community-based Services for People with Learning Disabilities.* London: King Edward's Hospital Fund for London.

Mansell, J. (1993) *Services for People with Learning Disabilities and Challenging Behaviour or Mental Health Needs: Report of a Project Group.* London: HMSO.

Mansell, J., De Kock, U., Jenkins, J. and Felce, D. (1982) *AM: the Activity Measure – a Handbook for Observers.* Southampton: Health Care Evaluation Research Team, University of Southampton.

Mansell, J., Jenkins, J., Felce, D. and De Kock, U. (1984) Measuring the activity of severely and profoundly mentally handicapped adults in ordinary housing. *Behaviour Research and Therapy,* 22(1), 23–9.

MENCAP (1991) *Employment Services Information Pack.* London: MENCAP.

MENCAP (undated) *Pathway Employment Service.* London: MENCAP.

Meyers, C.E., Nihira, K. and Zetlin, A. (1979) The Measurement of adaptive behaviour. In Ellis, N.R. (ed.), *Handbook of Mental Deficiency, Psychological Theory and Research,* 2nd edn. Hillsdale, NJ: Lawrence Erlbaum Associates.

Modell, B. (1986) Some social implications of early fetal diagnosis. In Brambati, B., Simoni, G. and Fabri, S. (eds), *Chorionic Villers Sampling: Fetal Diagnosis of Genetic Disease in the First Trimester.* New York: Dekker.

Moos, R.H. (1974a) *The Social Climate Scales. An Overview.* Palo Alto, CA: Consulting Psychologists Press.

Moos, R.H. (1974b) *Ward Atmosphere Scale: Manual.* Palo Alto, CA: Consulting Psychologists Press.

Moos, R.H. (1974c) *Community Oriented Programs Environment Scale. Manual.* Palo Alto, CA: Consulting Psychologists Press.

Moos, R.H. (1984) *Multiphasic Environmental Assessment Procedure (MEAP) Data Collection Forms.* Palo Alto, CA: Social Ecology Lab. and Geriatric Research, Education, and Clinical Center/Veterans Administration and Stanford University Medical Center.

Moos, R.H. and Lemke, S. (1982) The Multiphasic Environmental Assessment Procedure. A method for comprehensively evaluating sheltered care settings. In Jeger, A.M. and Slotnick, R.S. (eds), *Community Mental Health and Behavioral-Ecology. A Handbook of Theory, Research and Practice.* New York: Plenum Press.

Moos, R.H. and Lemke, S. (1984) *Multiphasic Environmental Assessment Procedure (MEAP) Manual.* Palo Alto, CA: Social Ecology Lab. and Geriatric Research, Education, and Clinical Center/Veterans Administration and Stanford University Medical Center.

Morreau, L.E. (1985) Assessing and managing problem behaviors. In Lakin, K.C. and Bruininks, R.H. (eds), *Strategies for Achieving Community Integration of Developmentally Disabled Citizens.* Baltimore: Paul H. Brooks Publishing Co.

Morris, P. (1969) *Put Away. A Sociological Study of Institutions for the Mentally Retarded.* London: Routledge and Kegan Paul.

MRC Social Psychiatry Unit (1986) *Evaluation of new services to be provided for residents of Darenth Park Hospital. Fifth Annual Report.* London: Medical Research Council

National Council for Voluntary Organisations (1991) *Working in Partnership. NCVO Codes of Guidance No. 1: Community Care Plans.* London: NCVO.

National Development Team for People with a Mental Handicap (1991) *The Andover Case Management Project.* London: NDT.

Netten, A. and Smart, S. (1993) Unit Costs of Community Care 1992/93. Canterbury: Personal Social Services Research Unit, University of Kent.

Nihira, K. (1969) Factorial dimensions of adaptive behavior in adult retardates. *American Journal of Mental Deficiency*, 73, 863–78.

Nihira, K. (1976) Dimensions of adaptive behavior in institutionalized mentally retarded children and adults: developmental perspective. *American Journal of Mental Deficiency*, 81, 215–26.

Nihira, K. (1977) Development of adaptive behavior in the mentally retarded. In Mittler, P. (ed.), *Research to Practice in Mental Retardation. Volume 2: Education and Training*. Baltimore: University Park Press.

Nihira, K. (1978) Factorial descriptions of the AAMD adaptive behavior scale. In Coulter, W.A. and Morrow, H.W. (eds), *Adaptive Behavior: Concepts and Measurements*. New York: Grune and Stratton.

Nirje, B. (1969) The normalization principle and its human management implications. In Kugel, R. and Wolfensberger, W. (eds), *Changing Patterns in Residential Services for the Mentally Retarded*. Washington, DC: President's Committee on Mental Retardation.

North-East CMH and Carle, N. (1986) *Talking Points No. 5. Helping People to Make Choices: Opportunities and Challenges*. London: Campaign for People with Mental Handicaps.

North Western Regional Health Authority (1990) *Together for an Ordinary Life*. Manchester: North Western Regional Health Authority.

Novak, A.R. (1980) Epilogue: a perspective on the present and notes for new directions. In Novak, A.R. and Heal, L.W. (eds), *Integration of Developmentally Disabled Individuals into the Community*. Baltimore: Paul H. Brookes Publishing Co.

O'Brien, J. (1987) A guide to life-style planning. Using *The Activities Catalog* to integrate services and natural support systems. In Wilcox, B. and Bellamy, G.T. (eds), *A Comprehensive Guide to the Activities Catalog. An Alternative Curriculum for Youth and Adults with Severe Disabilities*. Baltimore: Paul H. Brookes.

O'Connor, G. (1976) *Home is a Good Place: A National Perspective of Community Residential Facilities for Developmentally Disabled Persons*. Monograph of the AAMD, No. 2. Washington, DC: AAMD.

O'Neill, J., Brown, M., Gordon, W., Schonhorn, R. and Greer, E. (1981) Activity patterns of mentally retarded adults in institutions and communities: a longitudinal study. *Applied Research in Mental Retardation*, 2, 367–79.

Orlik, C., Robinson, C. and Russel, O. (1991) *A Survey of Family Based Respite Care Schemes in the United Kingdom*. Bristol: Norah Fry Research Centre, University of Bristol.

Pankratz, L. (1975) Assessing the psychosocial environment of halfway houses for the retarded. *Community Mental Health Journal*, 11(3), 341–5.

Passfield, D. (1983) What do you think of it so far? A survey of 20 Priory Court residents. *Mental Handicap*, 11, 97–9.

Pieper, B. and Cappuccilli, J. (1980) Beyond the family and the institution. The sanctity of liberty. In Apolloni, T., Cappuccilli, J. and Cooke, T.P. (eds), *Achievements in Residential Services for Persons with Disabilities. Toward Excellence*. Baltimore: University Park Press.

Pilling, D. (1990) The evaluation of PASS (Program Analysis of Service Systems) – report of first phase. London: Rehabilitation Resource Centre, City University.

Porterfield, J. (1988) Promoting opportunities for employment. In Towell, D. (ed.), *An Ordinary Life In Practice: Developing Comprehensive Community-based Services for People with Learning Disabilities*. London: King Edward's Hospital Fund for London.

Pountney, M. (1987) Training opportunities for real jobs. *Community Living*, July, 15.

Pratt, M.W., Luszcz, M.A. and Brown, M.E. (1980) Measuring dimensions of the quality of care in small community residences. *American Journal of Mental Deficiency*, 85(2), 188–94.

Prosser, H. (1989) *Eliciting the Views of People with Mental Handicap. A Literature Review*. Manchester: Hester Adrian Research Centre, University of Manchester.

Puddicombe, B. (1991) *Days. In Search of Real Alternatives to the Adult Training Centre*. Challenge to Consensus Booklet No. 4. London: Values into Action.

Qureshi, H. and Alborz, A. (1992) Epidemiology of challenging behaviour. *Mental Handicap Research*, 5, 130–43.

Raynes, N.V. (1988) *Annotated Directory of Measures of Environmental Quality for Use in Residential Services for People with a Mental Handicap*. Manchester: University of Manchester, Department of Social Policy and Social Work.

Raynes, N., Pettipher, C., Shiell, A. and Wright, K. (1990) *The Cost and Quality of Residential Care for People with a Mental Handicap*. York: Centre for Health Economics.

Raynes, N.V., Pratt, M.W. and Roses, S.S. (1979) *Organisational Structure and the Care of the Mentally Retarded*. London: Croom Helm.

Raynes, N.V. and Sumpton, R. (1987) Differences in the quality of residential provision for mentally handicapped people. *Psychological Medicine*, 17, 999–1008.

Renshaw, J. (1986) PASSING understanding. *Community Care*, 17 July.

Rivera, G. (1972) *Willowbrook. A Report on How It Is and Why It Doesn't Have to Be That Way*. New York: Random House.

Robinson, C.A. (1986) *Avon Short-term Respite Care Scheme Evaluation Study*. Bristol: Department of Mental Health, University of Bristol.

Robinson, C. and Stalker, K. (1989) *Time for a Break. Respite Care: A Study of Providers, Consumers and Patterns of Use*. Bristol: Norah Fry Research Centre, University of Bristol.

Robinson, C. and Stalker, K. (1991) *Respite Care – Summary and Suggestions*. Bristol: Norah Fry Research Centre, University of Bristol.

Robinson, J.W. (1987) *Architecture as a Medium for Culture: Public Institution and Private House*. Minneapolis: University of Minnesota Twin Cities, School of Architecture and Landscape Architecture.

Robinson, J.W., Thompson, T., Emmons, P. and Graff, M., with Franklin, E. (1984) *Towards an Architectural Definition of Normalization: Design Principles for Housing Severely and Profoundly Retarded Adults*. Minneapolis: University of Minnesota Twin Cities, School of Architecture and Landscape Architecture.

Roos, P. (1980) Dealing with the momentum of outmoded approaches. In Roos, P., McCann, B.M. and Addison, M.R. (eds), *Shaping the Future. Community-based*

Residential Services and Facilities for Mentally Retarded People. Baltimore: University Park Press.

Rosser, R. and Kind, J. (1978) A scale of valuations of states of illness: is there a social consensus? *International Journal of Epidemiology,* 7, 347–58.

Rossi, P.H. and Freeman, H.E. (1985) *Evaluation. A Systematic Approach,* 3rd edn. Beverly Hills, CA: Sage Publications.

Rotegard, L.L., Bruininks, R.H., Holman, J.G. and Lakin, K.C. (1985) Environmental aspects of deinstitutionalization. In Bruininks, R.H. and Lakin, K.C. (eds), *Living and Learning in the Least Restrictive Environment.* Baltimore: Paul H. Brookes Publishing Co.

Rotegard, L.L., Hill, B.K. and Bruininks, R.H. (1983) Environmental characteristics of residential facilities for mentally retarded persons in the United States. *American Journal of Mental Deficiency,* 88(1), 49–56.

Royal College of General Practitioners (1990) *Primary Care for People with a Mental Handicap.* Occasional Paper No. 47. London: RCGP.

Ryan, J., with Thomas, F. (1980) *The Politics of Mental Handicap.* Harmondsworth: Penguin.

Sandler, A. and Thurman, S.K. (1981) Status of community placement research: effects on retarded citizens. *Education and Training of the Mentally Retarded,* 16(1), 245–51.

Schalock, R.L., Harper, R.S. and Genung, T. (1981) Community integration of mentally retarded adults: community placement and program success. *American Journal of Mental Deficiency,* 85(5), 478–88.

Schalock, R.L. and Lilley, M.A. (1986) Placement from community-based mental retardation programs: how well do clients do after 8 to 10 years? *American Journal of Mental Deficiency,* 90(6), 669–76.

Secretaries of State for Health, Social Security, Wales and Scotland (1989) *Caring for People. Community Care in the Next Decade and Beyond.* London: HMSO.

Seevers, C.J. (1980) Assessing programmatic aspects of the problem. In Roos, P., McCann, B.M. and Addison, M.R. (eds), *Shaping the Future, Community-based Residential Services and Facilities for Mentally Retarded People.* Baltimore: University Park Press.

Segal, S. (1987) Parents' concerns for the future: the role of RESCARE in influencing plans for residential provision. *Mental Handicap,* 15(3), 105–7.

Seltzer, G.B. (1981) Community residential adjustment: the relationship among environment performance, and satisfaction. *American Journal of Mental Deficiency,* 85(6), 624–30.

Seltzer, M.M. (1985) Public attitudes toward community residential facilities for mentally retarded persons. In Bruininks, R.H. and Lakin, K.C. (eds), *Living and Learning in the Least Restrictive Environment.* Baltimore: Paul H. Brookes Publishing Co.

Seltzer, M.M. and Seltzer, G. (1987) Community responses to community residences for persons who have mental retardation. In Landesman, S. and Vietze, P. (eds), *Living Environments and Mental Retardation.* Washington, DC: American Association on Mental Retardation.

Seltzer, M.M., Seltzer, G. and Sherwood, C.C. (1983) The residential environment and its relationship to client behavior. In Kernan, K.T., Begab, M.J. and

Edgerton, R.B. (eds), *Environments and Behaviour. The Adaptation of Mentally Retarded Persons.* Baltimore: University Park Press.

Shaw, G., Naidoo, S., Wise, S. and Bateman, S. (1986) A home of their own. *Nursing Times,* November, 12.

Shearer, A. (1981) *Disability: Whose Handicap?* Oxford: Basil Blackwell.

Shearer, A. (1986) *Building Community with People with Mental Handicaps, Their Families and Friends.* London: CMH and King's Fund.

Shiell, A., Pettipher, C., Raynes, N. and Wright, K. (1993) A cost function analysis of residential services for adults with a learning disability. *Health Economics,* 2(3), 247–56.

Shinn, M. (1982) Assessing program characteristics and social climate. In McSweeny, A.J., Fremouw, W.J. and Hawkins, R.P. (eds), *Practical Program Evaluation in Youth Treatment,* Springfield, IL: Charles C. Thomas.

Sigelman, C.K., Schoenrock, C.J., Winer, J.L., Spanhel, C.L., Hromas, S.G., Martin, P.W., Budd, E.C. and Bensberg, G.J. (1981) Issues in interviewing mentally retarded persons: an empirical study. In Bruininks, R.H., Meyers, C.E., Sigford, B.B. and Lakin, K.C. (eds), *Deinstitutionalization and Community Adjustment of Mentally Retarded People.* Monograph No. 4. Washington, DC: American Association on Mental Deficiency.

Silverstein, A.B., McLain, R.E., Hubbell, M. and Brownlee, L. (1977) Characteristics of the treatment environment: a factor analytic study. *Educational and Psychological Measurement,* 37, 367–71.

Simons, K. (1986) Kirklees Relocation Project Information Bulletin No. 2. Interim report on progress. Sheffield: University of Sheffield, Department of Sociological Studies.

Simons, K., Booth, T. and Booth, W. (1989) Speaking out: user studies and people with learning difficulties. *Research, Policy and Planning,* 7(1), 9–17.

Smith, G. and Cantley, C. (1985a) *Assessing Health Care: a Study in Organizational Evaluation.* Milton Keynes: Open University Press.

Smith, G. and Cantley, C. (1985b) Policy evaluation: the use of varied data in a study of a psychogeriatric service. In Walker, R. (ed.), *Applied Qualitative Research.* Aldershot: Gower.

Smith, J., Glossop, C. and Kushlick, A. (1980) Evaluation of alternative residential facilities for the severely mentally handicapped in Wessex: client progress. *Advances in Behaviour Research and Therapy,* 3, 5–11.

Social Services Inspectorate (1989) *Inspection of Day Services for People with a Mental Handicap.* London: Department of Health.

Social Services Inspectorate (1990) *All Change from Hospital to Community. Inspection of Community Services for Former Long-stay Hospital Patients.* London: Department of Health, Social Services Inspectorate.

Spencer, L.D. (1981) On becoming a 'retarded' person. The institutional experience nine years later. In Haywood, H.C. and Newbrough, J.R. (eds), *Living Environments for Developmentally Retarded Persons.* Baltimore: University Park Press.

Sperlinger, A. (1987) Service evaluation of a staffed house for young people in Greenwich with learning disabilities. Paper presented at Quality of Life Assessment Meeting, Friern Hospital, 3 June.

Spreat, S., Roszkowski, M.J. and Isett, R.D. (1983) Assessment of adaptive behavior in the mentally retarded. In Breuning, S.E., Matson, J.L. and Barrett, R.P.

(eds), *Advances in Mental Retardation and Developmental Disabilities. A Research Annual (Volume I)*.

Spreat, S., Telles, J.I., Conroy, J.W., Feinstein, C. and Colombatto, J.J. (1987) Attitudes towards deinstitutionalization: national survey of families of institutionalized persons with mental retardation. *Mental Retardation*, 25(5), 267–74.

Stack, J.G. (1984) Interrater reliabilities of the adaptive behavior scale with environmental effects controlled. *American Journal of Mental Deficiency*, 88(4), 396–400.

Stainback, S. and Stainback, W. (1984) Methodological considerations in qualitative research. *Journal of the Association for Persons with Severe Handicaps*, 9(4), 296–303.

Sumarah, J. (1987) L'arche: philosophy and ideology. *Mental Retardation*, 25(3), 165–9.

Sutter, P. and Mayeda, T. (1979) *Characteristics of the Treatment Environment: MR/DD Community Home Manual*. Pomona, CA: Individualized Data Base, University of California/Los Angeles, Neuropsychiatric Institute Research Group at Lanterman State Hospital and Developmental Center.

Sutter, P., Mayeda, T., Call, T., Yanagi, G. and Yee, S. (1980) Comparison of successful and unsuccessful community-placed mentally retarded persons. *American Journal of Mental Deficiency*, 85(3), 262–7.

Taylor, J. and Taylor, D. (1986) *Mental Handicap Partnership in the Community?* London: Office of Health Economics.

Taylor, R.L., Warren, S.A. and Slocumb, P.R. (1979) Categorizing behavior in terms of severity: considerations for part two of the adaptive behavior scale. *American Journal of Mental Deficiency*, 83(4), 411–14.

Taylor, S.J. and Bogdan, R. (1981) A qualitative approach to the study of community adjustment. In Bruininks, R.H., Meyers, C.E., Sigford, B.B. and Lakin, K.C. (eds), *Deinstitutionalization and Community Adjustment of Mentally Retarded People*. Monograph No. 4. Washington, DC: American Association on Mental Deficiency.

Taylor, S.J., Racino, J.A., Knoll, J.A. and Lutfiyya, Z. (1987) *The Nonrestrictive Environment: A Resource Manual on Community Integration for People with the Most Severe Disabilities*. Syracuse, NY: Human Policy Press.

Thomas, M., Felce, D., De Kock, U., Saxby, H. and Repp, A. (1986) The activity of staff and of severely and profoundly mentally handicapped adults in residential settings of different sizes. *British Journal of Mental Subnormality*, 32(1), 82–92.

Thomason, C. (1986) Care in the community initiative: guide to the evaluation. Canterbury: Personal Social Services Research Unit, University of Kent.

Thompson, T. and Carey, A. (1980) Structured normalization: intellectual and adaptive behavior changes in a residential setting. *Mental Retardation*, 18(4), 193–7.

Tonkin, B. (1987) Voices in the wilderness. *Community Care*, 15 January, 26–9.

Towell, D. (1985) Residential needs and services. In Craft, M., Bicknell, J. and Hollins, S. (eds), *Mental Handicap. A Multi-disciplinary Approach*. Eastbourne: Baillière Tindall.

Towell, D. and Beardshaw, V. (1991) *Enabling Community Integration. The Role of Public Authorities in Promoting an Ordinary Life for People with Learning Disabilities in the 1990s*. London: King's Fund College.

Turner, F.J. and Turner, J.C. (1985) *Evaluation of the Five Year Plan for Closure of Mental Retardation Facilities. Southwest Region*. Ottawa: Province of Ontario Southwestern Region.

Twenty Two (1988) For people with learning difficulties, a study of services. *Twenty Two* 15, 10–11.

Twigg, J. (1992) Carers in the service system. In Twigg, J. (ed.), *Carers Research and Practice*. London: HMSO.

Tyne, A. (1986) Some practical dilemmas and strategies in values-led approaches to change. In Ward, L. (ed.), *Getting Better All the Time? Issues and Strategies for Ensuring Quality in Community Services for People with Mental Handicap*. Project Paper No. 66. London: King's Fund.

University of Minnesota Outreach Training Project (1976) *Minnesota Developmental Programming System. Training Materials*. St Paul: University of Minnesota.

Values into Action (1989) *Newsletter*, No. 59, Winter.

Wald, N.J., Cuckle, H.S., Densem, J.W., Nanchatial, K., Royston, P., Chard, T., Haddow, J.E., Knight, G.J., Palomaki, G.E. and Canick, J.A. (1988) Maternal serum screening for Down's syndrome in early pregnancy. *British Medical Journal*, 297, 883–7.

Walker, R. (1985) An introduction to applied research. In Walker, R. (ed.), *Applied Qualitative Research*. Aldershot: Gower.

Ward, L. (1989) For better, for worse? In Brechin, A. and Walmsley, J. (eds), *Making Connections. Reflecting on the Lives and Experiences of People with Learning Difficulties*. London: Hodder and Stoughton.

Welsh Health Planning Forum (1992) *Protocol for Investment in Health Gain: Mental Handicap (Learning Disabilities)*. Cardiff: Welsh Office.

Welsh Office (1991a) *The All Wales Mental Handicap Strategy*. Annual Report 1988/89. Cardiff: Welsh Office.

Welsh Office (1991b) *The Review of the All Wales Mental Handicap Strategy. Report on Consultation on the Key Issues*. Cardiff: Welsh Office.

Wertheimer, A. (1985) *Going to Work. Employment Opportunities for People with Mental Handicaps in Washington State, USA*. London: Campaign for People with Mental Handicaps.

Wertheimer, A. (1987) Towards a normal working life. New directions in day services. *Community Living*, April, 8–9.

Wilkinson, J. (1989) 'Being there': evaluating life quality from feelings and daily experience. In Brachin, A. and Walmsley, J. (eds) *Making Connections. Reflecting on the Lives and Experiences of People with Learning Difficulties*. London: Hodder and Stoughton.

Williams, A. (1985) The economics of coronary artery by-pass grafting. *British Medical Journal*, 291, 326–9.

Williams, P. (1978) *Our Mutual Handicap: Attitudes and Perceptions of Others by Mentally Handicapped People*. London: Campaign for People with Mental Handicaps.

Williams, P. and Salomon, A. (1980) *Make Us Citizens and See Us Grow* (A report of a study tour of services for mentally handicapped people in America). London: Campaign for People with Mental Handicaps.

Wing, L. (1989) Closing Darenth Park Mental Handicap Hospital: the effects on the residents. Paper given at the International Symposium on Mental Handicap, 'The Place of Special Villages', Middlesex Polytechnic, 20 March.

Witt, S.J. (1981) Increase in adaptive behavior level after residence in an intermediate care facility for mentally retarded persons. *Mental Retardation*, 19(2), 75–9.

Wolfensberger, W. (1972) *The Principle of Normalization in Human Services*. Toronto: National Institute on Mental Retardation.

Wolfensberger, W. (1975) *The Origins and Nature of Our Institutional Models*. Syracuse, NY: Human Policy Press.

Wolfensberger, W. (1983a) Social role valorization: a proposed new term for the principle of normalization. *Mental Retardation*, 21(6), 234–9.

Wolfensberger, W. (1983b) *Guidelines for Evaluators During a PASS, PASSING, or Similar Assessment of Human Service Quality*. Downsview, Ontario: National Institute on Mental Retardation.

Wolfensberger, W. and Glenn, L. (1975a) *Program Analysis of Service Systems (PASS) 3: A Method for the Quantitative Evaluation of Human Services. Volume 1: Handbook*, 3rd edn. Toronto: National Institute on Mental Retardation.

Wolfensberger, W. and Glenn, L. (1975b) *Program Analysis of Service Systems (PASS) 3: A Method for the Quantitative Evaluation of Human Services. Volume 2: Field Manual*, 3rd edn. Toronto: National Institute on Mental Retardation.

Wolfensberger, W. and Thomas, S. (1983) *Program Analysis of Service Systems' Implementation of Normalization Goals (PASSING): Normalization Criteria and Ratings Manual*, 2nd edn. Downsview, Ontario: National Institute on Mental Retardation.

Wright, K. (1986) *The Economics of Informal Care of the Elderly*. Discussion Paper No. 23. York: Centre for Health Economics.

Wright, K. and Haycox, A. (1992) Economics and the care of people with a mental handicap. In Baldwin, S. and Hattersley, J. (eds), *Mental Handicap Social Science Perspectives*. London: Routledge.

Wyngaarden, M. (1981) Interviewing mentally retarded persons: issues and strategies. In Bruininks, R.H., Meyers, C.E., Sigford, B.B. and Lakin, K.C. (eds), *Deinstitutionalization and Community Adjustment of Mentally Retarded People*. Monograph No. 4. Washington, DC: American Association on Mental Deficiency.

Yorkshire Television (1987) The Leftover Children. *First Tuesday Special*, TV documentary, 7 July (and leaflet).

Zarkowski, E. and Clements, J. (1988) *Problem Behaviour in People with Severe Learning Disabilities: A Practical Guide to a Constructional Approach*. Beckenham: Croom Helm.

Zigler, E. and Balla, D. (1977) The social policy implications of a research program on the effects of institutionalization on retarded persons. In Mittler, P. (ed.), *Research to Practice in Mental Retardation. Volume I: Care and Intervention*. Baltimore: University Park Press.

Index

economic analysis techniques, 22–5
efficiency in resource allocation,
  11–13
procedures, 10
production of welfare model,
  16–22
service interventions' rationale and
  objectives, 14–15
Evans, G., 10, 53, 97
everyday functioning, 81–8, 114–15
expectations, social, 84
experimental designs, 63–4
external outcomes (externalities), 52,
  59–60
production of welfare model,
  20–22
research dimension, 102
Eyman, R.K., 97, 100

family aide services, 159
family care, 37–40, 105, 108
costs of, 149–52
financial help, 39–40
professional support, 38–9, 121
short-term care, 37–8, 145, 157
see also carers
Family Fund, 40
Fanshel, S., 62
Felce, D., 89
funding, 46, 47
HIV, 154
use of staff, 158
Wessex community care, 146
Ferguson-Smith, N., 28
fetal screening, 27–31, 154
fieldwork, 76–9
final external benefits, 21
final outcomes, 52, 162
definition and methodology, 53–7;
  frame of reference, 53; starting
  point, 53–4
position statement, 104–15;
  de-institutionalization, 113–15;
  families, 108; institutions, 109–12;
  supported ordinary living, 112–13
production of, 57–8, 115–17
production of welfare model,
  17–18

research dimensions, 80, 81–94
user-level accomplishments, *see*
  user-level accomplishments
finance, 33
hindering development of
  community care, 157–8
policy background, 46–51
financial costs, 126–7, 132–4
financial help, 39–40
'fixed point' of action, 122
flexible staff teams, 120–21
Fogelman, C.J., 82, 83, 85
frame of reference, 53
freedom, losses of, 114–15
Freeman, H.E., 63, 67
friendship needs, 56
  see also personal networks
Frost, D., 93–4
functioning, everyday, 81–8, 114–15

general health care, 31–2, 155, 160
genetic counselling, 27
Gerard, K., 145
Gillygate Wholefood Bakery, York,
  124
Goffman, E., 32, 91, 95–6, 110
Griffiths, Sir R., 49
Grossman, H.J., 81, 82
grounded theory, 67

handicap, social construction of, 53–4
Haycox, A.
ante-natal care, 28, 29
cost measurement, 129, 135, 146
long-stay hospitals, 109
PASS, 97–8
health care
boundaries with social care
  blurring, 8
general, 31–2, 155, 160
see also National Health Service
health status, measuring, 62
hereditary conditions, 27
hidden costs, 129
HIV, 154
Holburn, C.S., 85
home care, *see* carers; family care
horizontal equity, 158–9

COORDINATING COMMUNITY CARE
MULTIDISCIPLINARY TEAMS AND CARE MANAGEMENT

John Øvretveit

This book is about how people from different professions and agencies work together to meet the health and social needs of people in a community. It is about making the most of different skills to meet people's needs, and creating satisfying and supportive working groups. It is about the details of making community care a reality.

The effectiveness and quality of care a person receives depends on getting the right professionals and services, and also on the support given to the person's carers. Services must be coordinated if the person is to benefit, but coordination is more difficult with the increasing change, variety and complexity of health and social services in the 1990s. This book challenges the assumptions that services are best coordinated by multi-professional and multi-agency teams, and that community care teams are broadly similar. It demonstrates when a team is needed and how to overcome differences between professions, and between agency policies and philosophies.

Drawing on ten years of consultancy research with a variety of teams and services, the author gives practical guidance for managers and practitioners about how to set up and improve coordination and teamwork. The book combines practical concerns with theoretical depth drawing on organization and management theory, psychology, psychoanalysis, sociology, economics and government studies.

Contents
Introduction – Needs and organization – Markets, bureaucracy and association – Types of team – Client pathways and team resource management – Team members' roles – Team leadership – Decisions and conflict in teams – Communications and co-service – Coordinating community health and social care – Appendices – Glossary – References and bibliography – Index.

240pp   0 335 19047 2 (Paperback)   0 335 19048 0 (Hardback)

COMMUNITY PROFILING
AUDITING SOCIAL NEEDS

Murray Hawtin, Geraint Hughes, Janie Percy-Smith with Anne Foreman

Social auditing and community profiles are increasingly being used in relation to a number of policy areas, including: housing, community care, community health, urban regeneration and local economic development. *Community Profiling* provides a practical guide to the community profiling process which can be used by professionals involved in the planning and delivery of services, community workers, community organizations, voluntary groups and tenants' associations. In addition it will provide an invaluable step-by-step guide to social science students involved in practical research projects.

The book takes the reader through the community profiling process beginning with consideration of what a community profile is, defining aims and objectives and planning the research. It then looks at a variety of methods for collecting, storing and analysing information and ways of involving the local community. Finally it considers how to present the information and develop appropriate action-plans. The book also includes a comprehensive annotated bibliography of recent community profiles and related literature.

Contents
What is a community profile? – Planning a community profile – Involving the community – Making use of existing information – Collecting new information – Survey methods – Storing and analysing data – Collating and presenting information – Not the end – Annotated bibliography – Index.

208pp   0 335 19113 4 (Paperback)

TOTAL QUALITY MANAGEMENT IN THE PUBLIC SECTOR
AN INTERNATIONAL PERSPECTIVE

Colin Morgan and Stephen Murgatroyd

TQM is a set of concepts, tools and applications which has been so successful in manufacturing industry that we are now witnessing experimentation in the transference of Total Quality Management to the public sector provision of government, health and education in North America, Europe and elsewhere. TQM is starting to set a new paradigm for management approaches in the public sector and 'not for profit' enterprises. All key public service managers will at least need to know the basics of TQM, its possibilities and limitations for the public sector, and particularly the types of applications which could work for them.

For all public sector managers this book provides: a clear understanding of the key concepts of TQM; a critical understanding of their fit and relevance to the public sector; empirical evidence of TQM applications in government, health and education; and exploration of the public sector TQM possibilities yet to be realized. It draws throughout on case examples from Britain, Canada, the USA and continental Europe which illustrate the application of TQM to the public sector.

Contents
Part 1: The nature of TQM in the public sector – Total Quality Management – Leading thinkers for Total Quality Management – Applying Total Quality Management in the public sector – Part 2: Applications of TQM to public sector organizations – TQM and health care – TQM and education – TQM and social services – TQM developments in government service – Issues and problems in adopting TQM in the public sector – Appendix – References – Index.

224pp   0 335 19102 9 (Paperback)   0 335 19103 7 (Hardback)

SOCIAL CARE IN A MIXED ECONOMY

Gerald Wistow, Martin Knapp, Brian Hardy and Caroline Allen

This book describes the mixed economy of community care in England and analyses the efforts and activities of local authorities to promote and develop it. It is based on national documentary and statistical evidence and on more detailed research with twenty-four local authorities; and includes a case study on the transfer of residential homes to the independent sector.

The roles of social services departments have been progressively redefined to emphasize responsibility for creating and managing a mixed economy. This entails a major cultural shift for departments which may be summarized as involving moves from providing to enabling, and from administration to management. It also implies the need for new skills and structures. *Social Care in a Mixed Economy* traces the historical changes; the local interpretations of central government policy; how authorities actually have been developing mixed economies; the main opportunities or incentives for promoting a mixed economy; and the main obstacles to its development.

Contents
Introduction: historical and policy context – Community care: markets and enabling – The mixed economy in 1991 – Local responses to the legislation and guidance – Building a mixed economy – Social care is different – Residential care home transfers – Conclusions – Appendix – References – Name index – Subject index.

176pp   0 335 19043 X (Paperback)   0 335 19044 8 (Hardback)